Gambling in America

Gambling in America meticulously breaks new ground by developing analytical tools to assess the benefits and costs of the economic and social changes introduced by casino gambling in monetary terms, linking them to individual households' utility and well-being. Since casinos are associated with unintended and often negative economic consequences, these factors are incorporated into the discussion. The book also shows how amenity benefits – for casinos, the benefit to consumers of closer proximity – enter the evaluation. Other topics include agent incentives and public decision making, conceptual clarifications about economic development, cost–benefit analysis, and net export multiplier models. Professor Grinols finds that, in considering all relevant factors, the social costs of casino gambling outweigh their social benefits.

Earl L. Grinols is Professor of Economics at the University of Illinois, Champaign–Urbana. He has previously taught at MIT, Cornell University, and the University of Chicago. Professor Grinols worked as a research economist for the Department of the Treasury and as Senior Economist for the Council of Economic Advisers. He has published in the fields of international economics, public finance, and macroeconomics, and is the author of two previous books, including an undergraduate text on microeconomics, and more than eighty other publications. He has testified before Congress and numerous statehouses on the economics of gambling. His work has been cited in numerous press accounts and he is often consulted by journalists and the media.

In 1994, Professor Grinols was one of the first academicians to recommend to Congress that it should create a national commission to study the impact of casino gambling. The National Gambling Impact Study Commission was established in 1996 and produced its final report in 1999 recommending a moratorium on gambling expansion. To spark awareness and greater interest, Dr. Grinols focused his research on the importance of a cost-benefit review of gambling, comparing the benefits of casinos to the social costs that they would create. Among the leading newspapers that have cited his work are the *New York Times, Wall Street Journal, Washington Post, Los Angeles Times, Boston Globe, Atlanta Journal and Constitution, Seattle Post, Congressional Quarterly Review, Chicago Tribune, The Economist, Time,* and *U.S. News and World Report.* News wire services covering his research include UPI, AP, Reuters, Copley, Gannett, Federal, Cox, Scripps, Howard, and Dow Jones Newswires.

Gambling in America

COSTS AND BENEFITS

Earl L. Grinols
University of Illinois, Champaign–Urbana

CAMBRIDGE
UNIVERSITY PRESS

PUBLISHED BY THE PRESS SYNDICATE OF THE UNIVERSITY OF CAMBRIDGE
The Pitt Building, Trumpington Street, Cambridge, United Kingdom

CAMBRIDGE UNIVERSITY PRESS
The Edinburgh Building, Cambridge CB2 2RU, UK
40 West 20th Street, New York, NY 10011-4211, USA
477 Williamstown Road, Port Melbourne, VIC 3207, Australia
Ruiz de Alarcón 13, 28014 Madrid, Spain
Dock House, The Waterfront, Cape Town 8001, South Africa

http://www.cambridge.org

First published 2004

Printed in the United States of America

Typeface Minion 11/15 pt.   *System* LATEX 2$_\varepsilon$ [TB]

A catalog record for this book is available from the British Library.

Library of Congress Cataloging-in-Publication Data
Grinols, Earl L., 1951–
    Gambling in America : costs and benefits / Earl L. Grinols.
        p.   cm.
    Includes bibliographical references and index.
    ISBN 0-521-83013-3
    1. Gambling – United States.   2. Gambling – Economic aspects.   I. Title.
    HV6715.G76   2003
    338.4′7795 – dc21   2003048554

ISBN 0 521 83013 3 hardback

For Anne

Contents

List of Tables and Figures   *page* xi

Acknowledgments   xiii

1   **Introduction**   1
    Conclusion   12

2   **Considerations**   13
    Background   18
    Freedom, Externalities, and Public Policy   24

3   **Agents and Incentives**   27
    The Proponents   28
        Owners   28
        Lobbyists   32
        American Indians   36
    The Players   45
    The Government   47
        Jurisdictional Conundrums   50
    The Opponents   52
    Summary   52

4   **Economic Development**   55
    Jobs and Economic Development   56
    "Major-League Losers' Fields of Schemes"   65
    Jobs   67
    Multiplier Models: Reliability   71

    Cannibalization   73
    Leakage   78
    Multipliers   79
  A Net Export Multiplier Model   79
  Industry-Sponsored Research: The Evans
        Group Example   88
  Conclusions   92

5 **Cost–Benefit Analysis**   95
  Theory   97
  Common Mistakes in Applying Cost–Benefit
        Analysis   108

6 **Social Benefits**   111
  Value Once Again   112
  Distance Benefits   114
  Profits and Taxes   125
  The Other Benefits   127
  Conclusions   128

7 **Social Costs**   131
  Social Cost Taxonomy   132
    Crime   133
    Business and Employment Costs   135
    Bankruptcy   139
    Suicide   141
    Illness   143
    Social Service Costs   144
    Direct Regulatory Costs   144
    Family Costs   145
    Abused Dollars   145
  Examples   146
  The Numbers   167

8 **The Present and The Future**   175
  Conclusion   181

Contents

A   **Cost-Benefit to the Locality: A
     Scenario**   189

     Revenue, Profits, Taxes   190
     Regional Income   191
     Cost-Benefit   193
     Lessons   195

     Glossary   197

     Notes   203

     References   215

List of Tables and Figures

Tables

2.1 Contrast between Nineteenth Century Constitutional Gambling Prohibitions and Gambling Acceptance in 2000 *page* 15
4.1 Representative Casino Use of Funds 80
4.2 Effect of a Casino on Local Income Flows 82
4.3 Net Export Multiplier Model 84
4.4 Casino-Induced Net Exports ($) 86
5.1 Summary of Casino Costs and Benefits 107
6.1 Distance and Demand Data: Casinos 117
6.2 Distance Benefits Estimated by Simulation 119
6.3 Gambling Demand Implied by Table 6.1 and the 30 to 35 Percent Rule 120
6.4 Distance Benefits Implied by Table 6.3 Gamblers 120
6.5 Regional Annual Casino Benefits for the Entire Economy 129
7.1 Social Costs per Pathological Gambler: 2003 $ 172
7.2 Social Costs per Problem Gambler: 2003 $ 174
8.1 National Costs of Problem and Pathological Gamblers, Adjusted by Prevalence Estimates Confidence Bounds (National Cost in $ Billion) 176
8.2 Iowa Replication Study: Problem and Pathological Gamblers (Percent) 178
8.3 Share of Problem and Pathological Gamblers in the Population by Distance from the Nearest Casino 179

Figures

3.1 Tribal Entities Recognized per Year by the Bureau of
     Indian Affairs   41
3.2 Gambling Shares: Las Vegas Residents   46
4.1 Jobless Growthlessness: Casino Employment Displaces
     Local Economy Jobs without Improving Resident
     Well-Being   60
4.2 Growthless Jobs: Casinos Append Jobs to the Local
     Economy without Improving Resident Well-Being   61
4.3 Jobless Growth: Resident Well-Being Is Improved by
     Casinos.   61
4.4 Multiplier vs. Cost–Benefit Analysis   62
4.5 Sectoral Winners and Losers 0–10 Miles from a Casino:
     Sales Change per $1,000 Increase in Casino Revenues   75
4.6 Average Losses by Distance from a Casino: General
     Merchandise, Miscellaneous Retail, and Wholesale Trade   77
4.7 Gains and Losses by Distance from a Casino: Revenue
     Change per $1,000 Increase in Casino Revenues, All Goods   77
4.8 Schematic Representation of the Three Relevant Sectors
     for Casino Net Export Modeling   81
4.9 The Evans Group Study, Reproduced Figure 4-1   90
4.10 Beginning and Ending Unemployment Rates for Counties
     with Similar Beginning Rates   91
6.1 Distance and Demand   115
6.2 Using Demand for Casino Gambling by Distance to Infer
     the Benefits of Proximity   117
A.1 Regional Geography for the New Casino   190

Acknowledgments

Portions of *Gambling in America* make use of previously published material. This is used with permission and acknowledged as follows. Chapter 3: Grinols, Earl L. (1996). "Incentives Explain Gambling's Growth," *Forum for Applied Research and Public Policy*, 11, 2, Summer, 119–124; Chapter 4: Grinols, Earl L. and J. D. Omorov (1996). "Who Loses When Casinos Win?" *Illinois Business Review*, 53, 1, Spring, 7–11, 19, Grinols, Earl L. (2003). "Cutting the Cards and Craps: Right Thinking About Gambling Economics" in *Gambling: Who Wins? Who Loses?*, G. Reith, ed. Prometheus Contemporary Issues Series: New York, Prometheus, Grinols, Earl L. and David B. Mustard (2001). "Business Profitability versus Social Profitability: Evaluating Industries with Externalities – The Case of Casinos," *Managerial and Decision Economics*, 22, 1, 143–162; Chapter 5: Grinols, Earl L. and David B. Mustard (2001). "Business Profitability versus Social Profitability: Evaluating Industries with Externalities – The Case of Casinos," *Managerial and Decision Economics*, 22, 1, 143–162; Chapter 6: Grinols, Earl L. (1999). "Distance Effects in Consumption: Measuring Distance Value with Application to Casino Siting," *Review of Regional Studies*, 29, 1, 63–76.

1 | Introduction

My object, I think, in this was to promote clear thinking on these matters.

John Maynard Keynes
To the Royal Commission on Betting, 1932

CHAPTER SUMMARY. Government decisions regarding economic development issues matter to the **well-being** of all of us. Knowing how to evaluate **economic development** requires a comprehensive framework to compare benefits and costs that is theoretically grounded and established prior to any choice being made, with reliable data obtained to fill identified information gaps. Without a coherent evaluation process, these decisions tend to be made in response to whichever group applies the most pressure. Fortunately, input from well-informed, unbiased parties can counterbalance this tendency. Here, we examine why the procedures typically employed to evaluate **casinos** as a means of economic development suffer from two deficiencies: lack of a valid framework, and lack of complete and trustworthy information. These problems are not special to casinos; what we learn from them has relevance to the evaluation of other economic development questions.

1

Two episodes stand out as reasons for writing this book. The first oc- curred at the start of the 1990s. A newspaper announcement appeared stating that an offtrack betting (OTB) parlor was slated for Champaign, Illinois, where I live. Knowing that OTBs generally drew 90 percent of their clientele from nearby residents; that their profit rates were higher than other businesses (I later learned the figure was 19 percent, includ- ing racing-industry payments); and that owners would be out-of-city investors taking their profits out of town, I was surprised and intensely interested to read that supporters believed it would bring 125 jobs to town. A **net export multiplier model** would show the opposite – a drain on community revenues and reduction in jobs. OTBs were not the only type of business that could drain a local economy (e.g., an out-of-area entertainer performing in town could do the same), but the fact that projections were backwards seemed to be valuable information that the city council and mayor would want to know. I appeared before a city council meeting where my offer to volunteer to work with city staff to produce an accurate economic impact study was rebuffed by the mayor.

At the time, it was incomprehensible to me that an offer to provide free service would be refused. I have since become less naive but, at the time, the rejection of evaluative data stirred me enough that I did the work anyway and published it as a newspaper commentary. This commentary was seen by the university news bureau and eventually led to other commentaries in St. Louis, Chicago, and Indianapolis – the nearest large cities. One of these commentaries was read into the Senate record by U.S. Senator Paul Simon. The commentaries led to questions about the effects of **gambling** expansions in other areas coming to me from coast to coast. I found that virtually no economists at that time were working on the question. Seeing that casino expansion was a topic likely to need independent research, I decided that the issue was worthy of further professional attention.

Forward the clock several years. The second episode occurred at a state-sponsored event hundreds of miles from home with invited speak- ers, including members of the gambling industry. I sat on a panel sand- wiched between a New York City gambling-industry consultant and a casino executive. My closing statement was that, apart from the harmful side effects and **social costs** associated with casinos – most operating through problem and pathological gamblers – there was little to object to about gambling. In the absence of such consequences, if some individuals liked to gamble, they should be free to do so; if others did not like it, they didn't have to gamble. At this time, the casino executives I had been exposed to portrayed themselves as well-meaning businessmen who did not want to hurt anyone by what they did for a living, but were saddled with the unfortunate fact of gambling addicts. At the conclusion of the panel, I turned to the young casino owner on my right, who appeared to be well under the age of forty and was already a wealthy man, (having offered to pay $10 million of his own money for a casino license in the state that had invited us). I pointed out that he looked like a well-to-do individual who probably did not need to work another day if he chose not to, an observation to which he assented. I then asked him the following question: If he knew that what he did to make his living unintentionally hurt people – really *hurt* them – would it be enough to make him change his line of work? He quickly replied that, of course, it would. I then drew from my briefcase a photocopy of a newspaper clipping titled, "Woman Gambles Away Family's Savings, Kills Self." He glanced at the title, waved his arm dismissively, blurted that she probably had had a problem before she began gambling, and walked away. In fact, this woman had no known prior problems before she began gambling; she used the house payments and eventually the family's savings in amounts of $150 and $200, one after the other. Her husband was called home from work one day to find a detective in his driveway. According to the newspaper account, "The detective told Steve two things: His mortgage was seventeen months behind, and the sheriff, there to evict him, had found Kate's suicide note."[1] This was the first that he or his two children knew there was any problem.

Of course, stories do not constitute the basis of good policy. The United States is a large country; one can find examples to support either side of virtually any issue. What these episodes graphically taught me was that there was a great unfilled need for an economist to study the costs and benefits of casinos in society and to identify which side of the ledger was predominant.

Policy triage suggests that there always will be those whose personal interests cause them to support casinos. Likewise, there will always be those who are against them without having to be convinced. It is the middle group, especially those in positions of public trust, who need independent information from sources who are not making money from the activity on which they are reporting. This is why the rudiments of a complete cost–benefit review of casinos was so essential; that is what I set out to collect. Since beginning research on the economics of gambling, I have been asked to testify on more than twenty occasions before statehouses and various national and state government commissions and committees, in addition to speaking publicly to chambers of commerce and other audiences. I was fortunate to be one of the first academicians to recommend to Congress (in 1994 testimony)[2] that it should establish a national commission to study the impact of casino gambling. I felt that rivalry between states could engender a **prisoner's dilemma** competition, whereby states that did not want casinos would feel forced to adopt them as defensive measures against bordering states that used casinos to target the populations of their neighbors.[3] A study conducted to determine the impact of gambling in Ohio and to review the desirability of casinos noted early in the report, "Casinos are within a few hundred yards of our border in Indiana, and within an hour's drive of Ohio in Detroit, Michigan, and Windsor, Ontario. Two West Virginia racetracks offer electronic gaming devices (EGDs; also often called video lottery terminals [VLTs]) also within an hour's drive of Ohio."[4] All states cannot gain at their neighbors' expense, but all will experience the impact of casinos, whether good or bad.

The nine-member National Gambling Impact Study Commission was formed in 1996 legislation and produced its final report in 1999. The report explains that the commission recommended

> ... a pause in the expansion of gambling in order to allow time for an assessment of the costs and benefits already visible, as well as those which remain to be identified.... What is most important, however,

is that these reviews take place and that whatever decisions are made are informed ones.[5]

The fact that the commission did not complete sufficient research to provide the elements of a cost–benefit assessment of casinos but recommended that gambling expansion be halted so that *others* could provide research is revealing. The commission had a significant research budget and, in many ways, was better positioned to conduct original inquiry on key questions than others. Many believe that the commission did not live up to its potential because it included members with financial ties to the gambling industry. On one occasion, for example, a commission member representing the gambling industry harshly criticized survey results presented to the commission that might be construed by some as unflattering to the industry, even threatening a lawsuit against the academics involved.[6] The commission chairman, after conclusion of the commission's work and its termination, stated that she "was not prepared for the venom, bigotry, prejudice, and stereotyping" that she experienced from progambling interests in leading the Congressional study commission.[7]

In an ideal world, policy would be determined by commissions and members of government dispassionately evaluating the alternatives, debating their merits, selecting the best, and then implementing. My travels confirmed for me that we do not live in an ideal world: instead, advocacy rules. Promoters produce proposals that benefit themselves. They and their government allies (who are sometimes promised various inducements[8]) urge their adoption. If there is no opposition – sometimes because no time has been allowed for input – the proposals may be adopted. Usually, however, groups that stand to lose have some opportunity to explain their case. This is a guarantee that both sides will be heard, not that the information will be in a meaningful form or that all of it will be accurate.

On one occasion, I was told privately by a gambling-addiction treatment specialist prior to a public hearing that her office did not take a public position on any form of gambling because in the previous year, one of their treatment specialists had made statements that were objected to by her state's casino industry, which promptly had treatment funding cut by the legislature. She said it was made clear to them that reprisals in the form of funding cuts could be expected in the future if similar episodes continued. Money is a carrot or a stick. Academics have been approached with offers to fund their gambling-related research and centers using gambling dollars, and a few have accepted such funding – even as the tobacco industry provided money to scholars and researchers in the smoking and health field for many years.[9] Providing money for gambling research and treatment is not a problem to the gambling industry, as long as what is said by those receiving it does not touch the core of the industry's interests.

Legislative committees tend to be unsatisfactory vehicles to solve the obvious need for independent, utilizable research to compare benefits and costs. In Ohio, the legislative Committee to Study the Impact of Gambling in Ohio reported that "the Committee had no budget, no permanent staff, and a short time frame within which to complete its work."[10]

> Because of limited time and the lack of a budget or full-time staff, this Committee could not conduct original research on gambling behavior and problem gambling behavior by Ohioans. Instead, we had to rely heavily on testimony from interested parties....[11]

The committee noted in its report that a cited study required 1-1/2 man years of professional economists' time, and spent $75,000 for data acquisition alone, and yet did not attempt to quantify the social costs of gambling.[12] In the same year, Maine's 2002 "Task Force to Study the Impact of a Maine-Based Casino" found its budget of $6,800 "wholly inadequate to address the task force needs," in the words of one member.[13] The task force concluded that limited resources and very complex issues did not allow it even to scratch the surface of the types of questions facing the state. In Connecticut, the state's study to identify the effects of legalized gambling on state citizens did not allow its authors "to address issues related to (1) the social costs of gambling, or (2) any of the important psychological, social, or treatment characteristics of intemperate gamblers in Connecticut," in the words of one reviewer. "This deficiency is remarkable, since the project's primary purpose was to complete 'A study concerning the effects of legalized gambling on the citizens of the state of Connecticut.'"[14] In South Dakota, the government's Legislative Research Council (LRC) had to insist on receiving more information from researchers, Deloitte & Touche, concerning social impacts although the original contract had called for such information. In its letter to Deloitte & Touche, the Council's director explains:

> Items J and N in the scope of the study specify social problems and social impacts. Module III [in your report] is titled "Identification of Social Issues." Later in the paragraph, the scope of the study in this respect is limited to costs expended by the state due to problem and pathological gambling addictions. Items J and N indicate that the LRC had in mind some information would be forthcoming relative to gambling and social phenomena as suicide, divorce, child neglect, failure in child-support payments, bankruptcy ... the LRC had in mind a much more extensive discussion relative to items J and N.[15]

In short, it is rare if ever that a valid framework of analysis is adopted, its elements understood relative to the overall question of well-being of the **citizens**, the information successfully acquired to fill the elements of the framework to undergo evaluation, and then evaluated.

So how should a proper assessment proceed? The question applies not only to the casino industry, but also to *any* industry believed to be associated with harmful social costs. Step One is to construct a framework of discourse. In this book, I take the well-being (i.e., **utility**) of the area's people as my starting point. An economic development proposal – this could be adding a new industry to the economy, as in the case of casinos, or something as far afield as choosing an immigration policy that decides whether to add new residents to a geographical nation – is desirable if it enhances the utility of existing residents. The focus on peoples' well-being has implications for how to measure benefits and costs, which are worked out in Chapter 5.

Chapter 2 presents background information about gambling as an activity and a number of considerations of which policymakers should be aware. Chapter 3 deals with an important preliminary issue, which is to explain why the incentives imbedded in the political and social process – at least in the case of casinos – are often not structured to make choices in the right way. Economics is the study of incentives and their consequences in the commercial interactions of people. Some extend the discipline to include the study of self-interest and incentives in peripheral areas such as political economy, which considers political policies and economic processes, especially as they relate to prevailing social institutions. The change in the social environment and in the institutions relating to the casino industry described in Chapter 3 created incentives that led to outcomes that no single agent controlled, but that all played a part in creating. How to evaluate the consequences of these actions is the subject of Chapters 4 through 8, which organize the process of translating a focus on residents' well-being into a correct **cost–benefit analysis**.

Chapter 4 reveals that it is difficult to keep economic development as it is usually discussed in proper context. Economic development is most often discussed in the halls of power in terms of **impact studies**, in which the focus is jobs and projections of taxes that will presumably be paid by new businesses. This emphasis is encouraged by the promotional studies that are provided to legislators and the public, but it is an emphasis that is decidedly wrong. Economic development in this guise is *not* synonymous with economic development in the sense of enhanced resident well-being. Another reason that there is a false emphasis on impact studies looking at jobs and tax payments is that they are easier to produce than cost–benefit analyses. One of the main themes of this book is that reliance on such studies is misplaced. Impact studies can show both job and tax increases at the same time that utility of the population falls. To appreciate valid cost–benefit analyses, one must understand invalid analyses based on impact studies. Chapter 4 describes how impact studies are invalid assessments for two main reasons: first, they are conceptually the wrong tool; and second, even for the questions they answer, they are prone to manipulation, misrepresentation, and error.

Chapter 5 begins the constructive process of relating costs and benefits to residents' utility. The pertinence of this process is wide-ranging, and it can be applied quite generally. Its specific application to the casino industry is particularly valuable because so many features relevant for casinos might not appear in other selected industries. For example, most entertainments do not generate **externalities** to any significant extent. The underlying concept for the conversion from utility to cost–benefit components is simple. Utility is generated by using income to purchase goods and services at available prices. Income derives from **value added**. Economic activity creates value added when it converts inputs into outputs of higher value. Because any increase in value added, including the value to residents of amenity changes that affect utility, must appear in some form in the post-change economy, performing appropriate budget identity manipulations allows the mathematics itself to identify the forms of increase.

Chapters 6 and 7 discuss what is known about the magnitude of the benefits and costs of casinos. There are certain conceptual issues to discuss because the form that benefits take depends on market structure. Chapter 8 concludes with an evaluation of the strengths and weaknesses of what is currently known.

There is inevitably difficulty in writing a book intended for multiple interested parties. In the case of casinos, this should include legislators and the public, in addition to academicians. Any subject – and economics is no exception – develops special argot. I have tried whenever possible to explain the necessary terminology and its significance whenever it could not be dispensed with. Some may find the material too technical in parts; others may find parts that are the opposite. It is my belief that people of intelligence, regardless of their own occupation or field, are capable of understanding the relevant issues in this book if they are clearly explained. My solution was to write at the level that I felt necessary to the topic at hand, but also to provide explanations to make the material as accessible as possible to all readers throughout. Where possible, I use boxes to separate material that was not essential to the discussion, but whose presence would add to it. I apologize to those who may find some explanations tedious, just as I urge others to bypass technical portions when not germane to their objectives.

Before concluding this chapter, I should explain my relationship to and personal views on casino gambling. I have studied the economic implications of casinos for twelve years. In that time, I have had to think carefully about the issues and determine fully my own views in light of the data and my research. I have received income neither from the gambling industry nor from its opponents. I do not accept honoraria for my testimony or public addresses, and my research has not been directly or indirectly funded or paid for by progambling or antigambling organizations or individuals. Thus, the time that I spend on this issue has no financial implications to me. This is one advantage of a research university as the provider of public services. Within the economics discipline, the study of the casino industry has not been on the list of professionally important or prominent activities. At best, the time devoted to it has been neutral to my career.

In view of this, why would anyone spend time studying the economics of gambling? One reason is curiosity. Early on, I felt that those making decisions about casinos needed to know what the consequences of introducing the new industry into their economy were, and I wanted to know what a cost–benefit study would find. Despite the longevity of casinos in Nevada, there was no good research available on casino costs and benefits. For example, the question of how much the opportunity to gamble nearer to home was worth had not been addressed, even though the issue has similarities to the question of what the value of creating a new amenity such as a national park might be.

Another reason is fascination with what I learned about the failings of the public decision-making process. It was a continual surprise to me how little reliable advice legislators tended to receive through the lobbying and hearing process and how confused was the information they did receive. I felt a certain degree of obligation to provide objective information.

The most important reason, however, came from the realization that the methodology of evaluating casinos had wider applicability. If one theme of this book is that legislators have difficulty inherent in the advocacy system in getting good information, another is that there is a pervasive lack of understanding among legislators and the business community – and even among the ranks of some economists – about what economic development is and how to evaluate it. Many accounting firms, consulting firms, and those academics who were often consulted on gambling issues have little or no understanding of how to construct the elements of a cost–benefit analysis and how to validate its components once they have done so. Many would be unable to differentiate the logical differences between the net export multiplier models they provide (i.e., jobs and income multiplier impact studies) and the related but different concept of cost–benefit. This is a shame because economic development is a subject of great importance. The environmental movement has reminded us that cutting down every tree in the land might create jobs but would be a foolish way to think about whether that should actually be done.

Previously in this chapter, I reported my view that if there were no social costs caused by gambling, there would be no reason to object to it. That is, when individuals understand risk and odds and want to gamble for enjoyment, budgeting and planning as they would for any other form of recreation, there is no argument, in my opinion, to object. I have no moral objections to gambling. However, a much misunderstood point is that *morality* is simply a term that refers to codified injunctions – often long-standing and ancient in origin – against activities that cause more social harm than good. Murder inflicts greater social costs than benefits; this has been known for centuries, and thus there exist widespread moral codes against murder. My approach is simple: Activities that create more social harm than good and, therefore, fail a cost–benefit test need to be regulated, monitored, and in some cases altered or banned to achieve greater social well-being. Rational agents will not choose to engage in an activity where social costs exceed social benefits and the costs are inflicted on the agents themselves. The need for public intervention occurs precisely when the costs are borne by one agent or group and the benefits by another.

CONCLUSION

Too often, public decisions are made with deficient information and evaluation. There is even a lack of agreement or understanding of what constitutes a proper evalution or review. This is especially true in the class of activities that falls under the rubric of "economic development." The incentives for government to seek out and receive unbiased and trustworthy assessments of proposed projects and to understand them in terms of their impact on the well-being of their citizens are unreliable. Those with significant money at stake are motivated to present only their own views.

However, the dictum that "you can fool some of the people all of the time, and all of the people some of the time, but you cannot fool all of the people all of the time"[16] suggests that truth and right thinking tend to be more persuasive in the long run. Good policy requires that some party generate an unfooled public by providing factual and accurate information. Because a casino promoter, an Indian tribe, or even local government places itself in the role of the house, thereby reaping benefits, does not mean that casinos are socially beneficial. Social benefits must take into account all stakeholders. There are benefits of casinos to players, to owners, and to citizens, and there are costs as well. Identifying a winner or loser from the social perspective requires understanding the complete picture and knowing which components should be compared.

The purpose of this book is to address this state of affairs by enunciating a framework for social evaluation and applying it to the casino industry. Precise numbers relating to gambling will undoubtedly change with the passage of time, but the framework for evaluating them – as well as many relative magnitudes and ratios – will remain accurate. Human nature and how it relates to gambling has not changed, nor will the requirements for right evaluation of social issues based on the well-being of households.

2 Considerations

We make progress slowly. Discredited institutions of one century, thought to have been permanently abolished after a long struggle, are revived in later centuries and the battle has to be fought all over again.

M. L. Walker (1934)

CHAPTER SUMMARY. For most of the twentieth century, casino gambling was criminalized in all states except Nevada. This situation was dramatically reversed, primarily in the last decade of the century. What lessons does this teach? Have we forgotten what our forebears once knew or is the nature of modern gambling different? Here, we identify a puzzle: Why does one generation judge gambling harshly and another embrace it? Those making decisions about gambling must understand its special features and decide whether or not it is appropriate for government to intervene. In any event, the present generation is embarked on a nearly perfect social experiment in most locations of the nation: comparing the complete absence of casinos on one extreme to their prominent presence on the other.

U.S. legal tradition is rooted in the value of personal freedom. A citizen has the right to do as he or she wishes, even to engage in activities that others might think dangerous or harmful to himself or herself, such as suntanning, smoking, or skydiving. Citizens' liberty to do as they wish is restricted only when their choices infringe on the freedom and rights of others. It is significant, therefore, that in 1909, after the last remaining state – Nevada – outlawed casino gambling, no state in America allowed casinos within its borders. New York closed its racetracks the following year and, at that moment, virtually all gambling anywhere in the United States was illegal – the only exceptions being a handful of racetracks in Kentucky, Maryland, and Illinois. Just as interesting as the actual presence of the ban is the fact that 76 percent of the states prohibiting gambling did so in *constitutional* provisions. Constitutions are intended to constrain behavior not only of individuals, but also of government; they are intentionally difficult to change. Even legislative simple majorities may not engage in constitutionally prohibited actions.

Table 2.1 lists states and adoption years of constitutions that prohibited gambling at the beginning of the twentieth century. The right-hand column lists the forms of gambling legally available at the end of the century. The language prohibiting gambling was generally written in terms of lotteries. A **lottery** is a scheme for the distribution of prizes by chance. The elements of a lottery are consideration (i.e., payment for play), prize, and chance.[17] Many court decisions establish that the term *lottery* applies to any game of chance and any game in which chance predominates.[18] The contrast between the large number of states that enforced constitutional prohibitions against any form of gambling in 1900 and the number that encourage multiple gambling forms today is remarkable. At this writing, only two states – Hawaii and Utah – authorize no form of gambling. Horseracing is allowed by Tennessee, but there are presently no operating tracks.[19] A sample of the constitutional provisions follows:

> "No law shall be passed, abridging the right of the people peaceably to assemble and to petition, on the government, or any department thereof, nor shall any office be granted, otherwise than by due judicial proceedings, nor shall any lottery hereafter be authorized or any sale of lottery tickets allowed within this State." (New York, 1846)

TABLE 2.1. Contrast between Nineteenth Century Constitutional Gambling Prohibitions and Gambling Acceptance in 2000

State	Year of Constitutional Ban in Effect in 1900	Gambling Allowed in 2000
Alabama	1875	Bingo, Parimutuel
Alaska		Bingo
Arizona		Bingo, Indian Casinos, Lottery, Parimutuel
Arkansas	1874	Parimutuel
California	1879	Bingo, Card Rooms, Indian Casinos, Lottery, Parimutuel
Colorado		Bingo, Card Rooms, Casinos, Indian Casinos, Lottery, Parimutuel
Connecticut		Bingo, Indian Casinos, Parimutuel
Delaware	1897	Bingo, Lottery, Parimutuel
Florida	1887	Bingo, Boats to Nowhere, Card Rooms, Lottery, Parimutuel
Georgia	1877	Bingo, Boats to Nowhere, Lottery
Hawaii		0
Idaho	1890	Bingo, Lottery, Parimutuel
Illinois	1887	Bingo, Indian Casinos, Lottery, Parimutuel, Riverboats
Indiana	1851	Bingo, Card Rooms, Lottery, Parimutuel, Riverboats
Iowa	1857	Bingo, Indian Casinos, Lottery, Parimutuel
Kansas	1857	Bingo, Indian Casinos, Lottery, Parimutuel
Kentucky	1891	Bingo, Lottery, Parimutuel
Louisiana		Bingo, Casinos, Lottery, Parimutuel, Riverboats
Maine		Bingo, Lottery, Parimutuel
Maryland	1867	Bingo, Card Rooms, Lottery, Parimutuel
Massachusetts		Bingo, Lottery, Paramutuel
Michigan	1850	Bingo, Casinos, Indian Casinos, Lottery, Parimutuel
Minnesota	1857	Bingo, Indian Casinos, Lottery, Powerball

(*continued*)

TABLE 2.1 (*continued*)

State	Year of Constitutional Ban in Effect in 1900	Gambling Allowed in 2000
Mississippi	1890	Bingo, Casinos, Riverboats
Missouri	1875	Bingo, Lottery, Parimutuel, Riverboats
Montana	1889	Bingo, Card Rooms, Lottery, Parimutuel, Sports Betting, Video Poker
Nebraska	1875	Bingo, Indian Casinos, Lottery, Parimutuel
Nevada	1864	Bingo, Casinos, Lottery, Parimutuel
New Hampshire		Bingo, Lottery, Parimutuel
New Jersey	1844	Bingo, Card Rooms, Casinos, Lottery, Parimutuel
New Mexico		Bingo, Casinos, Indian Casinos, Lottery, Parimutuel
New York	1846	Bingo, Indian Casinos, Lottery, Parimutuel
North Carolina		Bingo, Casinos, Indian Casinos
North Dakota	1889	Bingo, Card Rooms, Indian Casinos, Parimutuel, Sports Betting
Ohio	1851	Bingo, Lottery, Parimutuel
Oklahoma	1890	Bingo, Indian Casinos, Parimutuel
Oregon	1857	Bingo, Card Rooms, Indian Casinos, Lottery, Parimutuel, Sports Betting
Pennsylvania		Bingo, Lottery, Parimutuel
Rhode Island		Bingo, Lottery, Parimutuel
South Carolina	1895	Bingo
South Dakota	1889	Bingo, Card Rooms, Casinos, Indian Casinos, Lottery, Video, Parimutuel
Tennessee	1870	0
Texas	1861	Bingo, Lottery, Parimutuel
Utah	1895	0
Vermont		Bingo, Lottery, Parimutuel
Virginia	1902	Bingo, Lottery, Parimutuel
Washington	1889	Bingo, Card Rooms, Casinos, Indian Casinos, Lottery, Parimutuel

State	Year of Constitutional Ban in Effect in 1900	Gambling Allowed in 2000
West Virginia	1872	Bingo, Casinos, Lottery, Parimutuel
Wisconsin	1848	Bingo, Indian Casinos, Lottery, Parimutuel
Wyoming		Bingo, Parimutuel
Number of bans by Constitutional Prohibition	35 (76 Percent*)	

*Arizona, New Mexico, Alaska, and Hawaii did not become states until after 1900.

"Lotteries and the sale of lottery tickets, for any purpose whatever, shall forever be prohibited in this state." (Ohio, 1851)

"The legislature shall not authorize any games of chance, lottery, or gift enterprise, under any pretense, or for any purpose whatever." (Nebraska, 1875)

"The legislature shall not authorize any game of chance, lottery, or gift enterprise under any pretense or for any purpose." (Utah, 1895)

According to historians, there have been eras in which gambling in America was more prevalent, followed by periods of restriction, followed again by periods of resurgence. The growing movement in the early 1800s to oppose slavery, lawlessness on the frontier, and alcoholism also worked to curtail gambling. After the Civil War, a second wave of gambling occurred, including for a time an era of national lotteries that eventually led to so much corruption that policy moved in the reverse direction.

Consider Missouri:

- In 1814, gambling was prohibited in Missouri.
- In 1862, however, it was the only state except for Kentucky not to ban lotteries.
- It subsequently banned lotteries in 1875.
- In 1991, Missouri legalized riverboats, but allowed only games of skill.
- In April 1994, Missouri rejected full riverboat casino gambling, but legalized it in a second vote in November.

The pendulum has similarly swung in Nevada:

- In 1861, gambling was outlawed in Nevada.
- In 1869, it was made legal again.
- In 1909, Nevada banned gambling.
- In 1913, it legalized it again, but not commercial gambling.
- In 1931, it legalized commercial gambling.

Similar histories could be produced for other states. The social ambivalence about gambling is evident in Table 2.1. What one generation worked to permanantly eradicate, another generation resurrected.

BACKGROUND

SUMMARY. Any public position on gambling needs to accommodate a number of relevant facts. Gambling is an ancient practice and the nature of people's response to it appears to be similar through time, including its popularity, the associated tendencies for it to lead to harm for some, and for promoters to use it as a vehicle for fraud. Gambling needs government regulation, which is frequently an enticement to corruption. The bulk of gambling is done by 10 percent or less of the population. Furthermore, information from **problem and pathological gamblers** implies that they account for a disproportionate and sizable percentage of casino revenues. Thus, gambling differs in important ways from many other types of entertainment.

What really do we know about gambling? First, it has appealed to humankind from its earliest history. The first known six-sided dice reportedly date from 2750 B.C. and were found in Mesopotamia made of baked clay. Dice also appear at the same time in the Indus valley.[20] One of the earliest written documents about chance is the "Lament of the Gambler," written in Sanskrit in 1000 B.C. It is "a monologue by a gambler whose gambling obsession has destroyed his happy household and driven away his devoted wife."[21] Apparently, gambling affected some individuals then in much the same way it does today. Dostoyevsky's book, *The Gambler*, also comes to mind, as well as the 1828 novel, *The Gamesters*: "The duties of his profession had been for some time totally neglected" and "the hope of recovering what he had so inconsiderately lost plunged him still deeper in the abyss of ruin."[22] Adam Smith in *Wealth of Nations*, published in 1776, wrote "in the state lotteries the tickets are really not worth the price which is paid by the original subscribers, and yet commonly sell in the market for twenty, thirty, and sometimes forty per cent advance. The vain hope of gaining some of the great prizes is the sole cause of this demand."[23] The willingness to overpay that Smith noted in his time is still evident today. Assume that n people play a simple lottery that taxes t percent of proceeds, charging c per ticket. The value of the lottery is the sum of the probability of receiving the payout multiplied by the amount received and the probability of not receiving the payout multiplied by the nonpayout amount (zero): $V = \frac{1}{n}(nc - tnc) + (1 - \frac{1}{n})0$. The percentage by which the purchaser overpays is given by the extent to which the purchase price exceeds the value $\frac{c}{V} - 1 = \frac{t}{1-t}$. Overpayment reaches 40 percent for a lottery tax rate of 29 percent. Modern buyers of lottery tickets overpay by even more because higher tax rates usually apply to modern state lotteries.

Gambling has other enduring characteristics. For example, games of chance have traditionally been vehicles for fraud, often involving promoter scams and the inability of promoters to make promised payments. The *Encyclopedia Britannica* reports, "Much of the stigma attached to gambling has resulted from the dishonesty of its promoters, and a large proportion of modern legislation is written to control cheating."[24] The 1970 edition states, "As long as there has been gambling, there have been devices, such as dishonest dice and marked cards, to victimize opponents in a social game. . . . Nearly all casinos operate honestly up to a point, but if a plunger, or big bettor, seems likely to achieve a winning damaging to the casino, there is usually a dealer available with skill at prestidigitation equal to that of a stage magician who can manipulate cards or dice so as to recover the losses of the house."[25] Verifying that the odds applied and the payouts made are correct on Internet wagers presents new types of technological challenges.

It is well accepted, therefore, that gambling must be closely watched and regulated by government if it is allowed. The first major casino in

Nevada, El Rancho, was opened in the early 1940s, followed by others.[26] A short time later, in 1955, Nevada had to close a casino for the first time because of its links to organized crime.[27]

Because gambling requires public regulation, those who want favors for licenses or operating conditions must obtain them from government, which creates an enticement to public corruption. The Michigan Attorney General reported in 1995,

> such widespread bribery and corruption, all of which was done by gamblers to influence public officials, that we had indictments and convictions for felonies of the mayor... the superintendent of police... the sheriff of the county... and the prosecutor of the county.... And in the police department of the city at that time... the following numbers of officers were indicted for taking bribes: fifteen inspectors, thirty-nine patrolmen, and two superintendents.[28]

Edwin Edwards, Governor of Louisiana, became an example of the potential for dishonesty when he was found guilty in 2000 of seventeen charges of corruption in connection with extortion and awarding of casino licenses. The book *Bad Bet on the Bayou* by former *Times Picayune* writer Tyler Bridges documents the sad story, including how extremely hard it was to gather the necessary evidence for conviction.

From the policy perspective, the dilemma is this: free, unregulated gambling engenders the need for government oversight, but restricting and regulating it creates permanent incentives and enticements to subversion and government corruption. Sometimes government regulation takes the form of limiting the number of casinos that can operate. Restricting the number of entrants raises the return to financial capital invested in the gambling sector, leading to pressure for gambling expansion. Unregulated, free-entry gambling is allowed virtually nowhere. We must conclude, therefore, that most jurisdictions believe that if **laissez faire** prevailed, gambling could soon reach unacceptable bounds. This would lead to the need for restriction and the cycle starting over.

Another feature of gambling is related to the fact that Americans have many forms of recreation. Gambling is not a major activity for most of the population. Even in Las Vegas, a third of the population recently reported that they had not gambled at all in the past year.[29] Another 60 percent of the population might gamble occasionally, but most gambling is done by the remaining, relatively small percentage of the population. A Minnesota study found that 1 percent of gamblers accounted for 50 percent of the wagers.[30] According to the National Gambling Impact Study Commission, 5 percent of the population accounts for 51 percent of lottery revenues.[31] In an Illinois study, the top 10 percent of riverboat gamblers accounted for 80 percent of revenues.[32]

The use of the word *gaming* instead of gambling is meant by industry promoters to emphasize the recreational element of casinos. However, gambling appears to differ fundamentally from most forms of entertainment. Few suicides have been reported in the press and few family fortunes have been lost due to excessive opera attendance. Pathological bowling and pathological baseball attendance are not recognized disorders in the *Diagnostic and Statistical Manual of Mental Disorders - Fourth Edition (DSM-IV)*, published by the American Psychiatric Association; pathological gambling is. Speaking in 1984, the former Director of Gaming Enforcement for the State of New Jersey told a conference that the success of gambling depended on how well it sold its product.

> That product is not entertainment or recreation or leisure. It's really adrenaline: a biological substance capable of producing excitement – highs – and generated usually by anticipation or expectation of a future event, especially when the outcome of that event is in doubt.[33]

Medical research is still in the beginning stages of learning about the chemistry of gambling, but there does appear to be a bioligical connection. According to a 2002 report,

> Several studies were published last year looking at monetary rewards and dopamine.[34] Money is abstract but to the brain it looks like cocaine, food, sex, or anything a person expects is rewarding.[35]

The great majority of people who gamble develop no problems; however, according to researchers, the dopamine systems of pathological gamblers seem to be vulnerable. "The first time they win, they get a huge dopamine rush that gets imbedded in their memory."[36]

A natural consequence of the demographics and psychological factors of gambling is that casinos and other forms of gambling derive a disproportionate share of their revenues from the losses of problem and pathological gamblers. Whereas an average adult might lose about $300 per year at a nearby casino, problem and pathological gamblers report losing ten and twenty times as much. Lesieur (2002) reports that problem gamblers lose seventeen times more than nonproblem gamblers. The Australian Productivity Commission, which produced the government study *Australia's Gambling Industries* in 1999, reported that problem gamblers "lose around Aus$12,000 each year,"[37] compared with just under Aus$650 for other gamblers," a ratio of 18.5 to 1. A study conducted for the Gambling Impact Study Commission found that 2.4 percent of the population were problem or pathological gamblers among those who lived within 50 miles of a casino.[38] Using these numbers, if the average adult loses $X annually at casinos, and 2.4 of every 100 adults are problem or pathological gamblers who lose $17X per year, then 40.8 percent of casino revenues come from problem and pathological gamblers.[39] The Australian Productivity Commission estimated that 42.3 percent of revenues from gaming machines came from such gamblers, whereas overall, one third of gambling revenues came from problem gamblers.[40] A more recent study conducted in the Australian Capital Territory found that the share of gambling-machine revenue from problem gamblers was 48.2 percent.[41] In the United States, estimates have ranged from a low of 25 percent to as high as 50 percent in some locations.[42]

It would be naive to believe that gambling promoters are unaware of the source of so much of their income. One account

> ... recalls a storekeeper's account of the sales tactics employed by video-gambling machine manufacturers, who "promoted their product to convenience store owners by asserting that if you get one player 'hooked,' he'll pay your taxes. If you get two players 'hooked,' they'll pay your rent."[43]

The public's reaction to information of this type was tested in a 2002 telephone poll of six hundred people over the age of eighteen who were asked, "It has been shown that nearly half the income the Victorian Government receives from poker machines comes from problem gamblers. With this in mind, if a political party promised to reduce the number of poker machines in Victoria by half, from thirty thousand down to fifteen thousand machines, would you be more likely or less likely to vote for this party?" Of those polled, 54 percent said more likely, 12 percent said less likely, and 34 percent said they did not know or it would not affect their vote.[44]

For those and other reasons, gambling-industry promoters generally have had to find a "hook" to sell to hesitant communities the idea of allowing casinos in their cities and towns; jobs and economic benefits are the hook. From the president of a gambling company:

> My message to you today is very simple. Legalized and regulated casino entertainment is a proven job creator, a catalyst for economic rejuvenation, and a proven tourism draw that does not depend on asking taxpayers for handouts in the form of inducements, tax abatements, and infrastructure improvements.[45]

However, from the *World Book Encyclopedia* in the same year:

> The employment increases resulting from most gambling operations are illusory. The purchasers of lottery tickets and the patrons of racetracks are almost exclusively local residents. The money they wager comes from the local economy, and each dollar they spend on a lottery ticket or lose on a horse is a dollar they can no longer spend at a store or restaurant. This situation benefits the gambling operations but works to the detriment of other kinds of business.[46]

Can both characterizations be accurate? In some cases, casinos have become resort destinations, attracting patrons from great distances as in Las Vegas, which has world-class entertainment and a vacation atmosphere. However, in most cases, regional casinos are nothing more than "convenience" gambling to nearby residents. "Evidence shows that most gambling at riverboat casinos is from regional, or day-trip, patrons,"according to the National Gambling Impact Study Commission.[47] In a study of Illinois casinos,[48] 75 percent of patrons came from within 35 miles, and only a few percent from more than 100 miles.

The bottom line returns us once again to costs and benefits. There would be little or no concern over how much gambling there is – any more than government cares about golf or movie attendance – if the consequences of gambling were confined to those who chose to gamble. Unfortunately, this is not true. Bankruptcy and suicide, for example, are both examples of casino-industry consequences that impose costs on more than just the gambler.

FREEDOM, EXTERNALITIES, AND PUBLIC POLICY

SUMMARY. Here, we state the rationale for government to regulate or restrict an activity. The burden of proof is on those who would restrict an activity to show that its unrestricted existence creates more costs than benefits.

We have learned a number of interesting facts about gambling, but still are confronted by our original questions. Why did earlier generations want to prohibit games of chance "forever" and "under any pretense, or for any purpose whatever"? Were they biased? Were they misinformed? Did they misunderstand gambling? Did they restrict personal freedom unjustly?

In the remainder of this book, we attempt to understand the policy questions about gambling by taking an objective and comprehensive look at the economics of gambling, identifying and dispelling a number of misunderstandings about its economic effects, and providing a structure for discourse that has not been evident to this point.

How do freedom and externalities play a role in setting public policy in this recently expanded sector? We accept the view that personal liberty – in this case, the right of firms to offer casino gambling and the right of the people to engage in it – should not be curtailed without cause.

This is the "freedom" contribution to the debate. It places the burden of proof on those who would argue that gambling should be prohibited, even if the status quo already prohibits gambling. They must show that the social costs of casinos exceed their social benefits, and that the costs include those imposed on the nongambler by the gambler's choice to gamble.

The social benefits of casinos are conceptually similar in principle to the benefits from other industries, especially entertainment industries (explained in detail in Chapter 6). However, gambling is not just another entertainment industry. The Australian Productivity Commission, cited previously, asked this question in the section titled, "Just Another Industry?": "We don't seek to assess the costs and benefits of most other industries, so why do we do so for these industries?"[49] Despite claims by some who speak for the industry that there is little that is special, the commission reported that "Even within the gambling industries themselves, many of those with whom the Commission met accepted that their industry was indeed 'special'; in the words of one senior executive, gambling was seen as a 'questionable pleasure.'"[50] An economist would say that gambling is the source of negative externalities. A *negative externality* is a harmful effect that a firm or **household's** choices have on other firms or households and that does not operate through market prices. If my decision to dump my waste pollutes your drinking water, that is a negative externality. If my decision to water my lawn bids up the price of water, which you also purchase for your lawn, that is not an externality because the effect on you, although adverse, operated through market prices. It is in the nature of externalities that the causing agent does not take them properly into account when making decisions because, although they may affect others, they do not affect the agent's own profits or utility. In the case of casinos, if an increase in the number of pathological gamblers leads to social problems whose costs must be borne by those other than the casinos, there is an externality. If the presence of casinos creates conditions that lead to increase in crime that must be dealt with through money provided by public taxes, then that is an externality. Casinos get the profits; society gets negative externalities.

The contribution of externalities to the discussion, therefore, is to emphasize that one must assess the social costs, including externality costs, and compare them to the benefits of the gambling industry.

Public policy must be able to quantify and evaluate the impact of gambling by knowing how to perform the cost–benefit review without manipulation or mistake, and make the appropriate decisions in light of the common good. The remainder of this book provides the first conceptually complete cost–benefit assessment of an industry that was absent from the economy for most of the twentieth century and was reintroduced largely in the past dozen years. Casino gambling offers the researcher, scholar, and social observer an unusual experiment that is rarely available: the opportunity to observe the effects of an activity where the alternatives range from complete prohibition to free licensing. Prohibition and licensing are both feasible choices because both have been done: we successfully practiced prohibition for most of the twentieth century, and casinos operate in many places today. Why we should prefer one choice over the other is the subject of the rest of the book. In the next chapter, we review the incentives and social forces that play a role in the spread of gambling.

3 Agents and Incentives

Money is like fire, an element as little troubled by moralizing as earth, air, and water.

Lewis Lapham, American essayist (1988)

CHAPTER SUMMARY. In this chapter, we examine the social and economic forces that led the "players" in the casino drama – proponents, players, government, and opponents – to act as they did. The decision-making process has not always operated as it should. The main points of failure are lack of knowledge and good information, and the choice of the players to consider only a subset of the benefits and costs. There must be an informed agent that makes decisions based on all benefits and costs, however, if the social good is to be enhanced, and this must be the government in cases where externalities are present.

THE PROPONENTS

SUMMARY. Economics teaches that above-normal profit is an inducement for businesses to enter the market. Enormous casino profits, frequently based on government-granted monopoly rights, create pressure for gambling expansion that often finds expression in inappropriate attempts to influence government. Pressure for expansion will persist as long as entry is limited in any way so that casinos earn above-normal profits.

Owners

The evidence of tremendous casino profits is not difficult to find. In February 1993, The *New York Times* reported the success of investors in Argosy Gaming Company, which "has a monopoly on casino gaming in the St. Louis area through its Alton Belle riverboat."[51] According to the *Times*, "the insiders invested $201,000 for their stock, or roughly a penny a share. In the offering, they sold 8.3 percent of their shares for $31.7 million. Add in the $13 million of dividends they have received, and their investment looks pretty good." Finishing the story by doing the arithmetic, we find that $201 thousand had became $395 million in less than three years. "The insiders, including Jimmy Connors, the tennis star," had cleaned up. The message was not difficult to understand: If investors moved fast enough and played their cards right, there was big money to be had.

High profits provide incentives that sometimes seem to rival forces of nature in their intensity and ability to induce new promoters to enter the market. During a gold rush, the way to riches requires staking a claim. What else is required? Knowledge and skill, perhaps, but these are not the main requirements. It is unlikely, for example, that the investors in the Joliet Empress were seventy three times smarter than the average businessperson (see box); neither is developing a superior product a requirement. Gambling at expansion casinos is similar to gambling elsewhere. Rather, the main impediment in most states to a casino of one's own is the government license to a regional monopoly, much like the crown monopolies given to favored courtiers in the Elizabethan Era. High profits that reward socially valuable risk-taking, superior innovation, business

---

Incentives

In 1989, the state of Illinois was eager to enter the casino business. Iowa legislation that year allowed low-stakes casino riverboats on the Mississippi River. Not wanting to be left out, the Illinois legislature quickly followed suit with the Riverboat Gambling Act, effective February 7, 1990, allowing riverboats in Illinois. By December 1993, nine well-connected Illinois businessmen were feeling pretty good. They had put up the original money to finance the Joliet Empress casino riverboat in Joliet, which began operation in June 1992. Joliet is a nearby suburb of Chicago with access to a population in neighboring areas of more than 6.5 million. After just eighteen months, their starting investment, averaging $778 thousand each, had produced profits of $87.1 million.[1] Dividing the take nine ways, this translated into more than $1 million of profits per investor ... *every two months*! A typical stock-market return over the same length of time would have been 16 or 17 percent; 1,244 percent was more than seventy-three times better!

[1] Michael Hawthorne, statehouse reporter, "Report on Casino's Fortunes Shows Why Others Seek Boat of Their Own," The *News Gazette*, Champaign–Urbana, IL, May 1, 1994.

---

expertise, and the like are unobjectionable. However, there are other sources of profit; as the *Times* astutely noted, "In any business, a regional monopoly can be a very profitable thing."

Casino companies respond as expected. In 1996, midwestern newspapers, including the front page of the *Chicago Tribune*, reported that an out-of-state casino company offered to pay $20 million to two Illinois government insiders if they could obtain a state license for the casino.[52] One insider was a golfing buddy of the president of the state Senate, the other was a friend of the state Speaker of the House. Given the profits that earlier casinos had reaped, $20 million was a small price, even considering the additional lobbying effort that would add to the cost.

Rather than reflecting a sudden change in public attitudes about gambling, the expansion of casinos reflected more the coming together of events, leading to unintended market forces and incentives that emerged following the passage of the Indian Gaming Regulatory Act (IGRA) of 1988. No single agent – the proponents, the players, the opponents, or even the government – controlled the process. To a large extent, each was reacting to external forces that their collective behavior loosed.

According to Robert Goodman, professor of environmental design at Hampshire College, Massachusetts, in his study *Legalized Gambling as a Strategy for Economic Development*,

> There is no popularly-based movement for the expansion of legalized gambling; expansion has resulted from the efforts of gambling industry companies and public officials. There are no state gambling plans. Gambling has grown in an ad hoc, "copycat" manner as states follow each other's leads, responding to revenue shortfalls and the fear that neighboring states or Indian tribes will siphon off their gambling dollars.[53]

Goodman ends with a warning, "Once gambling ventures are legalized and governments become dependent on their revenues, the future form and spread of gambling within a state become extremely difficult to control."[54] An example is furnished by an incident in Missouri after the Missouri attorney general filed charges of perjury to regulators against members of the gambling industry. In response, legislation was created that would do away with the attorney general's authority to bring criminal cases related to gambling.[55] When a state Court of Appeals ruling[56] recognized the attorney general's jurisdiction to prosecute criminal gambling cases, a bill was put to the legislature for vote later *in the same day* to prevent him from exercising this authority. The approach taken, and the use to which influence on the legislature was put, makes this epsiode revealing. Missouri's legislators wisely turned down the bill.

Casino licensing can be treated in two ways. One model – followed by Nevada, Atlantic City, Deadwood (South Dakota), and the Gulf Coast of Mississippi – is to set standards for casino operators and effectively let all comers enter the market who meet licensing standards. The result of adopting this approach is that casinos will continue to enter the market until they have competed the profit rate down to ordinary business levels. Thereafter, there is less incentive for more casinos to enter; for example, the number of Atlantic City casinos has been relatively stable at twelve for many years.

The second regional licensing model – followed by states such as Minnesota, Illinois, and Michigan – is to license individual casino operators in separate geographical areas. This method creates regional monopolies and results in monopoly rates of profit. The examples at the beginning of this chapter showed how high such profits can be. With competition and entry limited by government, the fortunate owner of a casino monopoly stands to earn a very good return indeed. Profits earned in one market can then be used to influence the necessary legislation to expand in others. We do not mention this because successful businesses acquiring capital to expand is a cause for complaint; expanding business is a cause for complaint only if the business leads to more losses than gains for society, which is the subject of a cost–benefit analysis. Rather, we mention it because it is a predictable process and part of the resulting dynamic of the casino industry.

An example illustrates this point. As part of a day-long session organized by the government of an eastern state to discuss the pros and cons of gambling, I was able to meet the individual behind the proposal to expand gambling in the state. His father and he had worked on the construction of a riverboat for a project that was never completed at its original site. They bought the boat and floated it to the state of Mississippi, where they finished it and operated it as the first casino in its new home. They did well. A few years later, the son owned a racetrack in the East, had business operations in Nevada, and wanted to add slot machines to expand the gambling available at his racetrack. His offer was that he would write an up-front check to the state for $10 million in exchange for the permissions he sought. There was little doubt that he singlehandedly had the financial ability to make such a payment. Not bad for a man in his thirties who had started out in construction a short time earlier!

The response of local business owners to the arrival of outsiders with plans for casino projects mirrors the "fight or flight" dichotomy known in the animal world: they can either oppose the casino to retain the business they already have or, failing that, get a casino of their own to compete on equal footing. "If you can't beat 'em, join 'em" makes perfect economic sense. Consider the case of the Richmond, Virginia, restaurant owner who contacted me when a proposal to create a casino riverboat was presented to the state legislature. It was scheduled to dock near the downtown area not far from his successful multistory restaurant, which had been lovingly converted from an old and historic tobacco warehouse into a well-known and popular eatery. He understood his options well. The casino riverboat would be able to offer food and drinks in addition to gambling, but he could legally offer only food and drinks. Faced with unequal ability to compete, his restaurant would be at risk of becoming a victim like so many others that lost large portions of their business to a neighboring casino. His choice was to oppose the casino, but he made it clear that – although he did not like gambling – if a casino were approved, he would have little choice but to seek a license of his own to protect his livelihood.

Lobbyists

With so much money available to it, the industry would be foolish not to use its resources in lobbying and public-relations efforts. Lobbying can be both defensive and offensive. The American Gaming Association (AGA) was established to represent the industry. It selected Nevadan Frank Fahrenkopf, formerly associated with the leadership of the Republican National Committee, as its chairman. Under the AGA's leadership, the gambling industry successfully lobbied Congress to limit the subpoena power of the National Gambling Impact Study Commission (Public Law 104–169) to cover only documents and not individuals. This was a major coup for the industry because much more would have been learned from the ability to interview people.

According to Goodman, during the early 1990s the gambling industry quickly established itself as the most powerful lobbying group in many state legislatures.[57] In Illinois, a former governor, former attorney general, former director of the state police, two former U.S. attorneys, a former Chicago mayor, a former Senate president, and former House majority leader, and countless former state legislators have all been lobbyists for the gambling industry.[58] Business law professor John Kindt reported that in Virginia in 1995, casino proponents hired *forty-eight lobbyists* representing virtually every lobbying firm in the capital to prevent antigambling groups from hiring lobbyists to compete.[59] The industry spent between $18,000 and $24,400 per day ($820,000–$1.1 million total) during the forty-five-day legislative session in its attempt to legalize riverboat casinos. In Texas, seventy-four lobbyists were hired at one time for an expansion push.[60] In Louisiana, critics complained, "Gambling is going to supersede business, trial lawyers, the unions, and teachers as the lobbying force in the Louisiana legislature for the foreseeable future. They will be the 800-pound gorilla."[61] In the carefully selected words of a president pro tem of the senate for a large state (not Illinois, Virginia, or Louisiana) east of the Mississippi, "They own the legislature."[62]

The numbers tell the story. Between 1991 and 1996, the industry paid $4.5 million in national campaigns.[63] During the same period, it paid more than $100 million in donations to state legislators and lobbying fees.[64] The newly formed AGA paid its director an estimated $750 thousand salary[65] in contrast to the National Coalition Against Legalized Gambling, whose *entire* budget, raised primarily from donations, was $140 thousand.[66] The U.S. General Accounting Office (GAO) reported that total gambling donations to federal candidates and political parties rose from $1.1 million in 1992 to $5.7 million six years later, an increase of more than 400 percent.[67] In 2000, $13.4 million was spent lobbying in Washington alone.[68] In South Carolina, more than $3 million was spent by the industry to defeat Governor David Beasley, who "tried to ban South Carolina's $2.2 billion video gambling industry because it was the right thing to do, even though it cost him a second term," the press reported. "Hopefully, I can be a standing witness to any political figure in the nation to say it's worth risking it all for something you truly believe in.... I don't think there's any question that had we not touched video poker it would be elementary; we'd be here in a second administration," he was quoted as saying in the *Charlotte Observer*.[69]

The amount of gambling money brought to bear is impressive. The threat is that it will drown out the voices of ordinary citizens. In the words of Goodman,

> It is simply an issue of an industry that can buy politicians, that has more power than most industries, that operates on a national and international level, and is trying to expand gambling to everywhere in the United States. It is as simple as that.[70]

States such as Florida and Hawaii have been the ongoing focus of casino interests for obvious reason of the tourists that each attracts. Existing state interests recognize that because their states already attract tourists, casinos need Florida or Hawaii more than Florida or Hawaii needs casinos. Casino proposals have been rejected in a number of votes taken in the 1980s and 1990s. Unable to access land-based casinos in the 1980s, the first "boat to nowhere"[71] entered Florida in 1982, with others following in 1988, 1990, 1993, 1994, and 1995. In 1994, the gambling industry paid $16.5 million in an unsuccessful campaign to persuade the Florida legislature to legalize land-based casinos in the state. Whereas the gambling industry would be rewarded handsomely by its profits were it to win, opponents generally gain nothing by opposition except preservation of the status quo. It is true that an existing firm might sometimes contribute to public education – Disney World contributed in the case of Florida, for example – but the amounts are generally much smaller. In Florida, millions of dollars were pitted against fewer than $800 thousand – hardly a balance.

From contests played out in Missouri, Florida, Hawaii, Iowa, Virginia, Ohio, West Virginia, Pennsylvania, and other states, citizen groups worked from the rule of thumb that gambling interests would lose in their bids if they did not outspend their opponents by at least $75 to $1.[72] In Florida, for example, casinos were voted down, but the industry spent $16.5 million, which was only twenty times greater than its opponents. Even factors of 75:1 were not always enough. In Iowa, Casino America of Biloxi spent nearly $477 thousand – $73 for every vote it ultimately received – in its unsuccessful attempt to gain voter approval for a casino in Dallas County. It outspent opponents (who spent a total of $3,126) by more than 152:1.[73] Fortunately for gambling interests, they are often able to outspend their opposition by even greater factors. Consider the following account from California: "California tribes have been flooding the airwaves with TV and radio commercials as spending in the battle over Indian gambling topped $20.7 million just weeks before voters will decide the issue. The tribes had spent a total of $20.7 million by February 19, the close of the last reporting period, while the opposition campaign spent $3,783 by the same date."[74]

There also appears to be a one-way "ratchet effect" at work. In cases when the gambling industry loses a popular vote, it is often able to have additional votes taken a short time later. In Waterloo, Iowa, for example, casino gambling was rejected by voters on May 17, 1994. The issue reappeared for another vote on September 27, just four months later![75] In Missouri, voters turned down riverboat casinos in April 1994, only to find that gambling interests were able to have another vote placed before them in November. This time, gambling interests spent more than $7 million, compared to less than $600 thousand in the first campaign. The industry won the second vote. Six months later, no further vote was taken. If the industry had lost a second time, it is an interesting question whether Missouri would have gone eight years without another casino vote, as has been the case. In Ohio, "voters twice rejected, by about a 2:1 margin, proposed constitutional amendments to allow some form of casino (land-based or riverboat) in Ohio."[76] Other examples of closely repeated attempts are easily found.

Broadly speaking, these outcomes are predictable based on the money at stake and the resources available to gambling interests. As long as there is above-normal profit, there will be pressure for new casinos. The range of ways in which money can be used to acquire licenses will be limited only by the creativity of the human mind.

According to Nat Helms, a former high-ranking participant in the gambling industry's campaign to bring casinos to Missouri, "Because of the unlimited money it generates, gambling also generates unlimited potential for abuse.... I have never met anybody who could resist a full-court press by the gambling industry."[77] The concern, voiced by Congressman Frank R. Wolf, that the "flood of casino money into the states" will "drown out the voices of ordinary citizens and overwhelm state public officials"[78] is a real one, although to date it has not been universally borne out. Three of the fifty states (i.e., Hawaii, Tennessee, and Utah) have no legalized gambling, and further expansion has effectively been stopped in others. At this writing, however, another effort for casinos is being mounted in Hawaii.

A second ever-present threat, corruption, is exemplified in the case of Governor Edwards of Lousiana.

> Former Gov. Edwin Edwards was convicted today of extorting hundreds of thousands of dollars from businessmen applying for riverboat casino licenses. The former four-term governor was convicted of seventeen racketeering and fraud counts and acquitted on nine counts. His son, Stephen, was also found guilty of racketeering, convicted on eighteen counts and acquitted on five.[79]

In Missouri, casino lawyer, Michael Lazaroff, who pleaded guilty in federal court to multiple felonies, including misuse of more than $800 thousand, described his relationship with former Missouri Gaming Commission Chairman Robert Wolfson as "an illicit and 'tacit underttanding' that each would provide the other with useful information."[80] The casino executives involved challenged the Missouri Gaming Commission's investigative authority and refused to honor commission subpoenas.[81] Gambling requires government oversight, oversight creates the motive for periodic corruption, and large amounts of money create the means.[82]

American Indians

In 1992, the Mashantucket Pequot Indian tribe of Connecticut opened the Foxwoods Resort Casino in New London County, Connecticut.

A regional monopoly, Foxwoods was the only casino in all of New England. By 1995, it was the largest and most successful casino in the world, with annual revenues of more than $800 million and a payroll of $242 million.[83] A similar success story was playing out with the Mdewakanton Dakota tribe of Shakopee, Minnesota, a suburb only 15 miles from downtown Minneapolis. The casino is, therefore, the closest casino to the millions of adults who live in the Minneapolis–St. Paul metropolitan area. From the time of the casino's opening in 1992 to 1997, the enterprise converted 150 tribal members to millionaires through the distribution to its members each year of hundreds of thousands of dollars in casino profits.[84]

Although most Indian casinos are not of the Foxwoods or Mdewakanton Sioux "type" (meaning that most do not enrich their purveyors so copiously), casino owners and proponents both like to portray casinos as economic development tools. The truth of this claim depends on whether one considers net benefits to everyone or looks just at net benefits to a subset of individuals. The owner of a casino certainly benefits, as would a tribe that owns a casino, although experience shows that even the latter may not be true. Some casinos have been helpful to their tribes and/or communities; some have not. Whether the entire community that has the casino benefits depends on the size of the community relative to the casino's market. The fundamental reality is that within their market, casinos neither create nor destroy jobs. It is true that if unemployment is present, a new business might have the temporary effect of reducing unemployment below the level it otherwise would have taken; however, in the long run, employment and unemployment are determined by overall business conditions and macroeconomic policy. A region can have full employment with or without casinos. (Chapters Four and Five focus on issues of estimating and evaluating jobs and development impact.)

Expansion of the casino sector comes at the expense of other sectors whose revenues are diminished when they are diverted to the casinos. There is nothing unusual or wrong with shrinking other sectors – it is a normal feature of a flexible economy that is responsive to the changing desires of its consumers – but it does mean that the geographical extent of the casino market is the key to understanding its local effects. In the case of Foxwoods, the effective market is much of New England. Neighboring states and areas lose revenues to Foxwoods. The Mdewakanton Sioux casino serves a smaller area, but it just happens to include the largest metropolitan area in Minnesota and the neighboring states. Losses from Minneapolis–St. Paul are Shakopee's gain. Neither Foxwoods nor the Shakopee casino represent job creation for their markets, meaning the area from which clients come.

Indian owners of casinos are concerned about casino revenues and profitability. If the market area includes large numbers of people and major cities, a well-run casino will prosper; otherwise, it will not. This means that profitability to the owner and the effect of a casino on economic development to the local area are separate questions.

Despite the prominent examples just cited, most Indian casinos have *not* been particularly beneficial to their tribe or to the surrounding local area. Casinos like Foxwoods that are hugely profitable shift economic activity into the local area because they draw from a large population and their geographical market is large relative to the local area. Casinos like the Shakopee casino are profitable because they draw from markets with large populations, but have little or no effect on economic development in the surrounding areas because the surrounding areas (in Shakopee's case, the St. Paul–Minneapolis metropolitan area) include their markets. The third possibility includes casinos that are not particularly successful because their geographic market does not include a large population. They have little or no economic impact on development in their local area because the local area includes the casino's market.

The Apache Gold Casino of the San Carlos Apache Tribe, established in 1993 to "enable the San Carlos Apache Tribe to give a better quality of life to its tribal members" according to a plaque displayed outside the casino, did not stop the increase in reservation unemployment from 42 percent in 1991 to 58 percent in 1997, for example, nor did it prevent the number of tribal members receiving welfare from jumping 20 percent. "We get no help from the casino, no money, nothing," according to one lifelong resident of San Carlos.[85] An Associated Press (AP) computer analysis of federal unemployment, poverty, and public-assistance records indicated that the majority of American Indians has benefited little from casinos. Of the more than 130 tribes with casinos, "a few near major population centers have thrived while most others make just enough to cover the bills," according to the AP analysis. This agrees with what we would expect from the previous analysis.[86]

A Minnesota study also questioned the extent to which casinos had generally benefited the rural counties where most of them resided. Among the concerns of residents, for example, was the complaint that business volume fell at restaurants located within a 30-mile radius of casinos with food service.[87] Survey respondents estimated that the business drop was 20 to 50 percent. The numbers are similar to other experiences reported frequently in the press.[88] The 1990 Clark County [Las Vegas] Residents Study, conducted in conjunction with the Las Vegas Convention & Visitors Authority, asked residents who gambled in casinos if they usually ate in a restaurant outside the casino or in the casino itself. Only 18 percent reported that they ate in a restaurant outside the casino; the rest either ate at the casino (73 percent), did not eat (7 percent), or were unsure. Lack of general benefits to rural counties is consistent with the finding that the market for rural Indian casinos is commonly no larger than the host county plus part of the neighboring county or counties. Casino revenue, therefore, must come at the expense of other local sectors. The same is true of casinos in large metropolitan areas that draw patrons from nearby, although these casinos would be many times more profitable to their owners.

According to the IGRA of 1988,[89]

Class III gaming activities shall be lawful on Indian lands only if such activities are–

(A) authorized by an ordinance or resolution that–
    (i) is adopted by the governing body of the Indian tribe having jurisdiction over such lands,
    (ii) meets the requirements of subsection (b)[90] of this section, and
    (iii) is approved by the Chairman,

(B) located in a State that permits such gaming for any purpose by any person, organization, or entity, and

(C) conducted in conformance with a Tribal-State compact entered into by the Indian tribe and the State under paragraph (3) that is in effect.

In other words, Indian tribes must be sanctioned to operate **Class III gambling** facilities under a state-agreed compact if the state allows such gambling elsewhere in the state. It follows that a profitable Indian casino requires that the Indian promoters

- be a federally recognized tribe
- have land near a major population center
- be in a state that allows some form of Class III gambling

Although most prospectors do not strike it rich in a gold rush, the possibility of riches is enough to attract others. We expect, therefore, an assault on all three of these barriers to an Indian casino. What *should* constitute a valid tribe and how tribal land *should* properly be acquired if it is desired near a large population center are not intrinsically gambling-related questions. They become gambling-related matters, however, when incentives provided by casinos interact with them.

In 2000, sixteen states had tribal-state gambling compacts.[91] The first step to gaining such a compact and a casino is to be a recognized tribe. From 1960 to 1979, the Bureau of Indian Affairs (BIA) recognized eleven new Indian tribes. For this twenty-year period, the average number of recognitions was 0.55 tribe per year, or about one new tribe every two years.[92] In the 1980s, tribal interest in owning casinos rose, and the IGRA was passed on October 17, 1988. The December 29 *Federal Register* of the same year listed 309 federally recognized tribal entities in the lower forty-eight states, an increase of thirty-two – or 3.6 new recognitions per year. The noticeable upsurge in tribal recognitions continued in the 1990s at a reduced rate, but still 3.5 times the rate of the 1960s and 1970s. By March 13, 2000, the *Federal Register* list was up to 331 tribes, and 199 cases of the 210 new petitions received from 1978 to 2001 were in

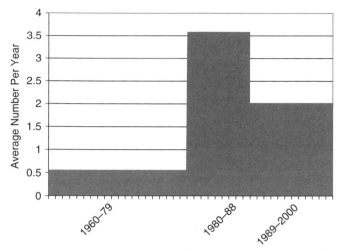

Figure 3.1. Tribal Entities Recognized per Year by the Bureau of Indian Affairs

some status other than resolved. Figure 3.1 shows the average number of recognitions per year for the three periods 1960–79, 1980–88, and 1989–2000.

The definition of what currently constitutes an Indian tribe is not consistently well defined. According to IGRA, the term *Indian tribe* means

> any Indian tribe, band, nation, or other organized group or community of Indians which
>
> (A) is recognized as eligible by the Secretary for the special programs and services provided by the United States to Indians because of their status as Indians, and
>
> (B) is recognized as possessing powers of self-government.

In at least one case, the "tribe" requesting recognition consisted of the descendants of a single individual, William Sherman, who died in Connecticut in 1875 and was listed in the 1880 census as an "Indian," but was identified in the 1850 and 1860 censuses as non-Indian. The "tribe's" land at one point dwindled to Sherman's quarter-acre lot in Trumball, Connecticut. According to the news account, "Quiet Hawk [the leader of the tribe, who was born Aurelius Piper, but began calling himself by the

Indian name] and many of his followers appear more African American than Native American, and he and others, including the Connecticut NAACP, have suggested that racial prejudice has played a role in opposition to his efforts."[93] Were Quiet Hawk's 324 followers to be recognized, "their preferred site [for a casino] would be on the Bridgeport [CT] waterfront – only 55 miles from New York City, and even nearer to the city's wealthy northern suburbs. Profits, gambling experts say, would be at least $1 million a day."[94] In its 2002 Special Report on Indian casinos,[95] *Time* reported the case of Maryann Martin, a one-person tribe, who was raised in an African American home and

> knew little of her Indian ancestry until 1986, when at age twenty-two she learned that her mother had been the last surviving member of the Augustine band of Cahuilla Mission Indians.

In 1991, the BIA conferred Maryann and her two brothers with tribal status. After the brothers were killed in street shootings, she became the sole member of the "tribe," which allowed her to develop and manage a casino.

In addition to tribal recognition, those wanting an American Indian casino must have land, and all land is not created equal. Rather than the casino economically developing whatever tract it occupies, land in proximity to a large population center – where reservations often are not located – is sought. According to IGRA, the term *Indian lands* means

(A) all lands within the limits of any Indian reservation; and

(B) any lands title to which is either held in trust by the United States for the benefit of any Indian tribe or individual or held by any Indian tribe or individual subject to restriction by the United States against alienation and over which an Indian tribe exercises governmental power.

Because reservation land is not always situated the best to attract the desired clientele, many Indian tribes have tried to acquire land to put in trust upon which to build their casinos. This land is generally selected with an eye to the urban and more populated market. New York was the target population in the previous example, but many areas such as Detroit, Milwaukee, San Francisco, and east-central Illinois have been the target of legal maneuverings. A 2001 AP story reported,

> Circumventing the Interior Department and the California governor, a congressman quietly pushed through a new law for a landless Indian tribe in his district that could open the San Francisco Bay area to Las Vegas–style gambling.... Miller's amendment places a 10-acre parcel that is a 25-minute drive from downtown San Francisco into reservation status for the Lytton Randeria band of 220 Indians. President Clinton signed the act containing the amendment in December.... Gambling opponents didn't spot Miller's [three-sentence] provision.[96]

The Miami Indians participated in ceding midwestern lands in Ohio and other states in the 1795 Treaty of Greenville and the 1805 Treaty of Grouseland with William Henry Harrison, later the nation's ninth president. In 1818, Illinois became a state. By 1846, the Miami were settled in Kansas, later moving to the northeastern corner of Oklahoma. In June 2000, 195 years later, the tribe decided that Illinois did not have title to the Wabash watershed serving 2.6 million acres in Illinois because the Miami had never ceded it; they sued to reclaim this territory in Illinois. Many question whether the Miami ever had any claim to the Wabash watershed. Legal experts may have to answer this question: If purchase was invalid and right of conquest and right of occupation do not grant valid title, then how do the Miami themselves prove valid title?

Illinois has had riverboat casinos since 1991 and has no Indian tribes. From the Indians' point of view, the land would be ideal for a casino and various spokespersons indicated the tribe would want to talk about a casino – although their true desire, they allege, is simply to reclaim the land that they avow is theirs. The suit alleged that the government violated the two treaties when it sold the Illinois land to settlers. This raises interesting legal questions because the treaties predate the federal grant of land to form the state of Illinois, under whose jurisdiction the current landowners reside.

The Indian Gaming Regulatory Act of 1988

The fact that the Indian Gaming Regulatory Act of 1988 was the turning point for expansion of Indian casinos all across the nation is significant in light of its legislative history. The stated purpose of the Act was to regulate Class III gambling on Indian lands for the benefit of Indian tribes, but its requirement of the need for a state compact also was intended to give states greater control over the gambling within their borders. In this respect, it had the opposite effect,[2] demonstrating Friedman's Law, named for Nobel Laureate economist, Milton Friedman. Friedman's Law says to write down the purposes of a piece of federal legislation; then write down the exact opposite of the purpose. The law will often more nearly accomplish the exact opposite than its original purpose.

[2] For example, the state of Ohio, citing the National Gambling Impact Study Commission's staff report, was aware of and so noted in its legislative report the fact that, in practice, the Secretary of the Interior under certain conditions may authorize an Indian casino even if the state opposes it. Committee to Study the Impact of Gambling in Ohio (2002), p. 44.

The story of the IGRA began with Indian bingo halls. According to Greene, the first was on the Seminole reservation in Florida.[97] The idea of bingo parlors spread to other states and, as tribes began to offer cash prizes too large for state laws, the states began to object.[98] Disputes between tribes and the states ended in court, culminating in California v. Cabazon Band of Mission Indians (480 U.S. 202 [1987]), in which the Supreme Court ruled that Indian sovereignty prevented states from regulating gambling on Indian land if it is permitted elsewhere in the state. To provide a structure for the process, and partly to rebalance the respective power of the states relative to the tribes, Congress passed the IGRA at the end of the following year. A state-tribal compact establishes the kinds of gambling that can be offered, the size of the casinos, betting limits, and security issues, and allows for revenue sharing with the state if applicable. Under IGRA, Indian tribes are exempt from the

Freedom of Information Act and do not have to report revenues or other financial information. Furthermore, tribes do not have to pay state or federal taxes on their gambling profits.

As would be expected, there are continuing conflicts over jurisdiction. States such as Florida have resisted being forced to sign compacts when the state allows no casino gambling elsewhere, even though Florida is home to "boat-to-nowhere" casinos that travel to international waters to gamble and then return to port. In Seminole Tribe of Florida v. Florida (116 S. Ct. 1114 [1996]), the Supreme Court ruled that the state's sovereign immunity prevented the tribe from forcing the state to have compacts. In Florida, California, and Washington, Indian tribes have opened Class III casinos without compacts. In other states, such as New Mexico, Indian tribes that began casino gambling illegally have been able to apply pressure on states to forge compacts. The history of Indian sovereignty and how it is treated in the courts has moved from one extreme to the other. Now that sovereignty issues matter to non-Indian and Indian casinos, it is likely that the last legal word on state versus Indian tribal sovereignty has not been heard.

THE PLAYERS

SUMMARY. Participation and interest in gambling is uneven. Although most individuals might enjoy it occasionally, they would barely miss it. The losses of a tiny percentage of gamblers account for a greatly disproportionate share of gambling revenues. Among this group are problem and pathological gamblers.

Whereas casino owners want profits, driving them to convince communities to give them places to make them, players are a more mixed group. Approximately one third of the population consists of nonbettors, meaning that if you ask, "Have you gambled in the past twelve months?," the answer will be "No." Even in Clark County, Nevada – home to Las Vegas, the gambling capital of the nation – the residents survey found that 33 percent did not gamble[99]; 46 percent gambled in casinos

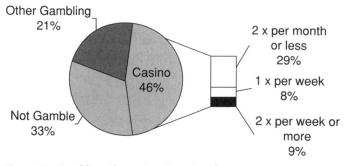

Figure 3.2. Gambling Shares: Las Vegas Residents

(69 percent of those who gambled) and 21 percent did other types of gambling. Breaking down further the number who gambled in casinos, 28 percent gambled twice per month or less, 8 percent once per week, and only 9 percent gambled twice per week or more. Figure 3.2 shows these percentages.

Based on their share of total gambling, the majority of the population is relatively indifferent to gambling. As noted in Chapter 2, one third do not gamble. Another 50 to 60 percent could be termed light bettors, frequenting casinos occasionally and not losing much. It is the remaining 10 percent who are heavy bettors, who are in the casinos frequently, and who account for the bulk of casino revenues. According to studies, the top 10 percent of gamblers account for approximately 61 percent of casino revenues in table games and gaming machines.[100] In lottery play, the top 10 percent accounted for 65 percent, according to Clotfelder and Cook's study of the same issue.[101] If 33 percent of the population does not gamble, the next 57 percent provides 39 percent of casino revenues, and the top 10 percent provides 61 percent, then for every $100 gambled by an average member of the first two groups, the heavy-bettor group must spend $1,408. The nonbettor, of course, would contribute zero percent of the total gambled by a group of three such gamblers, whereas the heavy bettor would contribute 90 percent.

For the third of the population that does not gamble or that gambles infrequently and who are unaware of the magnitude of gambling's social

---

Risk

Technical rock climbing, hang gliding, skydiving, and small-plane flying are risky activities. They are particularly unforgiving of errors in equipment, judgment, or execution, and people are regularly killed in each activity. Popular singer John Denver, flying his small experimental one-man aircraft, died in a crash due to running out of gas. John F. Kennedy, Jr., son of the former president, killed himself, his wife, and his sister-in-law in a crash off Martha's Vineyard, Massachusetts, caused by "spatial disorientation." Many technical climbers climb without aid (ropes are an aid; even the use of chalk to enhance grip – in some climbers' views – is a climbing aid). In all of these cases, Americans question whether it is the proper role for government – the rest of us – to interefere with these choices simply because they are dangerous or harmful.

---

costs, there is little reason to object to gambling by others. Even after a choice is known to be harmful, as in the case of smoking, there has been a reluctance to interfere until it was widely understood that significant costs were imposed on the public. It was increased awareness that led to the mega-lawsuits against the tobacco industry in the 1990s. Thus, unless Americans are aware of and believe that the social costs of casinos are high for themselves (including those who do not gamble), the votes of the uninformed, the indifferent, and the gambling enthusiasts will be to allow freedom of choice.

THE GOVERNMENT

SUMMARY. Government decision-makers need good information to make informed decisions. Unbiased information is difficult for them to identify and obtain. Often it is drowned out by a snowstorm of industry-sponsored claims and studies. Some participants in government have been co-opted by gambling industry money and appear no longer open to unbiased information.

The arbiter of most social issues that require expertise, wisdom, and judgment is government. Many city and state officials are sincerely interested in finding ways to develop the economies of their communities and states. They are ardent in their desire to do what is best for their constituents, including lessening for them the burdensome commitments to social spending that frequently strain their budgets. This group often perceives the granting of a casino license as a painless way to raise revenues without raising taxes. Casino promoters are eager to exploit this belief by promising tax dollars for little effort other than the granting of a license and permission to begin business. At public hearings held by the National Gambling Impact Study Commission, representatives of cities that took this route gave enthusiastic testimonials to gambling tax dollars. By becoming casino stakeholders, however, and focusing primarily on taxes collected, cities and states take on the mantle of partner or entrepreneur rather than impartial observer and benevolent regulator considering the benefits and costs to everyone. In the words of an Oregon state senator, "The state is a whore. The state wants revenues, and whatever game falls off, they're looking for new games to entice people to bet and play more."[102] "Governments used to be protectors that provided police and fire," according to Professor John Kindt of the University of Illinois. "Now they're predators, advertising to and preying on the public."[103]

The lavishing of gambling-industry attention on legislators and public officials invariably compromises a subset of them and separates them from their public loyalties and duties. We have already mentioned the corruption case of Louisiana Governor Edwin Edwards. "Gray" practices also result; the New York Law Journal, for example, describes a lawsuit alleging illegality in the way that gambling legislation was passed in New York State: "... an 81-page bill approved after midnight with less than an hour's debate, authoriz[ing] the Governor to enter into compacts with Native American tribes for the operation of up to six Las Vegas–style casinos."[104] The state constitution bans commercial gambling. Moreover, state law requires bills to be on the desks of lawmakers for three days, but the governor had waived that requirement using a "message of necessity" provision designed for situations in which immediate action is needed. "The proposed legislation was not subjected to committee study; there were no public hearings and no opportunity whatsoever for input by the average citizen. Instead, the impetus for the bill came from powerful gambling interests who mounted one of the broadest, most expensive lobbying campaigns in state history in order to obtain passage."[105] In the words of the attorney filing suit,

> It is a sad situation when representatives elected by the people don't get to see a bill and rank and file members don't see a bill that lobbyists have had a hand in preparing.... Who is representing the people, the elected representatives of the people or the paid lobbyists? It is a disgrace, and it is becoming common practice.[106]

In South Carolina, the Senate finance committee chairman "found a way to do secretly what could never have been done in an open democratic process."[107] By dropping the two words "or property" from the ban prohibiting any gaming machine from disbursing "money or property," he opened the way for video gambling machines in the state, even though they violated the state's constitution – as later action of the Supreme Court affirmed. The change would not have been passed had it been noticed among the hundreds that were made in the last phases of the budget process.[108] The *Indianapolis Star* reported the example of the House Ways and Means Committee chairman who "failed to report earnings he received while working indirectly for the gambling industry."[109] His career ended when his secret activity became known. Why was a legislator working indirectly for the gambling industry? The report goes on to document other cases such as the political-machine allies of an East Chicago mayor and former party chairman who "formed an investment group in order to reap millions of dollars from a riverboat casino license. They were never charged with a crime, but the political connections of the group suggested that gambling licenses were aimed as much at political payoffs as economic development."[110]

Jurisdictional Conundrums

The decisions of governments are hampered by regional considerations that often prevent proper and unencumbered decisions. One problem deals with unexamined consequences. In Joliet, Illinois, for example, casinos act as tax-collection "boxes" for the city. Gamblers come from the nearby Chicago metropolitan area and lose their money gambling, a part of which goes to the city of Joliet as taxes. City officials have no incentive to measure or even care what the harmful consequences might be that their casinos cause in the Chicago area. Their interests extend only to the visible effects within their small jurisdiction; taxes are visible. Social costs are more difficult to count, less visible, and easy to ignore.

Borders play a large role in the economics of casinos. Casinos are often intentionally placed near political boundaries to conduct "border raids" on the revenues of neighboring cities and states. The casinos in Tunica, Mississippi, are aimed at Memphis, Tennessee, for example; the casinos of Hammond, Indiana, are aimed at Chicago; and so on.

The process often works as follows. Imagine two identical regions, A and B. Originally, the unwritten social compact said, "We will not permit casinos in our jurisdiction if you will do the same." When this compact is broken, the first step frequently is a casino planned near A's border. The objective is to raid the money of B. Region A performs a cost–benefit calculation that finds its casino can collect money from Region B, leaving most of the social consequences across the border at the home base of the patrons. Reports and studies financed by the casino promoter reports to A's officials that economic development will take place because net new money will flow from B to A. The social costs to A are minimized in the report, either by not calculating them, assuming that they are small, or by ignoring those that accrue to B.

Time passes. The officials of Region B see that their residents gamble in Region A. B's government officials may not want gambling, but they feel they have little recourse except to create a dueling casino of their own: if residents are going to gamble and create social costs anyway, at least their money can stay at home. Casino promoters again produce a study, this time saying that the casino will create economic development because *it will return home the dollars now being spent across the border.* Because both areas are identical, however, the end result is that neither gets money from the other, but each suffers the social costs of gambling. The presence of border issues are often well known to casino promoters and exploited in their recommendations to government officials. In our example, the border considerations caused the "race to the bottom" to result in net losses to both regions, even though each had a study (correctly) pointing to gains if one accepts the different assumptions. Only if a consistent set of assumptions were used and an area encompassing both A and B applied would the cost–benefit studies show that the original social compact (i.e., no gambling in either region) was best.

Ultimately, the question of finding a proper government attitude about casinos devolves to finding the proper role of government in society: Should government present itself in the role of business owner in order to earn its money? There are many kinds of businesses that government could run to generate the money needed to supply services. Most political experts frown upon government-run industry because they believe government has less incentive to conduct business well than the private sector does. A private business must make a profit or disappear. Government can operate well or badly and still maintain its business presence through tax subsidies.

Presuming that government runs its enterprise well, however, still leaves the philosophical question as to whether government should engage in business at all. If legitimate government activity, such as the establishment of law and order, provision of **public goods** like national defense (but not publicly provided **private goods** such as shoelaces or ketchup), and enforcement of an environment of market competition as opposed to monopoly or firms operating in restraint of fair trade, are justified, then government is justified to collect taxes to accomplish those ends. The logical question becomes: What is the best way to collect the needed taxes? Experts agree that the social cost of an additional dollar of taxes collected through a conventional tax is more than one dollar, but undoubtedly less than $1.60. In the case of casinos, the cost of collecting the same dollar is likely to be more than $3.[111]

THE OPPONENTS

SUMMARY. Average nongambling citizens have little incentive to become educated about the costs and benefits of gambling. When they do, there is little incentive for them to spend their time and resources in public advocacy.

Finally, there are citizens who oppose gambling because they believe it is harmful social policy. Unlike commercial casino owners, Indian tribes, or tax-seeking governments, they have no direct economic stake. They do not stand to make large amounts of money if they succeed in halting the spread of gambling. These citizens and their groups are generally poorly funded and, as stated previously, hope only to maintain the status quo. Occasionally, such groups will be helped by businesses that feel they would suffer from casino competition, which sometimes includes other casinos or gambling outlets. The primary reward for such opponents is often nothing more than the sense of having done one's civic duty.

SUMMARY

An old Indian trick for killing buffalo was to stampede them over a cliff. The device worked because the buffalo in front, who knew danger was approaching, had no ability to stop; the buffalo in the rear, who had the ability to stop, had no knowledge that they should. A similar situation exists with respect to the various gambling constituencies. Dysfunctional arrangements of knowledge and incentives explain a great deal of the growth of casinos in the 1990s. The general public, which had most of the power to influence the spread of gambling often had the least knowledge of why it should want to influence it at all. Consequently, the general public was neutral to mildly in favor of gambling. The casinos owners, commercial businesses, and American Indian tribes, on the other hand, had – and continue to have – personal gain at stake if they can site casinos in locations near prominent population centers. They have the resources to finance studies to convince legislators to give them what they want. Legislators, taking much of their information from the casinos, usually want to do what is right, but are forced by competition with other states and jurisdictions to outcomes that they never planned or foresaw. Sometimes they are blinded by the need for tax dollars, and consider only that. Some legislators skirt the limits of legality and propriety to help casino interests that have bought their aid. A small group of civic casino opponents may have the desire to investigate and apply their knowledge to the decision-making process, but they have little means to fund the necessary research or make their voices heard. In addition, it takes time to organize volunteer effort, and time is frequently the least available commodity when legislation is rushed through. The end result is a process that drives itself to a social conclusion, but not necessarily to the public good.

4 Economic Development

> The focus of this study has been the determination of whether net new output (and jobs and employment) have been created statewide in Missouri as a consequence of casino gaming.
>
> *Leven, Phares, and Louishomme (1998)[112]*

> Build the Stadium – Create the Jobs!
>
> *Noll and Zimbalist (1997)[113]*

CHAPTER SUMMARY. Those who believe that they can evaluate the social desirability of casinos by the number of associated jobs have confused one question with another. More geographically local jobs may or may not have anything to do with economic development, which is defined as the increase in the residents' **welfare** or well-being. Net export multiplier models, which are easily manipulated, estimate the number of jobs that introducing a new business to an area will attract or lose. This is a different question than asking whether casinos increase or worsen the well-being of an area's residents. Here, we correct erroneous thinking about economic development and explain the reason why **job multiplier models** are an untrustworthy tool in the hands of a user with an outcome to justify. Many examples of misuse come from another public issue – the

building of major-league sports stadiums using tax dollars – showing
that the problem, though it is a concern in casino-industry studies,
is not special to them. In this chapter, we do two things. In addition
to explaining why jobs are independent of true economic development, we review the workings of multiplier models, which answer a
separate but valid question in their own context: What is the impact
of a business on the number of local jobs?

Economic development is often thought to be synonymous with job
creation. Yet, nowhere on the list of theoretically correct benefits and
costs of introducing casinos into an economy do jobs appear. According
to experts, "it is important to realize that a metro area's existing residents
may not benefit at all from net job creation."[114] An observer might be
excused, therefore, for being confused about why the focus of casino
proposals seems almost exclusively concerned with whether they will
create "jobs." Even economists have been drawn into making the same
mistake.

How does a jobs focus reconcile with true costs and benefits? This
chapter answers this question by defining what we mean by economic
development and returning to basics concerning the value of a job: what
the benefit to the average city resident is if an additional job is created
somewhere in town, and how the *real* benefits to society – profits, taxes,
direct consumer benefits, and improved prices – are related to the number of jobs, if at all. Chapter 5 then provides a theoretically accurate
foundation for cost–benefit analysis applied to the casino sector.

JOBS AND ECONOMIC DEVELOPMENT

SUMMARY. A faulty emphasis on jobs derives from an erroneous understanding of economic development. Jobs are neither necessary nor sufficient
for economic development, which is the enhancement of the welfare or utility of households from given resources. Jobs might sometimes be an input

into economic development – the means to an end – but they are not the end itself.

To answer the question, "What is economic development?," recall what the creation of **wealth** is. When individuals undertake productive activity, they engage in the creation of goods and services that provide greater welfare or satisfaction than the inputs used. Paint and canvas, for example, are rearranged in the hands of a master painter into a work of art that has more value than the components had previously. A barber provides grooming that is more valuable to the customer than the value to the barber of the time given up. Consumer utility rises when activities are pursued and productive assets are used in better ways. If society can reorganize so that someone is made better off without making anyone worse off in the process, the welfare of society is enhanced. Money and prices provide a convenient measure of the value of productive activity. When paint and canvas worth $100 become a painting worth $10,000 a month later, the painter has generated income of $9,900 over that month.

Income is a flow per unit time, whereas wealth is a stock. Wealth is the claim to something of value. Income that has not been used for consumption can be used to acquire wealth. Claims to some assets have value to buyers because of expectations about how the assets will produce a flow of income in the future. When these expectations change, the value of the assets may change up or down, leading to **capital gains or losses**. With proper accounting for capital gains and losses, wealth is the accumulation of unused (i.e., unconsumed) income.

Economic development is the creation of greater value by society from its available resources. Greater value can result from a greater quantity of activity, activity that is more valuable, or both. Economic development means greater income and wealth, which lead to greater utility for members of society. The following constructed examples show that job creation is neither necessary nor sufficient for economic development.

In the first example, let casinos be introduced into a community of ten thousand employed individuals. Residents are indifferent between frequenting a casino or one of the town's racetracks, and they are indifferent between eating at the casino or at one of the other available restaurants, so they choose randomly when they go out. The casino causes the demise of one of the nearby racetracks and takes business from neighboring restaurants. The casino hires 100 employees, but these are matched by the loss of 100 jobs at other businesses, and casino revenues are matched by reduced revenues at those other businesses. The net effect is the enlargement of the casino sector matched by an equal shrinkage of the rest of the economy. In this example, no economic development takes place because greater value is not created. Casinos in this example act much like another restaurant might in a town with many existing restaurants: the new entrant takes business from others, shifting the location of activity but not increasing it.

From this example, one might conjecture that hiring by a new business need not indicate an increase in jobs and that the failure to create jobs means there is no economic development. It is true that hiring by a firm may not represent job creation. However, the second and third examples show that economic development is not necessarily linked to job creation: development may occur with or without a net increase in jobs.

In the second example, assume that casinos attract clientele from the surrounding areas. Local residents do not gamble. Casinos hire 100 new employees who move in from surrounding regions, paying them out of casino revenues earned from outside clientele. In this example, the non-casino local economy continues to employ ten thousand people, whose earnings are unchanged and who buy and sell as before at unchanged prices.

In this case, regional net new jobs are created, but there is no economic development. The local economy is enlarged and employment rises 1 percent; however, this enlargement provides no benefits to residents. In a different example, we might have included discussion of **amenity benefits** or costs to the local residents. For example, if the casino caused congestion or noise problems to those living nearby, they would be harmed. On the other hand, if the presence of new residents due to the casino allowed a new shopping center to locate near the casino employees' homes, and some of the existing residents found it more convenient to shop there, this would be a positive amenity benefit that would need to be valued in some way. Although the conclusions of the example would not be as precise as before, the overriding point would be the same: the increase in jobs is not the measure of utility benefit.

In the second example, as originally constructed, casinos operate de facto like a tollhouse that uses the town as a platform for conducting its business. Money enters and money leaves. Although total economic activity *in the vicinity of the town* rises, shifting the location of jobs without an increase in well-being is not economic development, even though the local economy experiences enlargement. Viewed from the national perspective, this example could be consistent with casinos operating like restaurants in the first example: increased employment in the casino sector is matched by reduced employment in other sectors. It is generally accepted, for example, that employment in Nevada is larger at the expense of lower employment in California, from where many Las Vegas clients come.

The third example shows that economic development can occur without job creation. Assume that casinos begin operation and hire 100 employees, but cause the number of jobs in other sectors to shrink to 9,900. Because gambling is so desirable to residents and outsiders alike, the casinos earn higher profits than other businesses in town and bid up the prevailing wage rate. Housing prices also rise due to the willingness of casino owners to pay higher prices. Residents are better off because they can gamble nearer to home than before – this is an amenity benefit that provides them greater welfare – and they receive higher wages for their labor, which also makes them better off, and their housing experiences capital gains. Because the work of the 100 casino-sector employees generates greater profit than the profit lost from the businesses whose employment shrank, the total of wages and profits of all business is higher. Casinos have brought economic development without a net increase in jobs.

In the first example, casinos did not increase jobs or provide economic development; in the second, casinos provided jobs but no economic development; and in the third, casinos provided economic development

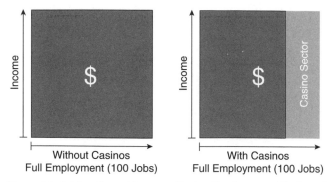

Figure 4.1. Jobless Growthlessness: Casino Employment Displaces Local Economy Jobs without Improving Resident Well-Being

but no net increase in jobs. Which principle explains the different outcomes? Anything that increases the value of social product leading to greater welfare of residents is economic development; anything that does not is not. Job creation is immaterial unless it happens to be a vehicle for increase in social value.

Schematic diagrams can be used to display the ideas presented. In Figure 4.1, the left-hand rectangle plots the number of jobs in a geographical region on the horizontal axis and plots income on the vertical axis. The area of the rectangle is the value of output – a measure of total well-being of the area's citizens. Holding other things fixed, economic development would be reflected in an increase in the height of the rectangle.[115] Residents are better off when they generate a higher value of output and, therefore, have higher incomes, which convert to greater value available for consumption. The right-hand rectangle in Figure 4.1 shows the same economy with a casino sector added. Casinos employ workers, so some of the area's jobs are now in the casino sector. However, in the figure, these jobs come one for one at the expense of jobs in the rest of the economy, and there is no increase in the height of the rectangle. Thus, there are no net jobs created and there is no economic development. Of the four logical possibilities determined by whether there is growth or no growth, job creation or no job creation, this case would correspond to our first example of "jobless growthlessness."

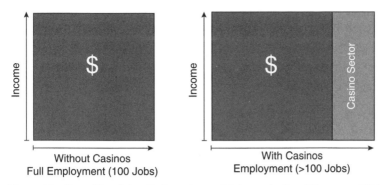

Figure 4.2. Growthless Jobs: Casinos Append Jobs to the Local Economy Without Improving Resident Well-Being

Figure 4.2 depicts the case of "growthless jobs," which corresponds to the second example. Casinos append jobs to the local economy, but they do not represent economic development because they have no impact on improving the conditions of residents. Casinos have shifted the geographic location of employment for those workers whose original employment was outside the region. If these workers were not casino employees previously, then their sectoral location was shifted as well.

Figure 4.3 shows the third possibility, in which the new industry – in this case, casinos – represents an improvement in well-being, true

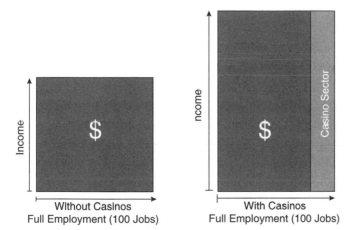

Figure 4.3. Jobless Growth: Resident Well-Being Is Improved by Casinos. (Growth is jobless in this example; net jobs are unchanged.)

economic development, and growth because casinos are a superior activity for providing utility relative to the products and activities for which the casino resources were previously used. In the example, the total number of jobs is unchanged. For the economy as a whole, however, the average job is a "better job" in the sense that the total value of those things produced is greater.

The fourth possibility – the case in which the value of local output increases at the same time the number of local jobs increases – needs no diagram. We employ it to make the additional point, however, that measuring improvement in citizen well-being is a different question from those asked by multiplier models.

Figure 4.4 presents the fourth case in which casinos cause both an increase in the value of output and in the number of local jobs. The left-hand portion of the diagram shows an increase in employment (i.e., enlarged horizontal dimension) and an increase in value of output (i.e., enlarged vertical dimension). The right-hand side of the diagram shows that some new jobs are in the casino sector and some are in the secondary sector. Secondary and/or casino jobs that displace jobs in the noncasino part of the economy do not represent net job creation. These are referred to as *cannibalized jobs* in the profession. In the case diagrammed in Figure 4.4, some of the secondary sector jobs come at the expense of preexisting jobs.

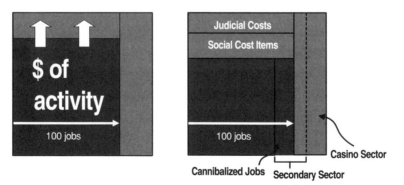

Figure 4.4. Multiplier vs. Cost–Benefit Analysis: A multiplier analysis may show job and output gains, whereas a cost–benefit analysis shows that costs of the new activity exceed benefits and society is harmed.

Figure 4.4 also introduces a new element to the discussion, which is that some economic activity in the postcasino economy may not represent an increase in resident well-being. In the diagram, the relevant portion for calculating resident utility is the darker shaded area. As is clear from the diagram, this has decreased in size, meaning that citizens are worse off in the postcasino situation. The reason is that casinos cause costs to be present that must be paid by residents. The types of costs that might be present are discussed in more detail in Chapter 7. For now, Figure 4.4 represents them by judicial costs and social service costs. Judicial costs – paying for more police, judges, and government bureaucracy – for example, are not a benefit to residents, but rather a cost to them paid by their taxes. Considering costs and benefits is the function of a cost–benefit analysis. Although a multiplier model shows that both employment and output have increased, a cost–benefit analysis would show a loss in the well-being of residents. The multiplier model is not wrong, it simply is designed to answer a different question.

Presuming that true economic development takes place, meaning that citizen well-being rises, the resulting increase in social value is distributed to the members of society in different forms depending on circumstances. It could appear as higher profits to firms, greater taxes provided by businesses to cover government provision of welfare-enhancing services, capital gains to residents on their property, or a combination of these. Gains might appear as direct amenity benefits to households, such as nearer access to an activity that was already available. They also could appear in the form of better prices for consumers for their purchases. We will refer to the former amenity benefit as **distance consumer surplus** to distinguish it from the latter, referred to simply as **consumer surplus**. A firm that is located closer to the consumer provides distance consumer surplus, whereas a market entrant that causes the price for its product to fall provides consumers with greater (price) consumer surplus. A new firm might cause wage rates to rise, also providing households with greater consumer surplus – in this case, in the household's role as labor supplier. Economic development could appear in other forms as well, such as improved functioning of markets. For example, the introduction of Internet auctions like eBay links markets, giving buyers lower prices and sellers higher prices for their goods. This also is an example of true economic development because both buyers and sellers are better off.

Nowhere in the preceding description of economic development is the creation of jobs an essential part of the discussion. Jobs matter only to the extent that they might in some cases proxy for one or more direct effects that benefit residents. Alternately, more jobs in an area might not be associated with *any* benefits to residents or even be associated with negative benefits. The point is that the worth of an additional job to residents is case-dependent.

The benefits and costs of a new business are precisely identified in Chapter 5. Using jobs as a shorthand or proxy for these other benefits and costs requires estimating how big the associated benefits and costs are, on a per-job basis. Promotional studies of the economic impact of a new business such as a casino frequently compute the effect on total jobs without completing the task of identifying how valuable to the economy the jobs are. Economists who have studied this question have found that the value to a metropolitan area of an additional job created could be zero, and tends to range from $0 to $1,500.[116] An increase in the number of local jobs may be associated with a rise in wages or house values. For those residents who are selling houses, a price increase is beneficial, just as a wage increase is beneficial to those selling their labor. Another area job, therefore, represents a gain to them. For those who do not own homes and are seeking to buy, higher housing costs represent a welfare loss. The $0 to $1,500 value per additional job represents an average over all of an area's residents. The value of a job could equal the lower bound of zero, and increased jobs in an area conceivably could even reduce the economic well-being of local residents.

Multiplier models – also sometimes referred to as *impact models, job multiplier models, net export multiplier models,* or *job impact models* – often conceptualize the economy as consisting of an export sector that sells to buyers outside the local region and the local sector that sells to buyers within the region. Expanding exports expands the **economic base** by bringing new money into the local economy. If that money is spent locally, it expands the sales of local-sector firms who, in turn, increase their hiring and spending. If the local component of *their* spending increases, then the cycle continues. Increasing the economic base ultimately leads to a new equilibrium, in which output and employment in both the export and secondary sectors are enlarged. The size of the enlargement is captured in the **multiplier** that gauges how much an increase in the base results in an enlargement of the economy. If an increase in exports of $100 leads to an increase in total output of $200, for example, the multiplier is 2. The greater the propensity of local income earners to spend their money in the local economy, the greater the multiplier. Sophisticated input–output models divide the economy into more sectors and trace what each sector does based on its needs for inputs and the demand for its output.

Having explained that multiplier and cost–benefit analyses do different things, we turn our attention in the remainder of this chapter to pitfalls in the practice of multiplier analysis. Multiplier analysis is justified in its own context. It is objectionable only when it is done incorrectly or when it is used to address a question that it was not designed to answer. Chapter 5 discusses cost–benefit analyses.

"MAJOR-LEAGUE LOSERS FIELDS OF SCHEMES"

SUMMARY. The decision by a community to host a major-league sports team is logically identical to the decision to host casinos: benefits are the presumed economic advantages that the new activity brings. Social costs are the expenditures on a stadium in the former case and the social costs of gambling in the latter. We can learn much that is relevant to the evaluation of casinos – indeed, any new industry – from studying the professional assessment of the decision to host a major-league team. In this section, we discuss why multiplier models are notoriously susceptible to manipulation, mistakes, misuse, and abuse.

Whether or not casinos cause jobs and whether or not jobs, in turn, represent economic benefits to residents is an empirical question. Like casinos, major-league sports teams have frequently been portrayed as economic-development tools, especially by their owners. A useful analogy exists between their economics and the economics of casinos. Books with titles such as *Major League Losers*[117] and *Field of Schemes*[118] discuss the economics of sports ventures.

The social benefits of major-league sports consist of the direct consumer value to fans of a local team plus the increase, if any, in local income due to a net increase in profits and taxes, plus the effects to local residents of beneficial changes in wages and prices. Pittsburgh residents, for example, were willing to pay between $0.83 and $2.30 per resident to keep the Pittsburgh Penguins ice-hockey team in Pittsburgh, suggesting that the Penguins provided direct benefits to consumers.[119] The list for a casino is similar, except that a casino is less likely to provide consumer benefits with public-good–like positive externalities. No one expects to spend their fall afternoons watching broadcasts of professional gamblers at the local roulette table, for example, but the same individuals might enjoy watching a broadcast of their town's major-league sports team or take pride in the team's performance discussed over the office water cooler.

The social costs of a major-league sports team typically include the taxes to fund construction of a stadium for the team, plus public expenditures to deal with congestion problems such as traffic and crowd control. Since 1990, more than two thirds of the $21.7 billion spent on stadiums has been contributed by the public.[120] The social cost of taxation exceeds tax collection by about 25 percent due to the economic distortions that taxes cause.[121] Hence, public expenditures financed by distorting taxes must be increased by 25 percent to accurately reflect the costs to society.[122] The social costs of casinos are not public payments for stadiums, but rather the cost of negative externalities such as crime, business and employment costs, bankruptcy, suicide, illness, social service costs, government regulatory expenditures, family costs, and the social costs of **abused dollars**. Chapter 7 discusses in detail the estimates of these social costs of gambling.

Major-league sports teams, therefore, bring entertainment to a community, but impose social costs in the form of subsidies to build and maintain stadiums. Casinos bring entertainment to a community, but impose social costs in the form of negative externalities. Both are social issues because the costs they burden the community with must be paid even by those who may not participate in the sports events or gambling. Because the economics of major-league sports teams is so well developed, it offers a useful vehicle for discussing the economic-development aspects of casinos.

JOBS

SUMMARY. Net export multiplier models are used to estimate the number of additional jobs in a region due to the introduction of casinos or other businesses. Additional jobs may or may not represent economic development. **Net exports** rise when a business causes more dollars to flow into a region than it causes to flow out. Applying a multiplier to the net-export number determines the impact on regional economic activity. For example, $100 more flowing into a region than out, with a multiplier of 2.5, implies that there will be $250 more income in the region and jobs will rise by the number needed to produce it.

Casinos, like sports teams, have relied heavily on the argument that they create jobs to counterbalance the perception that they create social costs. The previous discussion explained that jobs may or may not represent value to the area's residents. The same research has much to say about major-league sports teams – and, by implication, casinos – as creators of jobs.

It is possible that a casino could increase or decrease the number of jobs depending on how it operates and how it interacts with the existing economy. Consider again the different effects of a restaurant, a factory, or a tollhouse. We used these analogies when we showed that job creation is neither necessary nor sufficient for economic development. Now we use them to understand the different issue of when an industry or firm creates jobs within a specified geographical area.

A restaurant generally serves local residents and existing tourists. Adding another restaurant to a town that already has many increases employment in the new restaurant, but does not increase total employment. Because no new dollars are attracted from the outside, the restaurant redistributes money within the local economy: increased demand at one location comes at the expense of demand at another. A restaurant in Central Park of New York City, for example, would employ workers and, in a small circle including the restaurant, increase the number of jobs. Some might call this economic development, but enlarging the circle to include Manahattan would mean that there is no net increase in jobs if the demand was shifted from other area restaurants.

A factory that exports its product to buyers outside the local area operates differently. New money is brought in from buyers outside the area and the revenues are used to pay local workers' wages, suppliers, and owners' profits. This money, in turn, is recycled by being spent in the region. Secondary suppliers arise to serve the secondary demands. New local jobs are created – both directly at the factory and in the secondary sectors. These represent a true net increase in local employment. A variant of the factory is a business that serves local demand that would have flowed to the outside had the local factory not been present. Meeting demand that might otherwise have been met by imports is called **import substitution**. Import substitution also leads to a net increase in local jobs compared to the no-factory alternative.

A third possibility exists whereby the firm collects money from local buyers and those outside the region, but the positive effect is negated because an equally large or larger flow of money goes out. The net effect is that the local economy is reduced to the role of being a collection booth for the industry. The impact could either be to expand or to shrink the local economy. A variant on the tollhouse is the extractive industry – one can imagine a mining operation – that produces locally and sells to the outside, but whose primary impact is to leave negative externalities to the local region, such as polluted lakes and streams. Would existing residents be better or worse off with such an industry? A casino that employed many outside workers, with owners that took their profits elsewhere and created negative consequences for the local population, might very well fail to enlarge the economic base at the same time that it left the local economy with higher costs.

No single firm or industry is essential to the achievement of full employment. The American economy has and will achieve full employment in the long term with or without casinos present, with or without a particular restaurant present, and so on. This means that, *within its geographical market*, major-league sports teams and casinos have no effect on the long-term level of jobs. Restaurants, factories, and tollhouses differ in their effect on the local economy because their geographical markets differ. The geographical market for a local restaurant and the local economy coincide. The restaurant shifts demand within the local economy and market, but does not increase it. The factory's geographical market is larger than the local economy and its exports of goods, therefore, shifts employment to the local economy from the rest of the geographical market. The tollhouse's geographical market could be larger or smaller than the local economy, but it has no impact on jobs because it does not redistribute revenues between the two.

Could a geographical region be so small, so isolated, and/or so devoid of resources that it could not support productive activity, and yet have residents needing work? In rare circumstances, these types of situations have occurred, but they did not create permanent unemployment. Western ghost towns that closed when their silver mines ran out of ore had residents who gradually drifted to better prospects elsewhere. Full employment was restored by the linking of labor with gainful activity in a more advantageous location. Insisting that employment take place in a particular location that has obvious disadvantages and drawbacks imposes an artificial external constraint on the system that lowers the long-term well-being of the economy. Nevertheless, let us construct such a worst-case scenario by assuming such a constraint, and let us further presume that only one business could operate in the region (e.g., a casino), so that the choice is limited to accepting the casino for employment reasons or finding work in a different location. Knowing which solution is better requires comparing the short-term costs of moving versus the long-term costs of negative externalities of the casino. Which choice is better depends on the numbers; however, we are again led not to count the number of local jobs, but rather to perform a cost–benefit analysis (discussed in later chapters).

Let us return to the discussion of how to determine the number of local jobs. The restaurant, tollhouse, and factory analogies explicate the principles on which the models, called net export multiplier models,

---

The Bathtub Model[1]

The water level in a bathtub models the jobs-creation phenomenon. Taking water from one end of a bathtub and emptying it into the other has no effect on the tub's water level. (This is similar to the impact on jobs of a new restaurant in town that sells to preexisting demand.) If one adds more water to a bathtub than one removes, the level of water in the tub rises. The multiplier would correspond to supplementing the water in an amount proportional to the original increase. (This represents the impact of a factory in the factory example.) Finally, adding water to a bathtub and removing an equal or greater amount leaves the water level unchanged or lowers it. If water is lost to the bathtub, the multiplier works in reverse. (This explains the tollhouse case.)

[1] Thompson (1997b) discusses this analogy.

---

operate to predict the impact of a firm on the number of jobs in an economy. If a firm leads to an increase in the area's net exports (i.e., exports to the outside minus imports from the outside), and the net increase in money received is spent locally, there will be an increase in local economic activity. The increase will include the primary export activity, but it also will include the secondary businesses that spring up to meet the demand induced by the additional local spending. The net number of new jobs will include the jobs of the original enterprise plus the secondary jobs. The size of the secondary activity and the number of secondary jobs depend on the size of the multiplier, which reflects the way revenues earned by local businesses are spent in the local economy.

In the remainder of this chapter, we discuss several issues, such as reliability and manipulability, of which users of studies based on net-export models should be aware, and provide a detailed technical example of a multiplier model that incorporates relevant issues for describing the impact of a casino on area income and jobs including demand substitution (i.e., **cannibalization**), recovered expenditures (i.e., **recapture**), demand **leakages**, and inflated multipliers.

MULTIPLIER MODELS: RELIABILITY

SUMMARY. The reliability of studies based on multiplier modeling is an issue when backers (i.e., government or private business) of projects (i.e., major-league sports teams or casinos) produce the studies. Predictable abuses involve overstating the revenues gained, understating the revenues lost, and using inflated multipliers. The treatment of cannibalization, recapture, leakage, and inflated multipliers also has been criticized by outside expert reviewers.

Critiques of the ways in which net export multiplier models are misused are similar across applications. Knowing whether the business activity in question attracts more new money from outside than it causes to be lost to the outside requires knowing if the demand serviced by the business cannibalizes other local demand, whether the demand from local residents serviced by the business recaptures spending that would have gone outside the sector, how money obtained by the business is then spent outside the region (i.e., leakages), and how the entity is taxed and the taxes are used.

Errors in judgment can be introduced at each step. For example, industry promoters often treat all demand as if it were new. "The reality, however, is probably rather different."[123] According to the National Research Council, "economic impact studies often fail to explain the potential for one expenditure to displace another."[124] Goss & Associates concur that

> many studies have exaggerated the impact of casinos due to
>
> 1. their failure to recognize offsetting negative impacts for other businesses in the area ... [and] their recognition of each casino dollar as a "new" dollar for the area.[125]

Fort Wayne, Indiana, a medium-sized town of 675 thousand people, shows how this can happen.[126] The city is the site of a large portion of the region's recreation. A random survey of 786 households found that 39.9 percent had made a trip to another city for a sporting event; 12.7 percent said they would cancel some trips if Fort Wayne had its own minor-league sports team. Working from the number of games that respondents said they would attend implied that only 11.9 percent of the revenues gathered by a new stadium would be new revenues for Fort Wayne. The number actually reported by promoters of the stadium project could easily exceed this number by a substantial margin, without drawing resistance or particular scrutiny by city officials or citizen bodies.

Research on the job-creating effects of major-league sports teams overwhelmingly shows that there is a difference between what independent researchers say and what the promotional research funded by the teams and team backers says. "The obvious question that arises," according to Noll and Zimbalist in *Sports, Jobs & Taxes*, "is why such [publicly paid] subsidies [to sports stadiums] exist. . . . Part of the answer may lie in a widespread belief that sports facilities are an engine of local economic development. Most of this book is devoted to demonstrating that this belief is mistaken."[127]

Numerous researchers have reached similar conclusions:

> . . . Twenty-seven [of thirty cities studied] showed no economic impact on their local economy over a thirty-year period. . . . Far from generating new economic activity, as new stadium proposals continually assert. . . the new facilities at best seem to bring in dollars that otherwise would have been spent elsewhere in the immediate or general region.[128]

> Few fields of empirical research offer virtual unanimity of findings. Yet, independent work on the economic impact of stadiums and arenas has uniformly found that there is no statistically significant positive correlation between sports facility construction and economic development (Baade and Dye, 1990; Baim, 1992; Rosentraub, 1994; Baade, 1996; Noll and Zimbalist, 1997; Waldon, 1997; Coates and Humphrey, 1999).[129]

> Regardless of method, none of the academic studies has so far been able to find significant economic-development benefits sufficient to justify the large public outlays.[130]

[The conclusions of independent researchers] are in sharp contrast to the claims of the dozens of promotional studies that have been performed by consulting firms under contract with the affected city or team.... [The promotional studies] often confuse spending with spending that is diverted from other local activities ... attribute all spending by out-of-town visitors to the sports team regardless of the motive for the visit ... [overstate] the multiplier by ignoring crucial characteristics of sports spending ... apply the inflated multiplier to gross spending, rather than local value added ... [and] omit the negative effects from the taxation that is used to finance construction and operating deficits of the facility.[131]

[The commercial reports are] basically political documents.[132]

Cannibalization

Among the reasons why the new business claims about economic development may be false are cannibalization, leakages, and multiplier mistakes.[133] Cannibalized dollars are revenues to a business that are taken from other local businesses. Cannibalized revenues are not new activity and should not be attributed to a casino or sports facility as net exports.[134] In the words of three different experts, for sporting events

"there is considerable evidence that out-of-state sports fans at most sporting events do not come to town because of the game."[135]

"Economic research shows that people's total spending on entertainment is not affected by the presence of a professional sports team."[136]

"Most of the spending by fans at games is nothing more than the substitution of one form of entertainment (sports) for another (leaving the same number of dollars in the economy)."[137]

The importance of cannibalization varies. Among existing or proposed casino locations, New Orleans (especially during Mardi Gras), Hawaii, and Florida stand out as prime examples for cannibalization of outsider dollars. Jane Speyrer, economist at the University of New Orleans who worked on the study of New Orleans casinos, makes the point that "there's not new money falling from the heavens waiting to be spent at the casinos. The question is: Where are you going to take it from?"[138] Even if visitors to an existing or proposed New Orleans, Florida, or Hawaii casino were tourists, their demand should not be considered as new until the extent of cannibalization is known.

Eating out is particularly susceptible. "If a family eats dinner near the stadium or arena before a game, where did they not eat their dinner that night?"[139] Speaking for the restaurant industry, a food-industry executive expressed his concerns, "As it has evolved, I'm fearful for the [restaurant] industry. All over the country, restaurants are reporting 30, 40, and 50 percent declines. The dirty little secret is that [gambling] has become increasingly localized."[140] Several examples serve to make the point:

> A fifty-four-year-old Des Moines eatery closed this month after more than fifty years. Owner Sue Floyd blamed Prairie Meadows, saying her inner-city restaurant lost 50 percent of its clientele to the casino.[141]

> As soon as the casino opened a year ago, Marrero [former owner of Porto Coelli Cafe and Bakery a block from the casino] saw his business drop by half.[142]

> The North Island Bistro, located about a block from the casino, saw its average Saturday night crowd drop from about 120 people to about 50 as soon as the casino opened, said owner Jean True. The restaurant cut its waiting and cooking staff in half.[143]

There does not seem to be a single source from which gamblers get their money when they gamble. Revenues to other forms of entertainment suffer, but so can nonentertainment expenditure. For example, it was the concensus of metropolitan pastors in Des Moines that casinos had a detrimental impact on charitable giving.[144]

Evidence on Cannibalization from Tax Receipts
Some direct evidence exists showing how expenditures on other goods are affected by the presence of casinos and how far away these effects are felt.[145] To see which sectors are most affected by the opening of a casino, we obtained Kind-of-Business Tax receipts data collected by the State of Illinois. These data divide sales-tax collections into ten categories of expenditure: general merchandise; food; drinking and eating; apparel;

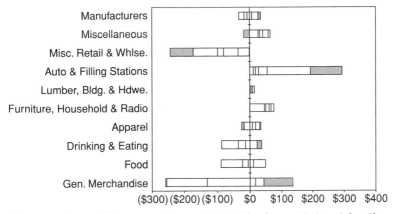

Figure 4.5. Sectoral Winners and Losers 0–10 Miles from a Casino: Sales Change per $1,000 Increase in Casino Revenues

furniture, household, and radio; lumber, building, and hardware; automotive and filling stations; miscellaneous retail and wholesale; other miscellaneous; and manufacturers. By knowing the tax rate, we can calculate total market expenditures in each category. We collected twenty-one quarters of data, much of it by laborious hand-transcription, going back to the beginning of 1989. We separated collections into taxes reported by establishments situated within zero to 5 miles of the casino and within 5 to 10 miles of the casino. In some areas, data were collected for distances 10 to 30 miles away. Quarterly tax collections, state tax collections for the same category of expenditure, and casino revenues were adjusted for price-level changes. The sample of casino locations included Alton, Aurora, Galena, Joliet, Metropolis, Peoria, and Rock Island.

Figure 4.5 shows the average effect of an additional $1,000 of casino revenue on the sales of the ten categories of merchandise. (The contribution to the average by each location is shown by the bar segments. Segments to the right of zero show gains; those to the left show losses.)

Three spending classifications show large effects. General merchandise as well as miscellaneous retail and wholesale trade stand out as the two categories of spending that show the greatest losses. Miscellaneous retail and wholesale revenues, showing an average loss of $247, are also notable in that all seven locations reported losses. General merchandise, showing a larger decrease among four locations, had three locations reporting positive effects. Net losses for the two sectors were $367.

Losses in general merchandise and miscellaneous retail and wholesale expenditures suggest that casino revenues tend to come from a broad range of alternative expenditures rather than from one particular type of spending. This differs from the situation for the only sector showing gains in all communities.

Automotive and filling-station sales showed an average gain of $295. Most of this effect is due to the two largest cases of Peoria and Joliet, suggesting that casinos enhance the sales of nearby gasoline stations in these locations. The impact for Peoria for this category of spending within zero to 5 miles of the casino was statistically significant, and for Joliet it was nearly so. The other locations reported smaller, statistically insignificant effects, but all were positive.

There does not seem to be an obvious pattern in the remaining seven sectors. The furniture, household, and radio category showed one positive and one negative statistically significant area, but the effects were relatively small; the other areas were statistically insignificant. More study will be needed before anything further can be said about these other seven sectors.

Figure 4.6 shows the losses in general merchandise and miscellaneous retail and wholesale trade in more detail by separating them by distance from the casino. The effect of an additional $1,000 in casino revenue is to reduce sales in these categories by $142 within zero to 5 miles of the casino, and an additional $217 for businesses 5 to 10 miles away. The figure also shows the effect on these categories for distances 10 to 30 miles away based on a sample of Alton, Galena, Metropolis, Peoria, and Rock Island. The effect is small enough to be viewed as negligible. In all, the average loss for an additional $1,000 of casino revenue was $381 in these categories.

Figure 4.7 shows average gains and losses across all goods by distance from the casino. Distances farther from the casino generally show losses, whereas closer areas are mixed. The average lost revenue was $195 for all

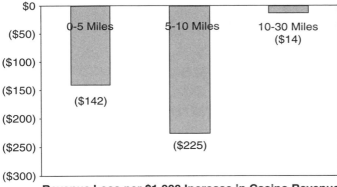

Figure 4.6. Average Losses by Distance from a Casino: General Merchandise, Miscellaneous Retail, and Wholesale Trade

sales between 5 and 10 miles from the casino. Gains occurring for sales within zero to 5 miles of the casino averaged $170 dollars. Of the gains, $112 is due to increased automotive and filling-station sales. The average loss for all goods zero to 10 miles from the casino is $25.

To measure the average long-term effect of the casino on revenues for businesses between 10 and 30 miles away, total sales-tax revenues were regressed on casino revenues, total state sales-tax collections, and lagged state and local sales-tax collections for businesses 10 to 30 miles from the casino. Average revenue losses 10 to 30 miles from the casino were $243 per $1,000 increase in casino gross revenue. More studies of this type would have to be conducted to establish with confidence the degree of demand shifting that occurs due to a casino. Results of the present

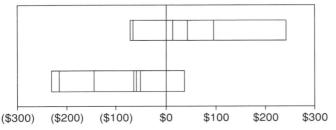

Figure 4.7. Gains and Losses by Distance from a Casino: Revenue Change per $1,000 Increase in Casino Revenues, All Goods (0-5 Miles on Top, 5-10 Miles on Bottom)

investigation, however, are consistent with economic theory. We did not find, for example, that consumers financed their gambling by choosing to reduce spending in a single category of spending. Rather, a range of alternative expenditures was affected. A consistent conclusion would be that sales in general near the casino tend to rise (or are mixed) at the expense of sales 5 to 10 and 10 to 30 miles away. It is possible in areas where eating and drinking *at* the casino form a part of the measured increase in revenues near the casino that eating and drinking establishments nearby actually suffer because our data do not distinguish between casino and noncasino sales.

Leakage

Leakages to the local economy include a large portion of spending to purchase goods and services outside the metropolitan area. Many employees also may live outside the local area.[146] Player compensation is 55 to 60 percent of National Hockey League (NHL), National Basketball Association (NBA), and National Football League (NFL), team revenues, for example, so leakage from players who live elsewhere matters.[147] Casinos face similar concerns. In one location, for example, 532 of the casino workers lived locally, but approximately 400 did not.[148]

Profits and operating expenditures are another source of leakage. "'These (casino) companies do not take their profits and throw them back into the local economy,' says Mr. Thompson, who has been a consultant to casinos."[149] State gambling commissions have taken to monitoring the share of expenditures that go out of state. In one case, 65 percent of vendor contracts for the state's casinos involved out-of-state purchases. The range over the state's casinos was 35 to 87 percent.[150] Two years later, a complaint by the state Racing and Gaming Commission found that only 11 percent of contracts put to the commission for approval were in-state.[151] The phenomenon is not restricted to one location. For instance, similar conclusions were reached in a study of casinos in Israel: "This *ex ante* evaluation shows that much of the output, income, and employment gains generated by a casino are likely to be captured outside the region, and that localized impacts are small."[152]

Multipliers

Once the effect on net exports is estimated, the net-export multiplier scales the effect to determine the ultimate impact on the local sector. Mistakes that lead to exaggerated multipliers are prevalent according to reviewers of the stadium literature. One device used to increase the multiplier involved changing the size of the area that is considered "local," making it smaller when defining "new" spending (i.e., so a larger fraction of spending is from the outside) and making the area larger when the area of multiplier effects on production is considered (i.e., so less of the spending goes to the "outside" and the multiplier is larger). Incredibly, these assumptions have been made even in the same study![153] As explained previously, if the amount spent by a casino outside the local area is underestimated (i.e., the leakage rate is high), the multiplier will be overstated. If the share of revenues earned by the casino that comes at the expense of other local spending is underestimated (i.e., cannibalization is high), the multiplier is applied to too great a base.

Moreover, multiple errors compound. If a 50 percent overstated multiplier is applied to 35 percent too high a base, the resulting estimate will be 100 percent too high. Greater errors have been made: "These studies assume that 2.5 total jobs are created for each initial observable job created from hosting a sports team. In contrast, the independent economic studies suggest that the appropriate local multiplier to apply to the gross jobs created from hosting a sports team is probably no more than 1.25."[154] In a different example provided for a hypothetical baseball team, the multiplier model predicted an impact of $760,000 where the true impact was only $22,200, off by a factor of 34.[155]

A NET EXPORT MULTIPLIER MODEL

SUMMARY. Although jobs multiplier analyses can be manipulated, are fraught with hazards, and do not measure what we commonly mean by economic development – the enhancement of the welfare or utility of households – we still might want to know whether a particular casino venture will increase or decrease the number of people employed in a defined geographical area.

TABLE 4.1. Representative Casino Use of Funds

Expenditures	Percent of Revenue
Payroll	32
Taxes	12
Depreciation	8
Interest & Profit	12
Other Operating Expenses	36
Total	100

Source: Arthur Andersen & Co., 1996. *Economic Impacts of Casino Gaming in the United States, Volume 1: Macro Study.*

Under what conditions does a casino create or destroy local jobs? The answer depends on the source of its revenues and how it uses its winnings.

Table 4.1 lists expenses for a typical casino. Approximately 32 percent of casino revenues goes to payroll; 32 percent goes to taxes, profits, interest, and depreciation; and the remaining 36 percent goes to other operating expenses, which include food and beverage for resale; administrative expenses; food, beverage, retail, and entertainment expenses; energy and utilities; advertising; retail goods for resale; and hotel-related expenses.

We will refer to profits plus depreciation plus interest as **gross profits**. Gross profits play an important role in the effect of a casino on the local economy. Precisely how gross profits are used in a given situation depends on how much was borrowed and what the local tax rates are. A casino operating without debt and with low taxes, for example, would pass more in profits to owners, whereas one with higher debt would pass less. In states such as Nevada, taxes on casinos are as little as 6.25 percent, whereas in states like Illinois, they are higher: in 2000, wagering taxes were $474 million out of total revenues of $1.66 billion, a rate of 28 percent.

To track the casino's effect on income, Figure 4.8 divides the economy into three sectors: (1) the casino sector, (2) the local (noncasino) sector, and (3) the outside sector (everything else). We are primarily interested

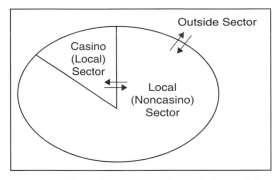

Figure 4.8. Schematic Representation of the Three Relevant Sectors for Casino Net Export Modeling

in the flows in to and out of the local sector. Table 4.2 summarizes these flows before and after the casino enters the market. The change between before and after is the effect of the casino.

A number of possibilities emerges. First, the casino might cause spending by locals that used to go to the outside to return home. Such dollars are called *recaptured dollars*, designated by R in Table 4.2. Recapture might occur, for example, if locals gamble on the outside but switch to the local casino when it begins operation. Another possibility is that spending by locals in the casino sector may be diverted from other local spending. This spending, C_L, would be cannibalized local dollars because the casino sector gains at the expense of other local firms. Spending in the casino by outsiders also may be cannibalized. For example, an area with visitors and tourists may find that they diminish their spending on other local attractions and spend it in the casinos instead. Cannibalized dollars $C = C_O + C_L$ remove money from the local sector.

The presence of the casino may require increased police presence or infrastructure spending and maintenance by local government. This spending is captured in Table 4.2 by the term I. Next, the casino itself may leak money to the outside. Gross revenues of the casino go for operating expenses E, profits P, the wage bill W, and for taxes T. The share of each of these $\sigma_e, \sigma_p, \sigma_w, \sigma_t$ that go to the outside represent leaked dollars L that must be subtracted from gross revenues before the remainder goes to the local sector. There may be direct taxes T_D paid to governments outside the local sector because of the casino. In our

TABLE 4.2. Effect of a Casino on Local Income Flows

Sectoral Flow Being Tracked	Before Casino	After Casino	Net (After−Before)
Local → Outside	$-R$	0	R (*Recaptured $*)
	0	$-T_D$	$-T_D$ (*Direct Taxes to Outside*)
Local → Casino	0	$-C_L$	$-C_L$ (*Cannibalized Local $*)
	0	$-I$	$-I$ (*Infrastructure $*)
Outside → Local	V	$V - C_O$	$-C_O$ (*Cannibalized Outside $*)
Casino → Local	0	$G - \sigma_e E - \sigma_p P$ $-\sigma_w W - \sigma_t T$	$G - L$ (*Casino Gross Revenue − Leakage to Outside*)
Total			$G - L - C + R - I - T_D$ (*where* $C = C_L + C_O$)
Multiplier Effect			$m(G - L - C + R - I - T_D)$

model, we assume that a small admission tax is charged that is paid to the outside. The net of all these flows, Gross Revenues − Leakages − Cannibalized Dollars + Recaptured Dollars − Infrastructure Spending − Direct Tax Payments $(G - L - C + R - I - T_D)$, is multiplied by the net export multiplier m to determine the change in local economic activity: $m(G - L - C + R - I - T_D)$. The number of jobs needed to produce this change in economic activity is the jobs impact of the casino. In more detailed analysis, different multipliers might be applied to selected components of the net flows, depending on how far the reviewer wants to track the details on how different flows enter the economy. These refinements are not necessary for our demonstration.

Based on Table 4.1, we assign the share of casino revenues G going to gross profits, taxes, payroll, and other expenses by the weights

$w_p = 0.2$, $w_t = 0.12$, $w_w = 0.32$, and $w_e = 0.36$, respectively. Taxes paid from casino revenues based on w_t are separate from direct taxes T_D; in our example, direct taxes are an admission tax of $2 per patron visit. To simplify, we assume that local gamblers and those from outside spend similar amounts per visit. Thus, revenues from outsiders equal θng, where n is the number of gambler visits and $g = \$87$ is the amount spent per visit.[156] The casino of Table 4.3 admits 1,149.4 representative individuals so that its gross revenues are $100 thousand. θ will be a parameter that we adjust in our analysis, so we do not assign it a single value. We set the fraction of gambling by locals who would have gone to casinos outside the area if there were no local casino at 5 percent, $s_R = 0.05$; hence, recaptured dollars are $R = s_R(1 - \theta)ng$. This number is intentionally small, but we include it to retain the effect it represents in the model. Many visitors to a city might be there for other purposes, stopping into a casino if one is available rather than finding other entertainment. In our example, we assume that 75 percent of gambling revenues from outsiders is spending above and beyond what they would have spent otherwise, implying that the share of cannibalized outsider dollars is $s_O = 0.25$. Following the literature, we set consumers' marginal propensity to consume out of income at $mpc = 0.7$.[157] Because the amount of gross profit that owners spend locally varies – owners often use money acquired in one region to finance their ventures in other regions, for example, or must pay off borrowing from outside lenders – we consider a range from zero to one for the share of gross profits, σ_p, spent outside. The local economy retains 25 percent of the taxes on casino gross revenue (e.g., the majority goes to the state), spending 90 percent locally, $\sigma_t = 1 - 0.9 \times 0.25 = 0.775$. We assume that 90 percent of payroll income is used locally: $\sigma_w = 1 - 0.9 \times mpc$. Casinos spend 14 percent of gross revenues on other expenses outside the local economy,[158] hence, $\sigma_e = 0.14/w_e$. We set infrastructure spending for the benefit of the casinos (e.g., crowd control by local police) at 1 percent of revenues: $I = 0.01G$.

The infrastructure figure does not include the social costs of harmful externalities caused by casinos; these are treated separately. If we use the

TABLE 4.3. Net Export Multiplier Model

	Variables
G	Casino gross revenues
w_p, w_t, w_w, w_e	Revenue shares for profits, taxes, wage bill, other operating expenses
T_D	Direct tax payments to outside
θ	Share of gambling by outsiders
n	Number of gambler visits
g	Casino revenue per visit
s_R	Recovered local $ (share of local gambler revenues that would have been spent outside if no local casino)
s_O	Cannibalized outsider $ (share of outsider gambler dollars that would have been spent locally anyway if no local casino)
mpc	Marginal propensity to consume out of income used locally
$\sigma_p, \sigma_t, \sigma_w, \sigma_e$	Shares of profits, taxes, wage bill, and operating expenses spent by casino outside local sector
I	Infrastructure spending for benefit of casino
C_L	Cannibalized spending from locals
C_O	Cannibalized spending from outsiders
V	Tourist spending by visitors

	Flows into Local Sector
$G = ng$	Casino gross revenues
$R = s_R(1 - \theta)G$	Recovered dollars

	Flows Out of Local Sector
$L = \sigma_e E + \sigma_p P$ $+\sigma_w W + \sigma_t T$	Leakage to outside from operating expenses, profits, wages spent outside, and taxes
$C = C_L + C_O$	Cannibalized dollars
$I = .01G$	Infrastructure expenditures
$T_D = n2$	Direct taxes

	Identities	
$E = w_e G$	$P = w_p G$	
$W = w_w G$	$T = w_t G$	
$C_O = s_O \theta G$	$C_L = (1 - \theta)G$	

figure for average number of visits per adult from Chapter 6 for those living near casinos of 3.64, 1,149.4 visits would represent 315 adults. Assuming that 1.3 percent of these adults become pathological gamblers – a not-unrealistic selection (see Chapter 8) – implies 4.1 pathological gamblers. Multiplying this by the annual crime, bankruptcy, and social service costs per pathological gambler in Chapter 7 implies social costs of $17,454. Were all social costs including those borne just by the gambler included, the figure would be higher. Although these represent real re-sources removed from the local sector that can no longer be used for other productive purposes, the treatment specialists, lawyers, criminal justice personnel, and others whose work time must be devoted to dealing with harmful consequences of casinos do represent a part of the postcasino economy. Therefore, we continue to count their jobs and output as social product. However, the social costs are not ignored when well-being is considered. They are subtracted from the final postcasino, postmultiplier tally of domestic product. For example, assume that the casino leads to an increase in net exports of $8 thousand and the multiplier is 2.0, so that the output of the local economy is increased by $16 thousand. If social costs were not considered, this would look like wanted economic devel-opment. Because $17,454 of the postcasino output represents the value of resources devoted to social costs, however, the net effect is that the remainder of the economy is smaller by $1,454. The fact that the casino expanded the economy but required more than the expansion to pay for social costs is important for evaluating the desirability of the casino.

Table 4.3 lists model information and defines the variables and equa-tions.

Table 4.4 shows the degree to which the local sector expands or shrinks, depending on the share of casino patrons who are visitors from outside and the share of gross profits spent outside the local sector. At one ex-treme, when casino patrons are entirely local residents and owners spend their profits outside the community, the model predicts that the casino drains the local economy of $53,889 for every $100,000 it takes in in revenues. Assuming a multiplier of 2.2 – this number might apply to a large city[159] – implies that the economy experiences a drop in income of

TABLE 4.4. Casino-Induced Net Exports ($)

		Percent of Patron Visits from Nonlocals				
		0%	25%	50%	75%	100%
Percent of Gross	100%	−53,889	−36,389	−18,889	−1,389	16,111
Profits Spent Out-	50%	−43,889	−26,389	−8,889	8,611	26,111
side Local Sector	0%	−33,889	−16,389	1,111	18,611	36,111

Notes: Representative patron visits = 1,149
Casino gross revenues = $100,000

more than $118 thousand and loses the number of jobs needed to produce that value added. The local sector does not experience positive net exports. In fact, the break-even point for positive net exports is reached only when 77 percent or more of the gamblers come from outside the region. It was scenarios of this type that prompted *USA Today* to editorialize, "You can't endlessly suck money from the pockets of local gamblers, send 20 percent or more to out-of-state operators, and not disrupt the local economy."[160]

If the share of profits spent locally rises to 50 percent, then break-even occurs when 62 percent of gamblers are from the outside. If owners spend their profits entirely in the local sector, break-even occurs when 49 percent or more of gamblers come from outside the region. This is why it is so important to know what owners will be doing with their profits, information that is often lacking in industry impact studies and that may change over time.

Whether a casino shrinks or enlarges the local sector is sensitive to other parameters as well. For example, making a number of small adjustments – any one of which in isolation might plausibly be within the range of ignorance about the true figure, but each selected to show favorable effects of the casino – can lead to quite different conclusions. In our example, assume that the number of recaptured dollars contained in the gambling of locals is 10 percent of their spending instead of 5 percent, that cannibalized dollars from outside gamblers are 20 percent of their expenditures instead of 25 percent, that the marginal propensity to consume out of income is 10 percent higher, that operating expenditures to the outside are 10 percent instead of 14 percent, and that all profits are spent locally. Making these combined changes would imply that just 33 percent of revenues must come from nonlocal gamblers for the casino to break even in creating net exports for the local sector.

Relative to publicized rules of thumb that two thirds or more of casino demand should be nonlocal if casinos are going to be engaged in more than redistribution and displacement of existing demand,[161] our model presents a more favorable assessment of casinos if we assume that profits are spent 50 percent or more locally. In general, the effect of a casino remains an empirical matter. The evidence in many cases is that demand does *not* meet even the modest bounds just identified. For example, in Montreal a study for Societe des Casinos Du Quebec found that just 9.4 percent of visitors were from outside greater Montreal and only 4.4 percent were from outside Quebec.[162] If the region being considered for job increase was Quebec or greater Montreal, this casino would come far short of increasing jobs. In Council Bluffs, 68 percent of casino clientele came from the Omaha Metropolitan Statistical Area and 91.7 percent from inside Iowa and Nebraska.[163] In Minnesota, when losses from all gamblers totaled $590 million, only $40 million, or 6.78 percent, was lost by gamblers from out of state.[164] A later study in the same state found that 80 percent of revenues in Indian casinos was from residents.[165] Survey research in Illinois found that about 80 percent of customers live within 35 miles of the casinos.[166] In the case of Elgin, only 2 to 3 percent of the Grand Victoria's customers come from out of state, according to the casino's own figures.[167] The concensus is expressed well in the words of a Chicago reporter: "Hopes for a tourism boom run counter to what industry experts have learned in recent years: gamblers stay close to home if given the chance."[168]

Although some casinos obviously do lead to increases in local jobs – Las Vegas is certainly larger at the expense of California – the claim must be examined on a case-by-case basis and the numbers carefully scrutinized. Unfortunately, studies of the economic-development effects of casinos often do not state which assumptions they are making about necessary flows – yet, as the simulation shows, this matters greatly to the outcome. The model presented herein clarifies that the effect of a casino on local economic activity and the jobs that go with it depends on who the gamblers are, what casino owners do with their profit, and the way government uses tax proceeds. By the cumulation of small adjustments in assumptions, most or all of which the study's users would have no way to evaluate, such models can be made to give large or small predictions. Reporting to the National Gambling Impact Study Commission on the use of impact studies to evaluate the economic implications, Adam Rose and Associates (1998) commented on the lack of necessary data, imperfection of models, biased assumptions, and failure to report enough.

> Most of the studies contained biasing assumptions or serious omissions. The most prevalent was the absence of negative impacts from external economic costs or substitution effects.[169]

They cited the use of inflated multipliers as another questionable practice,[170] a complaint also frequently voiced by academic reviewers of the studies of major-league sports stadiums.

INDUSTRY-SPONSORED RESEARCH: THE EVANS GROUP EXAMPLE

SUMMARY. Multiplier models are prospective, predicting what impact a proposed business project may have. After the fact, data can be accessed using statistical and regression procedures to see if impacts materialized. The emphasis for such studies is often employment. According to research not sponsored by the casino industry, commercial casinos nationwide generated job losses in more than 42 percent of the counties with casinos.[171] On the other hand, no promotional study seen by the author has ever reported that a proposed casino would generate job losses. Here, we present an example of a study conducted for a member of the gambling industry, which readers can evaluate for themselves.

International Game Technology (♠IGT), a manufacturer of computerized casino gaming products and video gaming machines, and operator of proprietary gaming systems, commissioned The Evans Group, an econometric consulting firm, to produce a study of the impact of the gambling industry in 1996. The September 9, 1996, press release for the resulting report entitled *A Study of the Economic Impact of the Gaming Industry through 2005* issued by ♠IGT reported:

> States and localities that permit casino gaming have improved their overall economic performance.... The study...reports that **wherever casino gaming has been implemented, employment has risen, unemployment fallen**, and additional tax revenues have been generated. [Emphasis added.]

The Evans Group study describes impacts for individual states. We will briefly examine the findings related to Illinois, the state where the author resides. On page 4-3, the report states:

> Based on these data, **it would appear that the opening of a casino reduced the unemployment rate** in that county in both the year it was opened and in the following year. The average employment in these eight counties...implies a total of 37,000 extra jobs. These multiplier figures are much higher than ordinarily obtained, and employment in these counties might have risen for other reasons as well. Nonetheless, **the figures do indicate that casino gaming has been a boon to these counties**, especially those that are more rural. [Emphasis added.]

Most casinos opened after 1991. The period 1991–96 covered by the study, therefore, coincided with the nationwide economic expansion coming out of the recession of 1990–91. Employment was rising and unemployment was falling in many counties, with or without the introduction of casinos. The authors, therefore, were right to feel uneasy. Their caution that "employment in these counties might have risen for other reasons" shows they knew that simple before-and-after comparisons finding declining unemployment and increasing employment proved nothing about the effects of casinos in a country recovering from recession. Figure 4.9 reproduces Figure 4-1 provided in the original study. The authors explain that the observed drop in casino-county unemployment rates exceeded the state average by 0.3 and 0.2 percentage

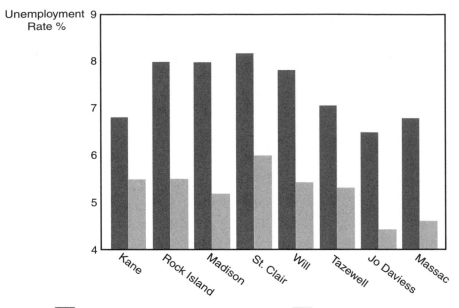

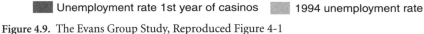

Figure 4.9. The Evans Group Study, Reproduced Figure 4-1

points on average in the first and second year after introduction, respectively. The authors' conclusions are noted previously; the rest of the story follows.

The study gives the impression that counties that opened casinos experienced better economic performance than those that did not. However, Illinois contains 102 counties. We can select other counties that had the same unemployment rate (within 0.1 percentage point) as the casino county in the inital period and compare their performances directly (Figure 4.10). As shown in Figure 4.10, the unemployment rate dropped in all counties with similar initial unemployment. Some counties did better than casino counties, some counties did worse. From left to right, bottom row to top, the casino counties are numbers 6, 1, 3, 3, 3, 7, 3. Nineteen counties performed better than their casino cousins, nineteen performed worse.

A statistical test confirms that the drop in unemployment of casino counties is statistically insignificant from the drop experienced by the

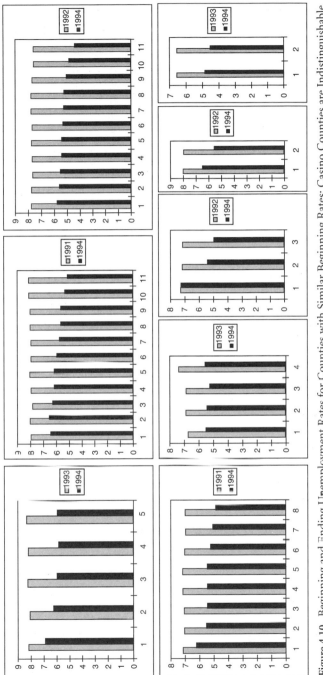

Figure 4.10. Beginning and Ending Unemployment Rates for Counties with Similar Beginning Rates: Casino Counties are Indistinguishable from Noncasino Counties

comparable noncasino counties shown in Figure 4.10. Let ΔU denote the change in county unemployment rate minus the change in state unemployment rate for the same period, and let *Casino* identify counties that introduced casinos in the initial period (*Casino* $= 1$ if a county introduced a casino, 0 otherwise). Then running the following regression

$$\Delta U = a + b \; Casino + \epsilon$$

reveals that coefficient b is 0.275 (consistent with the 0.2 and 0.3 percentage-point differences reported by The Evans Group), but with a standard error of 0.856, implying a P-value of 0.4. Coefficient b is, therefore, statistically indistinguishable from 0 at conventional levels.

CONCLUSIONS

Confusion about economic development, jobs, and the social desirability of casinos is widespread. A similar confusion exists regarding the logically identical issue of the value of major-league sports teams to a community. A net export multiplier model, or a jobs multiplier model, asks:

- What is the effect on the number of jobs of introducing casinos into the economy?

A cost–benefit analysis asks:

- What are the economic costs and benefits of introducing casinos into the economy?

The first question is well defined and valid, but it is not an economic-development question because it does not ask about the well-being of area residents. The second question, phrased in cost–benefit language, *is* an economic-development question because it asks about the effect that the new industry has on the people. Net export multiplier models answer the first question by measuring the impact of the industry in question on revenue flows to the geographical area. If more revenues come in than leave, the industry expands the number of jobs in the geographical area.

Because it is *net new* flows that should be counted, it is easy to mistake or misrepresent flows that are not net or new for those that are and *vice versa*, making the models easy to manipulate. We constructed a model that explained the role of cannibalization, recapture, and leakages.

The difference between counting jobs and conducting a true cost–benefit analysis is easier to understand by considering that among the jobs a new industry might cause to come into being could be jobs that represent costs to society. Enlarging an area's employment base by 5 percent is not a welcome change if the new jobs are required for increased social caseworkers and police, for example. More social workers and police indicate problems that need attention. In short, counting jobs counts jobs; economic development is concerned with higher welfare. Chapter 5 discusses the question of how to measure the costs and benefits in a consistent, theoretically sound way.

5 Cost–Benefit Analysis

Nothing in all the world is more dangerous than sincere ignorance and conscientious stupidity.

Martin Luther King (1963)

CHAPTER SUMMARY. Properly done, cost–benefit analysis is a precise process for measuring the increase or decrease in household well-being attendant upon a change in economic circumstances. Cost–benefit analysis identifies and separates the components of utility change so that they are exhaustive and mutually exclusive. Here, we construct a theory to do that, interpret it, and explain how the derived forms apply to the expansion of casinos, an application that needs to allow for externalities. This chapter is notationally demanding, but the benefit is that once the methodology is completed, and the mathematics have done the work for us, we can be confident in the results. The main contribution of this chapter is the accurate listing of costs and benefits.

The literature on the costs and benefits of casino gambling is fraught with inadequacy and confusion. Even studies that purport to evaluate the economic impact of casinos commonly exhibit a great deal of misunderstanding about what should be included among benefits and costs, and provide little or no guidance about how the costs and benefits relate to one another or should be computed. In general, the costs and benefits discussed are casually listed, vary by study, and are presented with little or no justification of how they were selected. There is no appeal to theory to explain why other potential costs or benefits were excluded. We saw in Chapter 4 why the claim that jobs are an economic benefit of casinos confuses the means to social welfare with the ends.

One discussion of the costs and benefits of gambling identified three principal benefits of casinos: (1) gain in utility (for those gambling in moderation for entertainment); (2) ancillary economic benefits such as "job creation, investment stimulation, tourism development, economic development or redevelopment, urban or waterfront revitalization, or the improvement of the economic status of deserving or underprivileged groups;" and (3) additional revenues to the public sector.[172] The author listed two principal costs: (1) "moral disapproval," and (2) "fears of adverse social impacts," such as pathological gambling, crime, or political corruption.[173] The net increase in profits to business, unless it is meant to be part of ancillary economic benefits, is absent from the list of benefits.[174] Although this author listed gain in utility (clearly internal to the individual or household) as a benefit, he wrote that "many of the costs identified are internal to the individual or the household, as opposed to external – borne by society – and are therefore difficult to place into a cost–benefit framework." This view of costs (including the references to moral disapproval and fears of consequences instead of the actual consequences) suggests that the author believes costs are more subtle and possibly less tangible than benefits. However, because the process that was used to determine how items were included was not explained, there is little theoretical guidance about how the identified cost–benefit components relate to one another or how competing costs and benefits are reconciled.

This chapter shows how cost–benefit components based on utility are derived in a proper evaluation framework. The theory generates a taxonomy for costs and benefits that is exhaustive, internally consistent, utility-based, and theoretically sound. Although the primary purpose of Chapter 5 is to apply cost–benefit theory to evaluating casinos, the methodology applies generally to the evaluation of other industries.

THEORY

SUMMARY. Cost–benefit analysis measures citizen well-being in common units that can be added and compared. It is possible to separate the components of the change in individual well-being into mutually exclusive and exhaustive components. The benefits, if present, of a new business activity include the following:

- net increase in profits measured across all businesses
- net increase in taxes measured across all taxpayers
- consumer surplus (benefits to consumers from lower prices)
- distance consumer surplus (consumer benefits from nearer access to a casino)
- capital gains to consumers induced by the activity
- gains from relaxation or elimination of nonprice constraints on consumer choices

The costs of a new business activity, if present, are as follows:

- real resources consumed to deal with harmful externalities

(Note: Benefits with a negative sign are traditionally counted as costs. Thus, some items on the benefit list also could be costs.)

Our cost–benefit framework can be as comprehensive and general as desired, although our use of it in this chapter provides just enough detail to include all of the major elements commonly thought to be relevant to the economics of gambling. We will supply enough explanation to allow a more detailed application of the framework, if desired.

Our starting point is the individual household's change in utility, $u_i^1 - u_i^0$, where subscript i identifies the household, u is the numerical level of utility, and superscripts 0 and 1 applied here and to other

---

Multiple Types of Gambling

For simplicity's sake, we presume that gambling is a standardized good and that casinos offer gambling on essentially the same terms as casinos in other locations. That is, the returns to playing roulette, slot machines, or a blackjack game are approximately the same regardless of where offered. The framework can be modified at the cost of more detail to allow for different qualities of gambling. In this case, the model would deal with multiple imperfectly substitutable goods.

---

variables throughout the analysis distinguish the "before" and "after" situations, respectively. To fix ideas, we will assume that casinos are geographically widespread in the final situation (Alternative 1) and less widely spread initially (Alternative 0). We assume that $u_i(x_i, x_i^g)$ is a utility function satisfying standard properties[175] defined on consumption bundle (x_i, x_i^g), where x_i is a listing of the economy's private goods, of which there are K types, and x_i^g is a listing of public goods, of which there are L types. A positive element of (x_i, x_i^g) denotes consumption of a good or service by the household, whereas a negative component indicates that the household is a provider of the good or service. In this, we follow standard general equilibrium accounting conventions for describing inputs and outputs. For example, the provision of 10 hours of labor by the individual would appear as -10 in the labor component of x_i, whereas consumption of 6 pounds of fish would appear as a positive number in the fish component.

The spread of a new business sometimes provides advantages to households in the form of amenity benefits. By these, we mean changes to the environment of the consumer that directly improve his or her well-being, but that do not operate through prices or the consumer's income. For example, in the case of casinos, the primary advantage to the household of more casinos is better proximity to the nearest one. Distance consumer surplus, introduced in Chapter 4, captures the consumer's value for this amenity. Distance consumer surplus refers to the amount of money the consumer could give up when a casino is a shorter distance away and be no worse off than the alternative situation when the casino was farther away. From the household's perspective, proximity is a given feature of the economic environment, as are the available public goods x_i^g provided by noncasino sources and the prices that the household faces in the marketplace. All three need to be accounted for.

Next, relate utility to dollars as follows. Define the expenditure function $e_i(d_i, x_i^g, p_i, u_i)$ as the minimum expenditure needed to achieve utility u_i when prices are p_i, d_i is the distance to the nearest casino, and public goods are provided in the amount x_i^g. The expenditure function increases for larger u_i for fixed choice of d_i, x_i^g, and p_i. The sign of $e(d_i^1, x_i^{g1}, p_i^1, u_i^1) - e(d_i^1, x_i^{g1}, p_i^1, u_i^0)$ is identical to the sign of $u_i^1 - u_i^0$. Given distance, public goods, and prices, therefore, $e(d_i, x_i^g, p_i, u_i(x_i, x_i^g))$ is itself a utility function that reports utility in dollar units. That is, $100 of utility is the utility that can be achieved by optimally spending $100 at prices p_i with nearest casino d_i miles away when public goods x_i^g are provided.

We want to compare social welfare between situations 0 and 1. By definition, the changes in welfare that result for all households in the move from the original situation to the final one are the social costs and benefits of the change. The approach described thus far provides the framework for analyzing this change:

$$\Delta W = \sum_i w_i \left[e_i \left(d_i^1, x_i^{g1}, p_i^1, u_i^1 \right) - e_i \left(d_i^1, x_i^{g1}, p_i^1, u_i^0 \right) \right] \quad (5.1)$$

where w_i are the social weights accorded to the utility of each household, $\sum_i w_i = m$, $m_i > 0$, and m is the number of consumer households. In applying Equation 5.1, we must identify how we handle a number of issues.

- We assume that a dollar of value to one household is equal to a dollar of value to another. With respect to Equation 5.1, this implies that w_i is the same for all households. The transfer of wealth in gambling is generally from relatively poor to relatively wealthy. Therefore, if we believed that a dollar generates more utility for rich than poor, our assumption would understate the social benefits. If we believed that a dollar generates more utility for the poor than the rich, our assumption understates the social costs of casinos. The assumption of equal value across households also implies that firm profits do not need to be assigned artificial premia or discounts based on which individuals or households happen to own them.[176]

- One desirable implication of our assumption is that firm profits are equally important to social welfare regardless of which firm generates them. For example, casino profits are valued the same as the profits of a noncasino firm.

- To allow for regional tax differences, households and firms may face different prices. In an extreme case, each firm and household could have a different, personalized set of prices. Household i faces prices p_i, firm j faces prices p_j, and endowments ω (i.e., goods of the K types available in the economy that are not produced in the current period but are inherited from nature or the past) are traded at prices p_ω.

- We allow for the possibility that consumers may be constrained in their market decisions by factors other than price and income. We often refer to these as **transactions constraints**. The most important example would be constraints on labor supply that result in unemployment. People have a reservation wage above which they are willing to work, but cannot always find a job at that wage, and lowering their asking wage will not increase the chances of their getting a job.

- Firms and economy endowments ω are owned by households. Household i owns share θ_{ij} of firm j, $\sum_i \theta_{ij} = 1$, and endowment ω_i, where $\sum_i \omega_i = \omega$, the economy endowment vector.

- The government uses tax revenues to buy goods and services and to provide public goods.[177] The government does not publicly provide private goods, although this complication could be added to the model. The relevant feature for the analysis is that real resources are used to produce the goods provided by the government. Hence, taxes paid by casinos and other firms are a social benefit because they make available more resources to provide utility-raising goods to the public. Holding the quantities of public goods constant, taxes *paid* by the public reduce their welfare by shrinking their ability to consume goods and services.

- In addition to direct benefits and costs, casinos may generate positive or negative externalities. In general, positive externalities are helpful effects from an activity on an agent different from the one undertaking the activity that do not operate through markets and that are not reaped by the agent creating them. Negative externalities are the same as positive externalilities, except that their effects on other agents are harmful. For example, if a casino's presence reduces crime in an area, leading to less need for police presence, this frees resources to the rest of the community and represents a positive externality. The firm creating the positive externality does not personally benefit from the effect. If the reverse is true, and the casino increases the need for police, real resources are removed (paid for by the public in taxes), which is a negative externality.

- Although it is not strictly necessary for deriving a working cost–benefit measure, sketching some of the background details of the production side of the economy may be helpful to some readers. Production is conducted by firms and government. The production choice of agent j is described by its list of inputs and outputs $(y_j, y_j^g, -y_j^G) \in Y_j$, where Y_j is the $(K + 2L)$-dimensional set of feasible production choices. The production set is assumed to satisfy standard assumptions, such as being nonempty, closed, and convex. y_j is the K-dimensional vector listing private goods. Following the usual convention, an element in y_j with a positive sign denotes an output and an element with a negative sign denotes an input. y_j^g in L-dimensional space is the vector of public goods produced by agent j. y_j^G, also L-dimensional, lists the public goods available for use as inputs in the production of agent j. The capital letter G denotes the publicness of the list of public goods; all firms can use the same public-good inputs. The negative sign before y_j^G indicates that y_j^G are inputs to the firm.

Social accounting in real terms requires that

$$x + r = y + \omega + z \tag{5.2}$$

$$x_i^g = \sum_j y_j^g = -y_j^G \tag{5.3}$$

where $x \equiv \sum_i x_i$ is aggregate consumption of private goods, and $y \equiv \sum_j y_j$ is aggregate current production of private goods. Consumption of public goods by households x_i^g and use of public goods as inputs by firms y_j^G each equal the available economy supply $\sum_j y_j^g$ because of their public-good feature. z is the economy trade vector. Although it, too, is not central to our discussion, we include z to be consistent with the general framework we develop. Components of z are economy excess demands for traded goods. A zero denotes a nontraded good, a positive entry denotes imports. The vector r of nonnegative numbers in K-dimensional space denotes resources taken out of the productive system. These are resources used to deal with harmful externalities and to produce public goods. A car used by police, and not available to provide utility to households, would come from the car services component of r, for example. Because utility depends on (x_i, x_i^g) and not r, the drain of goods and services implies real utility cost to households.

Consider the following carefully chosen identity, a telescoping sum where each term cancels part of the preceding term:

$$\sum_i \left[e_i \left(d_i^1, x_i^{g1}, p_i^1, u_i^1 \right) - e_i \left(d_i^1, x_i^{g1}, p_i^1, u_i^0 \right) \right] =$$

$$\sum_i \left[e_i \left(d_i^1, x_i^{g1}, p_i^1, u_i^1 \right) - p_i^1 \cdot x_i^1 \right] \tag{5.4}$$

(Transactions Constraints in Situation 1)

$$+ \sum_i \left[p_i^1 \cdot x_i^1 - p_i^0 \cdot x_i^0 \right] \tag{5.5}$$

(Income Effects)

$$+ \sum_i \left[p_i^0 \cdot x_i^0 - e_i \left(d_i^0, x_i^{g0}, p_i^0, u_i^0 \right) \right] \tag{5.6}$$

(Transactions Constraints in Situation 0)

$$+ \sum_i \left[e_i \left(d_i^0, x_i^{g0}, p_i^0, u_i^0 \right) - e_i \left(d_i^0, x_i^{g1}, p_i^0, u_i^0 \right) \right] \tag{5.7}$$

(Public Good Effect)

$$+ \sum_i \left[e_i \left(d_i^0, x_i^{g1}, p_i^0, u_i^0 \right) - e_i \left(d_i^1, x_i^{g1}, p_i^0, u_i^0 \right) \right] \tag{5.8}$$

(Distance Consumer Surplus)

$$+ \sum_i \left[e_i \left(d_i^1, x_i^{g1}, p_i^0, u_i^0 \right) - e_i \left(d_i^1, x_i^{g1}, p_i^1, u_i^0 \right) \right]. \tag{5.9}$$

(Consumer Surplus)

We now explain what the components in Equations 5.4 through 5.9 tell us. Start with Equation 5.4. Recall that $e_i(d_i^1, x_i^{g1}, p_i^1, u_i^1)$ by definition is the *least* costly way of achieving the utility u_i^1 that was actually achieved in Situation 1. Consumption bundle (x_i^1, x_i^{g1}) satisfies $u^1 = u(x_i^1, x_i^{g1})$ and thus is one way to achieve utility u^1. If bundle x_i^1 – the choice actually made by the consumer in Situation 1 – is not the cheapest way to achieve utility u_i^1, then Equation 5.4 is positive and the consumer's choice must have been constrained. Otherwise, why would the consumer choose a more costly bundle to achieve the same utility? Thus, the cost difference in Equation 5.4 is the amount of money the individual would be willing to pay to remove the constraint.

We will interpret Equation 5.5 at the end of the discussion because it needs one more manipulation before we are ready to give it meaning.

Equation 5.6 measures the welfare impact of transactions constraints on the consumer in Situation 0. Its interpretation is the same as Equation 5.4 was for Situation 1.

The telescoping sum requires the presence of Equation 5.7, which measures the value to households of the change in public goods provided between the initial and final situations.[178] The government pays for the public goods it provides with tax dollars. The formula in

Equation 5.7 allows for the worth of those public goods to be above or below the cost of the inputs needed to make them. Government using \$100 to pay for public goods that the public values at \$65, for example, would constitute inefficient or wasteful government. It is not our purpose to discuss whether getting more taxes to the government increases the amount wasted, for example, so we will speak as if additional taxes produce public goods of value equal to the cost of the resources used to produce them. We could also allow for the possibility that the government rebates some tax dollars in a lump-sum fashion back to the private citizens who use them to purchase private goods and services. Either way, the additional taxes received by government and paid by business represents a benefit to consumers.

Distance consumer surplus, Equation 5.8, measures the value to the consumer of having the nearest casino distance d_i^1 away compared to distance d_i^0. For example, in the initial situation, the consumer needed $e_i(d_i^0, x_i^{g1}, p_i^0, u_i^0)$ to reach initial utility. When the nearest casino is closer, distance $d_i^1 < d_i^0$, the income needed to maintain original utility, $e_i(d_i^1, x_i^{g1}, p_i^0, u_i^0)$, is smaller (presuming the individual likes to gamble). The difference in Equation 5.8, therefore, is the amount the consumer would be willing to pay to have the nearest casino closer.

Equation 5.9 is the conventional measure of consumer surplus. It measures the amount of money that the consumer would be willing to give up to have better prices. The only difference between the two terms in Equation 5.9 is the price vector. If prices p_i^1 are better for the household than prices p_i^0 (i.e., lower for goods purchased and/or higher for goods sold, such as labor), then Equation 5.9 is positive.

We now turn to Equation 5.5, which we postponed. To revise it, use the aggregated household budget identity

$$\sum_i p_i \cdot x_i = \Pi + p \cdot \omega + T - E \tag{5.10}$$

where Π is the after-tax profit of firms in the economy, $p \cdot \omega$ is the income from endowments, T is taxes collected, and E is expenditure on resources r used to deal with externalities and provide public goods.[179]

The key consideration is that E represents expenditure on real resources taken from the economy. Differencing Equation 5.10 between the initial and final situations[180] yields

$$\sum_i \left[p_i^1 \cdot x_i^1 - p_i^0 \cdot x_i^0 \right] = \Delta \Pi + \Delta p \cdot \omega + \Delta T - \Delta E. \quad (5.11)$$

Thus, Equation 5.5 measures benefits appearing as net increase in profits to firms, increased value of household endowments, the net change in taxes collected, and the increased use of economy resources by government due to the shift from the initial to the final situation.[181]

Substituting Equation 5.11 into Equation 5.5, writing the distance effects in differential form, and rearranging gives the following overall taxonomy of cost–benefit elements that we seek:

$$\Delta W \equiv \sum_i \left[e_i \left(d_i^1, x_i^{g1}, p_i^1, u_i^1 \right) - e \left(d_i^1, x_i^{g1}, p_i^1, u_i^0 \right) \right]$$

$$= \sum_j \Delta \Pi_j + \Delta T + (5.9)$$

$$+ \left(\sum_i \int_{d_i^0}^{d_i^1} \frac{\partial e_i}{\partial d_i} dd_i \right) + \Delta p_\omega \cdot \omega + (5.7)$$

$$+ (5.4) + (5.6) - \Delta E$$

$$= \text{Change in Profits} + \text{Change in Taxes} \quad (5.12)$$

$$+ \text{Consumer Surplus} + \text{Distance Consumer Surplus}$$

$$+ \text{Capital Gains} + \text{Public Good Effect}$$

$$+ \text{Transactions Constraints}^1 + \text{Transactions Constraints}^0$$

$$- \text{Externality Costs}.$$

The nine components in Equation 5.12 are an exhaustive and exact tabulation of the elements that measure the economic effects of a new industry – in this case, casinos. Moreover, Equation 5.12 with Equations 5.4–5.9 shows precisely *how* each term should be computed. Whether a component is a cost or a benefit depends on the sign. Normally, profits are

---

Unemployment

The introduction of a new industry or business might be able to temporarily reduce unemployment below what it would have been otherwise. Discovering what the time path of unemployment would have been with and without the industry present is extremely difficult to do.

A significant amount of promotional material purports that casinos decrease unemployment, but fails to prove what employment *would have been* in the absence of casinos. Most casinos were introduced after 1991, when the country was recovering from the recession of 1990–91. The period from 1991 to 2001 also coincided with the longest economic expansion in American history. As the country emerged from the recession, unemployment declined in areas with and without casinos. If casinos *temporarily* reduced unemployment faster than it would have fallen otherwise, this transitory effect could correctly be counted as a benefit of casinos. However, we know of no study that has made this case. On the contrary, the failure to account for the decline in unemployment that would have occurred anyway leads to a classic *post hoc, ergo propter hoc* fallacy of logic. An example appears in Chapter 4, which discussed The Evans Group (1996). Although The Evans Group argued that casinos reduced unemployment, its study did not report that areas without casinos with comparable starting unemployment rates experienced comparable and, in many cases, larger reductions in the unemployment rate.

---

expected to be a benefit because introducing a new activity is expected to create profits for the entering firm. The term in Equation 5.12 requires something different, however. The introduction of the new industry must cause the profits summed over all firms to rise. Only if net profits increase is the contribution of profits positive. Higher net profits, of course, is beneficial because it implies that there is more income available for the purchase of goods and services to those who own the profits. Increased taxes are also typically expected to be on the benefit side of the ledger because taxes collected from casinos enter government coffers and are used to provide utility-enhancing goods to citizens. Better access to casinos is a benefit to those who gamble, but consumer surplus is typically

TABLE 5.1. Summary of Casino Costs and Benefits

Benefits	Costs	Cost or Benefit as Applicable
Higher Profits	Externality	Transactions Constraints
Higher Tax Collections	Costs	Capital Gains
Distance Consumer Surplus		Consumer Surplus

not a consideration because prices of gambling or other products are not usually lower because of gambling. The primary costs are the externality costs associated with gambling.

The effect of introducing casinos on improving or worsening the extent of constraints on household market transactions varies. The main way that this might apply is through gambling's effect on unemployed workers. In the long term, most economists believe that quantity demanded equals quantity supplied. In the labor market, therefore, full employment will be reached with or without a given industry present in the economy. In that case, the contribution operating through the transaction term in the long term is zero.

A new regional business could change prices enough to matter to local residents. We noted in Chapter 4 that if casinos increased employment, the demand for local housing could increase, thus raising housing prices and providing capital gains for residents. The *reduction* in demand for residential property and capital *losses* in the areas from which the new residents came would have to be accounted for as well. Over time, if new housing was built to respond to the increased demand, the prices of the existing stock of housing also would be affected. Because gambling does not create new people (it can only move them from one place to another), a reasonable first approximation is that the net effect of a casino on capital gains and consumer surplus considerations is small. If firm and household prices are invariant to the amount of gambling ($p_i^0 = p_i^1$, $p_j^0 = p_j^1$, $p_\omega^0 = p_\omega^1$), the two terms in Equation 5.12 related to capital gains on endowments and consumer surplus drop out.

COMMON MISTAKES IN APPLYING COST–BENEFIT ANALYSIS

SUMMARY. Cost–benefit analysis tends to be misused in predictable ways. Chapter 4 discussed the tendency to state an industry's impact on regional jobs as an economic benefit without computing its significance in terms of value to area residents. Other common mistakes are to confuse business profitability with social profitability; to focus on the profits of the industry being added to the economy and to neglect to account for lost profits of other businesses; to count taxes paid by the industry as being added to the economy without accounting for reduced tax collections elsewhere; to make unsubstantiated claims about unemployment; and to neglect to consider externality costs.

Equation 5.12 allows us to address some common errors and mistakes of cost–benefit analysis in the case of gambling. The first obvious error is the tendency to identify business profitability, $\sum_j \Pi_j$, and its improvement, $\sum_j \Delta \Pi_j$, with "social profitability"; that is, passing a cost–benefit test. Business profitability is clearly important to social profitability and contributes to a true cost–benefit evaluation, but the two are not synonymous. Failure to account for all of the components of social profitability is perhaps the most common failing. Casino profits are visible and prominent; costs and other benefits may be less so.

Another error is to evaluate the economic impact of gambling with respect to the profits and taxes of a subset of firms – typically, the profits and taxes of firms in one state or region and sometimes the profits and taxes of local gambling firms only. Net profits and taxes are calculated by determining the casino profits and taxes, minus the reduction in profits and taxes of other businesses caused by casinos. Although casino profits and taxes are highly visible, they are invalid measures of *social* benefits because they do not adjust for the entire economy for the lost profits and taxes of competing businesses. This point is not special to casinos. Any business – be it Wal-Mart or a drugstore chain – that attracts consumer sales, employs labor and other inputs, and displaces competing businesses should be evaluated on the same basis. Equation 5.12 sums profits over all firms, not just casinos or firms in one location.

Ignoring firms that lose profits and pay lower taxes due to the expansion of gambling is equivalent to selecting weights for them in Equation 5.1 that are zero. Because households own these other firms, this violates the assumption that households are treated equally.

With respect to social costs, it is not uncommon for studies to omit them entirely or to focus only on costs within the state, even though casinos that border another state have ramifications for citizens of the neighboring jurisdiction. Equation 5.12, discussed previously with respect to firms, also sums over *all* households and regions. Evaluations that consider only the costs or benefits of a subset of households or regions are inaccurate and incomplete. For example, the cost–benefit measure in Equation 5.12 does not treat the impact of a job in one location as more valued than the same job in another. Employment is not a benefit to the economy unless it increases one or more of the components in Equation 5.12.

Regional competition across jurisdictions often suffers from the problems just discussed. When the benefits – often profits and taxes – go to the jurisdiction with the casino but the social costs go to another, the winning jurisdiction has no incentive to care about the costs. Implicitly, it is weighting the costs as zero because they accrue elsewhere, when a true cost–benefit analysis would count them. A similar circumstance applies to production externalities. The town that has a factory that creates tremendous pollution and damage to the residents in some other location, or a factory that produces a defective good that damages users of the good, may still extol the desirability of the factory. In explaining why political decisions may not match up with social desirability, we should consider the failure to count the damage imposed on others, as well as lack of knowledge about costs.

6 Social Benefits

Everything is worth what its purchaser will pay for it.

Publius Syrus, (42 B.C.)

CHAPTER SUMMARY. The demonstration in Chapter 5 that the benefits of casinos are described by profits, taxes, distance consumer surplus, consumer surplus, induced capital gains, and elimination of transactions constraints, if any, may surprise some who expected to see jobs ("economic development") figure prominently in the discussion. This chapter elaborates and expands our discussion of economic benefits, followed by numerical estimates. Here, we estimate the benefits of casino expansion in three ways: by using economic theory to construct a bound for measuring benefits using information on how much consumers gamble when they are different distances from the casino; by applying the bound to a rule of thumb about how casino demand drops off with distance; and by simulating the gambling choices of a representative consumer. The three estimates produce similar answers, giving us confidence in the estimates.

VALUE ONCE AGAIN

SUMMARY. Consumers value things that improve their well-being. The benefits in a cost–benefit analysis are the identifiable components of anything that leads to the consumer's improvement in well-being. In the case of casinos, the main benefit to expansion is the value to consumers of closer proximity to casinos.

For a short time in the 1980s, there was a rage surrounding "pet rocks." Customers at retail store checkout counters could find ordinary field stones for sale. The size that would fit into one's pocket or purse, the rocks had names cut into their surface or sometimes happy faces. They were the ideal pet, so the story went, because they required no feeding, no care, and no training, yet their happy demeanor provided love and companionship on demand when removed from one's pocket or purse. Eventually, the fad died away, leaving the interesting question: How did pet rocks represent economic value and what economic benefit did they provide?

The phenomenon of selling apparently worthless rocks provides an interesting parallel to gambling, which many describe as shifting money from one person's pocket to another's without creating anything in the process. It would be easy to dismiss both activities as socially wasteful. Because of their simplicity, however, pet rocks offer a useful object lesson for identifying economic benefits.

Value is a statement about what people want – how they think about a particular arrangement of objects or services. Stones in the field generally have zero value. If a field stone is collected, carved with a face or name, and boxed and distributed to retailers for sale at checkout counters, economic benefits result *if* consumers see the rocks as desirable and are willing to pay for them at least as much as it cost to make them available. For a short time, pet rocks passed this test; therefore, they represented a bona fide part of gross domestic product.

A similar description applies to gambling and popular entertainment, which are services. Services get their value from the worth that people ascribe to them. Passing a cost–benefit test means tallying all of the values from a set of activities and learning that the sum is higher than for the next best set of activities.

Chapter 5 identified increased profits and taxes as two forms that an increase in well-being could take. To be sure that an activity making profit represents a true social gain, we must identify what would have happened if the activity had not been undertaken. In the case of pet rocks, producers could have used their time and resources elsewhere. If their profits in pet rocks were equal to their foregone profits, then their pet-rocks profits did not represent a net gain to society. Other forms that benefits may take must also be considered. For example, a monopoly producer might supplant competitive producers of a good. Competitive firms earn zero profits and a monopolist earns positive profits; however, the monopolist's profits imply losses to consumers in the form of higher prices, so that there is a net social *loss*.

Producers and sellers pay taxes. Government (i.e., all of us collectively) is a beneficiary of business expansion through the additional taxes paid. Again, only the *net increase* in taxes represents additional value (i.e., benefits) to society from the cost–benefit perspective and, as discussed in Chapter 5, only if the taxes are used by government in a constructive fashion. Here, we do not get into the debate about the value of government expenditure, but presume that tax revenues are social benefits.

Some of the benefits in cost–benefit analysis also may take the form of price improvements and greater convenience to consumers. Both can be measured in dollar terms. If you normally pay $1.00 for your morning coffee and then learn that you can get the same coffee for $.80, you are better off by at least $.20 because you can have your coffee and whatever $.20 will buy. Your *consumer surplus* has increased by the savings on your coffee purchases. Consumer benefits also can result from getting the object under more favorable conditions. A grocery store opening nearer your home might sell at the identical prices as one farther away, but you receive value because of the greater convenience – convenience that you would be willing to pay for if it were necessary to guarantee that the grocery store would open nearby. The fact that the opening took place without the need for you to pay means that you retained the increased value. When consumer benefits of either or both type (i.e., price and convenience) are present, they should be summed over all of society. The latter form of consumer benefit, distance consumer surplus, applies to the geographical expansion of an industry such as casinos.

DISTANCE BENEFITS

SUMMARY. Reducing the distance needed to travel to the nearest casino from 500 or more miles to 5 miles generates consumer benefits that are less than $43 per person per year, according to a procedure that produces an upper bound. An exact simulation using a representation of consumer preferences produces a number of $34 per person per year. This figure is adjusted for the fact that one third or more of casino revenues typically come from problem and pathological gamblers.

Adults in the United States have been able to gamble in casinos in Nevada since 1931. What is different in Atlantic City since 1978 and in many other locations since 1990 is the ability to find casinos nearby. Gambling in one casino is much like gambling in another. Typically, 70 percent or more of casino revenues derive from slot machines. Blackjack, roulette, and other table games are also available in most casinos, played according to standard rules. With the exception of destination resort locations, such as in Nevada and Atlantic City – where the reason for travel often has as much to do with the nongambling attractions of world-class entertainment and dining as it does the gambling – the expansion of regional casinos of convenience in the past fifteen years provides comparable gambling opportunities to one another. The primary *gambling-related* benefit of casino expansions to consumers, therefore, takes the form of closer proximity.[182] In this section, we discuss the social benefits to consumers of this improved proximity.[183,184]

The connection between distance and consumer welfare includes many considerations. One consumer might enjoy a moderately long drive to a ski resort, for example, whereas another views it as a burdensome inconvenience. In this chapter, we take the "representative consumer approach," which models the behavior of a single individual whose choices

Distance and Demand

Information about how demand varies with price allows the benefits to the consumer of lower price, *consumer surplus*, to be calculated. Figure 6 shows hypothetical demand for visits to a recreation site as a function of price per visit and distance. The curve labeled $m = 500$ miles is a demand curve. When the distance is 500 miles away, for example, and the price is g_1, the consumer chooses consumption at Point a. Lowering price from g_1 to g_2 with no change in distance causes the consumer to choose Point b. The benefit to the consumer from the price reduction is measured by the shaded area bounded by the demand curve and the two price levels.[1]

When we consider demand for casino gambling, the amount spent per visit becomes a choice of the consumer, as well as how many visits to make per year. Presuming now that Figure 6 refers to demand for casino gambling, the consumer selects Point a when the nearest casino is 500 miles away, Point c when the nearest casino is 100 miles away, but Point d when it is only 5 miles away. The consumer makes more visits when the casino is closer, spending less per visit but more in total per year.

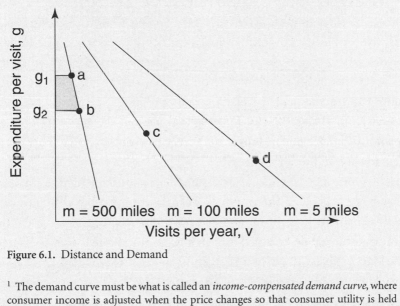

Figure 6.1. Distance and Demand

[1] The demand curve must be what is called an *income-compensated demand curve*, where consumer income is adjusted when the price changes so that consumer utility is held constant.

represent the average consumer's behavior. This approach is common in *macroeconomics*, the study of economy behavior.

Information about how demand for a product varies with distance can be used to infer the value of closer proximity to consumers. A direct approach is generally preferred for measuring the consumer benefits of amenities such as nearness. Bockstael and McConnell (1993) consider a direct approach to measuring the value of water quality at a beach by the way demand for associated private goods (e.g., use of the beach) change with the level of the water quality. This scenario has similarities to measuring the benefits of proximity (distance is an amenity like water quality), but differs from the casino-siting problem because prices for the private good in the Bockstael and McConnell analysis are constant. In gambling, both the number of visits (i.e., quantity) and the amount spent (i.e., price) are choice variables of the consumer. Therefore, we need to allow for differences that apply to gambling.

The skier who anticipates having to make a long trip to enjoy skiing generally plans to ski several days instead of the afternoon he or she might ski if the slopes were a few minutes down the road. Increased distance causes the skier to take fewer trips per year but to do more skiing per trip. We would expect total annual expediture on skiing to be higher for the skier living close by, however. He or she would be more likely to buy a season lift ticket and be on the slopes more frequently. This pattern appears to apply to a large number of leisure activities, whether it is visits to Disney World, hunting and fishing, skiing, or gambling: greater distance leads to longer, less frequent trips and declining total expenditure on the activity.

The consumer benefit of having nearby casinos versus ones farther away is the answer to the question: What would you be willing to pay each year for the benefit of having a casino located nearer to you? The same question could be asked for other recreational sites, such as Disney World or a ski resort. Assuming truthful answers, the average of all such responses would be the per capita **distance benefit** of casino expansion. Such a survey has not been conducted, but by using information on how

TABLE 6.1. Distance and Demand Data: Casinos

Distance (miles) d	Expenditure per Visit g	Vists per Year v	Expenditure per Year gv	Expenditure per Year (2000 s) gv
0–35	$35.31	3.56	$125.70	$166.37
35–75	$62.39	1.56	$97.33	$128.82
75–150	$64.54	0.73	$47.11	$62.36
150–300	$85.45	0.48	$41.02	$54.29
Over 300	$143.01	0.10	$14.30	$18.93

demand for casino services varies by distance from the casino, we can infer how big the benefit is.

Table 6.1 provides data showing gambling expenditures averaged for Las Vegas, Atlantic City, and Illinois casinos.[185] The right-hand column adjusts dollar values for price level changes to 2000. We take advantage of data relating distance and demand in three ways. First, we use it to construct information of the type shown in Figure 6.2. As the distance from the nearest casino is reduced from 500 to 5 miles, it causes the expenditure per visit, g, and the number of visits per year, v, to vary with it. The area of the shaded portion of the figure is a dollar number that is greater than the value to the consumer of reducing the distance to the nearest casino from 500 to 5 miles. Other starting and ending distances would be handled comparably. Thus, constructing a curve of the type DD in Figure 6.2 and calculating the shaded area produces an upper bound for the distance benefits of nearer casinos.

The second way we use the data is to perform an exact calculation of the benefits of closer casinos by simulating consumer behavior for a representative consumer whose choices mimic the data. Results of the simulation are reported in Table 6.2.

The third method uses the rule of thumb that casino demand drops by 30 to 35 percent for each doubling of distance to provide a continuous relation between distance and demand that is consistent with the main

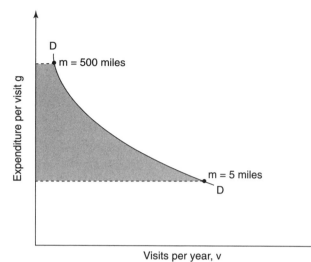

Figure 6.2. Using Demand for Casino Gambling by Distance to Infer the Benefits of Proximity: The Shaded Area Provides a Dollar Upper Bound on the Consumer Benefits of Nearer Casinos

elements of Table 6.1. Table 6.3 was constructed this way. Integrating the area under the corresponding demand schedule produces upper-bound estimates of the distance benefits reported in Table 6.4.

The procedures reach similar conclusions. Rounding to the nearest dollar, the first method suggests that the distance benefit from reducing the distance needed to travel to the nearest casino from 500 to 5 miles is less than $43 per adult annually. The second method based on the exact simulation indicated that the amount is less than $48. The third method finds that the yearly distance benefit of reducing the distance from 500 to 5 miles is less than $41. The distance benefits for other combinations of distance reductions can be seen in Table 6.4.

Taking the highest benefit of the three, $48, and adjusting for the fact that one fourth or more of casino revenues comes from problem and pathological gamblers, suggests that the benefit for *nonproblem and nonpathological* gamblers is less than $34 per adult.[186] For the interested reader, more details about the three methods are provided in the box.

TABLE 6.2. Distance Benefits Estimated by Simulation: The amount by which income can be reduced when $m = 0$, holding utility at its $m = 500$ level, is the distance benefit.

| Variable | Benchmark | Additive | | Multiplicative | |
(1)	(2)	(3)	(4)	(5)	(6)
Distance (miles) — m	0	500	0	500	0
Expenditure/Visit — g	$55	$112.96	$55.00	$110.46	$55.00
Visits/Year — v	3.6363	0.1	3.6321	0.1	3.63206
Expenditure — gv	$200	$11.30	$199.77	$11.03	$199.76
Annual Income — Income	$40,000	$40,000	$40,000–$46.63	$40,000	$40,000–$47.36
Utility — $u(x,v,E(g,m))$	100	99.947	99.947	99.882	99.882

119

TABLE 6.3. Gambling Demand Implied by Table 6.1 and the 30 to 35 Percent Rule

Distance (miles) d	Expenditure per Visit g	Vists per Year v	Expenditure per Year gv
0	$71.83	10.580	$759.93
3	$71.83	10.580	$759.93
15	$77.59	3.669	$284.63
35	$80.80	2.101	$169.73
55	$82.57	1.560	$128.82
75	$83.81	1.272	$106.61
150	$86.64	0.806	$69.84
300	$89.56	0.511	$45.75
Over 300	$100.36	0.100	$10.05

TABLE 6.4. Distance Benefits Implied by Table 6.3 Gamblers

Starting Distance (miles)	2000	1000	500	100	50	20	10	5
3000	$0.25	$0.84	$1.75	$6.14	$9.84	$17.87	$27.74	$42.81
2000	$0.00	$0.59	$1.50	$5.89	$9.59	$17.62	$27.49	$42.56
1000		$0.00	$0.91	$5.30	$9.00	$17.03	$26.90	$41.97
500			$0.00	$4.39	$8.09	$16.12	$25.99	$41.06
100				$0.00	$3.70	$11.73	$21.60	$36.67
50					$0.00	$8.03	$17.90	$32.97
20						$0.00	$9.87	$24.94
10							$0.00	$15.07
5								$0.00

Final Distance (miles)

Estimate 1: Using Data on Distance and Gambling Demand to Find a Bound on Distance Consumer Surplus

The connection between data on distance and demand and the value to consumers of the greater convenience of gambling nearby is established as follows. Assume that there are two goods: casino visits, v, and a composite good, x, which represents consumption of all other goods. All else held constant, assume that the enjoyment derived from a casino visit combined with traveling a shorter distance is greater than the enjoyment for the same visit coupled with traveling a longer distance.[7] For fixed distance, assume that the enjoyment per visit rises with expenditure per visit. The overall quality of a visit – the enjoyment factor – is a function of both distance and expenditure, $E = E(g, m)$, where E rises with the amount gambled on the visit g and falls with the distance traveled in miles, m. We represent satisfaction in terms of *utility*, which depends on the quantity of x, the number of gambling visits, and the enjoyment factor

$$u = u(x, v, E(g, m)) \tag{6.1}$$

where $\frac{\partial u}{\partial x} > 0$, $\frac{\partial u}{\partial v} > 0$, $\frac{\partial u}{\partial E} > 0$. If consumers adjust their number of visits and amount gambled in such a way that visit for visit, the enjoyment attached to visits coming from farther away are nondecreasing in distance, then we can show that

$$\frac{\partial e}{\partial m} dm \leq v dg. \tag{6.2}$$

In other words, the area under the curve relating number of visits and the amount gambled per visit that was created by varying the distance to the nearest casino provides an upper bound on the consumer benefits of reduced distance. This is what Figure 6.2 shows by relating demand and distance information to consumer benefits.

The construction of the bound in Equation 6.2 is as follows. Let $e(p, m, u) = p_x x + g v$ be the minimal expenditure needed for the consumer to achieve utility $u = u(x, v, E(g, m))$ when the price of goods x is p, m is the number of miles to the nearest casino, v is the number of casino visits, and $E(g, m)$ is the enjoyment factor associated with a casino visit. We assume that $\frac{\partial E}{\partial g}$ and $-\frac{\partial E}{\partial m}$ are both positive.

The Lagrangian associated with the minimization problem forming e is

$$L = px + gv + \lambda[u - u(x, v, E(g, m))] \tag{6.3}$$

where λ is the Lagrangian multiplier, interpreted as the marginal cost of an additional unit of utility. The first-order conditions to the minimization are as follows:

$$\frac{\partial L}{\partial x} : \quad p = \lambda u_x \tag{6.4}$$

$$\frac{\partial L}{\partial v} : \quad g = \lambda u_v \tag{6.5}$$

$$\frac{\partial L}{\partial g} : \quad v = \lambda u_E E_g \tag{6.6}$$

where subscripts denote partial derivatives. Applying the envelope theorem to expenditure,

$$\frac{\partial e}{\partial m} = \frac{\partial L}{\partial m} = -\lambda u_E E_m. \tag{6.7}$$

Equation 6.7 shows that expenditure rises with distance to hold utility constant because u_E and λ are positive and E_m is negative. Presuming that $v(m)$ and $g(m)$ are the optimizing choices of v and g, $E(g(m), m)$ varies according to

$$\frac{dE}{dm} = E_g \frac{dg}{dm} + E_m. \tag{6.8}$$

Substituting into Equation 6.7 gives

$$\frac{\partial e}{\partial m} dm = -\lambda u_E E_m dm \tag{6.9}$$

$$= -\lambda u_E \left(\frac{dE}{dm} - E_g \frac{dg}{dm} \right) dm \tag{6.10}$$

$$= \lambda u_E E_g \frac{dg}{dm} dm - \lambda u_E \frac{dE}{dm} dm \tag{6.11}$$

$$= v dg - \lambda u_E dE \tag{6.12}$$

$$\leq v dg \tag{6.13}$$

where the last inequality follows from the behavioral assumption that $\frac{dE}{dm}$ is nonnegative, meaning that the enjoyment connected to a visit for which the consumer spent more because he or she had to travel a greater distance is more than the enjoyment attached to one of frequent short visits where the distance traveled was short. Adding up all of the values vdg, which is what taking the area to the left of the curve in Figure 6.2 does, produces the desired upper bound for distance consumer surplus.

[7] We assume this because it is the usual case. For some individuals, of course, traveling to a resort location might become an enjoyment in its own right. The fact that most people use airplanes rather than cruise ships or cars, however, suggests that time in travel is minimized.

Estimate 2: Simulating the Benefits of Distance

Exact simulation is an alternative to the method of constructing an upper bound on distance consumer surplus. This chapter reports results of a simulation for an indivual whose utility, $u = u(x, v, E(g, m))$, depends positively on the number of casino visits, v, and on $E(g, m)$, an enjoyment factor that depends positively on the amount gambled, g, and negatively on the miles needed to travel to the casino for each visit, m. It also depends on the consumption of other goods, x. We benchmark the consumers' preferences so that they make their choices in a way that represents the behavior we observe in Table 6.1.

We report simulations for two versions of utility,

$$u = c_0 \left[c_1 x^{\frac{\sigma-1}{\sigma}} + c_2 v^{\frac{\sigma-1}{\sigma}} \right]^{\frac{\sigma}{\sigma-1}} + E(g, m) \tag{6.14}$$

$$u = c_3 \left[c_4 x^{\frac{\sigma-1}{\sigma}} + E(g, m) v^{\frac{\sigma-1}{\sigma}} \right]^{\frac{\sigma}{\sigma-1}} \tag{6.15}$$

where $E(g, m)$ is a polynomial in m of the form $c_5 g^2 + c_6 g + c_7$ and the c's are parameter constants. Both Equations 6.14 and 6.15 are modifications of the widely used constant elasticity of the substitution utility function. In Equation 6.14, $E(g, m)$ enters additively and in Equation 6.15, it enters multiplicatively on the gambling visits term. In Equation 6.14, for example, a change in distance from the nearest casino does not influence the marginal utility that the consumer receives from an additional visit to a casino. Both Equations 6.14 and 6.15 are natural ways to modify the standard constant elasticity of the substitution utility function.

We choose constants c so that the consumer has \$40,000 annual income,[8] gambles \$55 each visit to the casino, visits 3.64 times per year, for a total gambling expenditure of \$200 when the casino is next door (\$198.84 was lost to casinos by the average adult living within zero to 35 miles of Atlantic City casinos in 1991. See Deloitte & Touche (1992), pp. 137, 162. Mirage Hotel (1993) also uses $200 as its estimate of demand for spending by adults near the casino), and generates benchmark utility of 100. Moreover, when the casino is 500 miles distant, the consumer visits 0.1 time per year, matching the visit frequency for the over-300 distance (bottom row) of Table 6.1. Without loss of generality, we also assume that the price of goods x is 1. These requirements are enough to specify the parameters of Equations 6.14 and 6.15 and to generate interior solutions for the consumer's optimization problem. Certain restrictions apply to the range over which the polynomials for $E(g, d)$ apply. Details are in Grinols (1999a).

After constructing a gambler who makes choices about how much to gamble in a representative way, we adjusted the consumer's distance from the casino to see what the resulting utility value was of having the casino at $m = 0$ miles versus $m = 500$ miles. The numbers computed this way will be exact, not upper bounds. Table 6.2 reports the results.

Columns (1) and (2) list the variables of interest: the consumer has $40,000 annual income, visits the casino 3.63 times per year, and spends $200 gambling when casinos are zero miles away. Columns (3) and (4) show what happens when the casino is 500 miles away and zero miles away for the additive version of the utility function. The key calculation is shaded in the income row. The consumer would be willing to give up $46.63 to have the casino at zero distance rather than 500 miles away. Performing the same experiment for the multiplicative version of the utility function (Equation 6.15) reveals that the consumer would be willing to give up $47.36.

[8] This nearly perfectly matches median household income in 1999, which was $39,657.

Estimate 3: The 30 to 35 Percent Rule

A general rule of casino demand is that it falls by about 30 to 35 percent when the distance from the casino is doubled.[9] Table 6.3 used this information, for example, to construct a distance and demand schedule in which each doubling of distance, m, reduced expenditure by 34.5 percent. In the constructed table, consumers 35 to 75 miles away from a casino have average expenditures per year of $128.13; those 150 to 300 miles away have average expenditures of $54.29, which closely approximate the figures in the right-hand column of Table 6.4.

For very small or very large distances, the general rule that demand declines by 30 to 35 percent for each doubling of distance, or increases by 43 to 54 percent for each halving, is not credible. For example, such consumers would have average gambling losses of more than $1,485 if they were 1 mile from the casino, and this supposedly would rise to $5,283 if they were 220 yards away. In Table 6.4, we reported advantages to the consumer of reducing proximity of the casino to 5 miles in the right-hand column, other distance combinations are to the left. Large distances do not present as much of a problem. The amount gambled falls quickly for large distances because people take fewer trips and so the estimates do not matter much to the comparisons in which we are interested. The last row of Table 6.3 reports the averages for consumers 300 or more miles away (actually, 300 to 6,400 miles). At those distances, visits per year match the figure in Table 6.1.

[9] Christiansen Capital Advisers, LLC (2000): "The 'distance factors' estimated for these models are, technically, the 'elasticities' of spending with respect to distance. Based upon survey data from several jurisdictions, rates of casino visitation appear to decline in proportion to about the 0.5 to 0.6 power of the distance to the casino, yielding distance factors of about 0.5 to 0.6." (p. 5) Let us use the midpoint, 0.55. In other words, if demand is proportional to $m^{-0.55}$, where m is distance, then demand at twice the distance is $(2m)^{-0.55} = 0.683m^{-0.55}$, or 31.7 percent less.

PROFITS AND TAXES

SUMMARY. The form that economic benefits such as profits and taxes takes depends on market structure. If we assume **perfect competition**, the profits of the casino industry will be competed to the same level as other businesses in general. When the net increase in profits and taxes from a new industry is zero, it does not imply that there are no social benefits; it just means that social benefits appear in a different form.

The most direct way to discuss casino profits and taxes would be to tally the profits of all casinos, estimate and subtract the reduction in profits to other businesses that are due to the presence of casinos, and produce a net profit figure. Because many casinos do not need to report their profits to anyone – American Indian tribal casinos are generally in this category

– such an approach is doomed from the beginning. Fortunately, there is an alternative that we can motivate in terms of the underlying theory.

Recall that we are interested in comparing two situations. One is the situation in which gambling is allowed to expand to the point of market saturation. *Market saturation* is a nontechnical term for a market in which casinos are free to enter and the market has reached equilibrium where the number of casinos and the amount of gambling present are not expanding. Saturation implies that the profits of casinos have reached ordinary business levels so that no further entry is desired. The second is the situation in which casinos are banned, as they were in all but two states before 1990. These alternatives provide a good comparison because casino benefits are at their maximum level in the first alternative. The two extremes are also easier to evaluate well in economic terms.

Apart from government regulation, most economists would agree that the casino industry would be a *free-entry* industry, meaning that the barriers to entry and exit would be small. Free entry and exit – competition *for* the market as distinct from competition *in* the market – is one of the most important attributes that characterizes perfect competition. Casinos tend to offer a similar product – another primary condition of perfect competition. Perfect information, a third characteristic of perfect competition, describes the casino industry in the sense that information is not a significant impediment to competition, either to buyers or sellers. In places where government has allowed it – such as the Gulf Coast of Mississippi; Deadwood, South Dakota; Atlantic City, New Jersey; and Nevada – casinos have continued to enter the market until profits have been reduced by competition to ordinary business levels and no further casinos seek entry. In Atlantic City, for example, the number of casinos has been stable at twelve for many years.

In short, apart from the current regulatory environment, the casino industry would likely be characterized by perfect competition with many entrants. In 1994 congressional testimony, I reported that "apart from government control, gambling is a free-entry activity. It requires little knowledge or high technology to offer gambling. This means that it is physically and economically possible to introduce gambling anywhere.

Gambling could be franchised on every street corner in the nation, like McDonald's hamburger stands."[187] The same sentiment was echoed by the National Gambling Impact Study Commission in its 1999 final report:

> With little stretch of the imagination, it is conceivable that someday gambling enterprises may be franchised and, at least in part of the country, become as common as fast-food outlets are today.[188]

Few economists would disagree.

The end result of perfect competition is that profits converge to the ordinary level of profits. In the United States, manufacturing profits as a percent of sales averaged 8.8 percent in 1999[189] and as a percent of stockholder equity, 5.9 percent. In that event, the best estimate of the *net* increase in profits and taxes caused by casino expansion is zero. This docs not mean that casinos in a perfectly competitive regime provide no benefits. Rather, it means that the benefits they provide have been maximized and that all of the benefits will be captured by consumers as price-related benefits, consumer surplus, and distance benefits.[190]

THE OTHER BENEFITS

SUMMARY. As described in Chapter 5, some of the benefits of casinos may appear as price effects, such as consumer surplus and capital gains. The ability of casinos to reduce consumer constraints such as unemployment relative to what they would have been is another potential benefit. This benefit is temporary because, in the long run, the economy can have full employment with or without casinos present.

In general, the terms on which casino gambling is offered are the same in different locations. We have already noted that EGDs in one location are much the same as in another, and the rules of roulette, poker, blackjack, and most games are the same. To a first approximation, therefore, the spread of casinos does not alter the prices to consumers of gambling.[191] In most cases, casinos are not large enough relative to the economy to affect many other prices, nor do they pay well enough that they regularly raise the level of wages for the entire labor market. In other words, price effects tend to be small or negligible except in special cases, implying that consumer surplus and capital-gains price effects are approximately zero. In cases where we are looking at regional effects only, the consumer surplus and capital gain-related benefits are captured in the $0 to $1,500 value per job numbers from the major-league sports teams literature.

This leaves the potential role of casinos as eliminators of consumption constraints. When short-term unemployment is present, for example, it is theoretically possible that there may be a period during which the introduction of a particular type of product or activity leads to a transitory reduction in unemployment compared to what would have happened otherwise. The U.S. economy has experienced full employment in the past without casinos and almost surely can do so again in the future. Thus, unless we believe that full employment in the long term requires the presence of casinos, unemployment reduction is a short-term benefit that is not captured in the list of other benefits. As noted previously, I am aware of no study at the time of writing that makes this claim about unemployment and estimates the value to existing residents of its temporary reduction.

CONCLUSIONS

SUMMARY. If one compares an economy where casinos are prohibited to the same economy where casinos are legalized and casino entry is free, the long-term benefits appear to be on the order of $34 per adult per year. These benefits take the form of distance consumer surplus. From a narrower regional perspective, benefits also may include price-related elements: consumer surplus and capital gains to residents. These benefits vary with circumstances, but are on the order of $0 to $1,500 per job added regionally. In the short term, some benefits may take an additional form: casinos may help eliminate unemployment faster. There are no figures available on the value of this temporary benefit to the existing residents of the region.

To some degree, any generalized estimate of the economic benefits of casinos must remain partly unsatisfactory for two reasons: (1) First, benefits take different forms depending on market structure and other considerations that vary with conditions. If casinos are granted regional

TABLE 6.5. Regional Annual Casino Benefits for the Entire Economy: Compares an economy with no casinos to the same economy with free entry of casinos

	Regional (Short Term)	Regional (Long Term)	Economy (Long Term)
Profits and Taxes	$\dfrac{\$0}{\text{adult}}$	$\dfrac{\$0}{\text{adult}}$	$\dfrac{\$0}{\text{adult}}$
Distance Consumer Surplus	$\dfrac{\$34}{\text{adult}}$	$\dfrac{\$34}{\text{adult}}$	$\dfrac{\$34}{\text{adult}}$
Consumer Surplus and Capital Gains	$\dfrac{\$0-\$1,500}{\text{job}}$	$\dfrac{\$0-\$1,500}{\text{job}}$	$\$0$
Transactions Constraints and Temporary Unemployment Reduction	?	$\$0$	$\$0$
TOTALS	$\dfrac{\$0-\$1,500}{\text{job}}+\dfrac{\$34}{\text{adult}}+?$	$\dfrac{\$0-\$1,500}{\text{job}}+\dfrac{\$34}{\text{adult}}$	$\dfrac{\$34}{\text{adult}}$

monopolies, for example, the list of benefits includes positive net profits and taxes, but distance consumer surplus would be diminished relative to the alternative where casinos are introduced in a regime of free entry. The largest benefits to the economy are generated if free entry of casinos is permitted. In this case, competition limits net profits and taxes, but increases distance consumer surplus. (2) Second, the price effects – consumer surplus and capital gains – and the transactions constraint benefits are intrinsically difficult to estimate. We have borrowed our estimates for price-related benefits from the literature on major-league sports teams. There, recognizing that the number could be negative under certain conditions, it was found that an additional job in a region tended to provide benefits to existing residents of between $0 and $1,500 per job added to the region. Casinos can be the cause for both additional jobs and a decline in jobs in a region, depending on how the net export multiplier mechanism functions (see Chapter 4). Table 6.5 condenses the discussion of benefits of this chapter into the entries shown.

7 Social Costs

The price of... gambling is turning out to be every bit as high as opponents had said it would be – not only for those who get caught directly in its web, but for everyone else as well.

Editorial, Minneapolis Star Tribune *(1995)*

CHAPTER SUMMARY. The social costs of casinos are the real resources used to deal with their negative externalities – the harmful by-products of gambling that affect both those who gamble and those who do not – as well as the hard to measure and often immeasurable direct harm done to individuals. This chapter classifies the main kinds of social costs and summarizes what is known about their magnitude. We arrange costs in units commensurable to benefits to answer the following hypothetical question: What are the benefits and costs of moving from a policy of no casinos on one hand to the alternative policy of free-entry laissez faire regarding casinos on the other? Based on available numbers, costs exceed benefits by a factor of more than 3:1. Even when better estimates are available, it is likely that they will show that casinos fail a cost–benefit test.

Riva Wilkinson, wife of the Anoka County, Minnesota, sheriff,[192] was responsible for accounts receivable at the elite Guthrie Theater, a well-known performing arts theater in Minneapolis. According to information later made public, her gambling compulsion caused her to begin to "empty the cash from the theater safe onto the blackjack tables at Mystic Lake Casino in Prior Lake, hand after losing hand."[193] Discovering a deficit, accountants eventually learned that she had stolen $418,000 in twelve months, but not before requiring 1,062 hours of Federal Bureau of Investigation (FBI) investigation; services of local police; Guthrie accountants' time; services of the U.S. attorney's office; judicial time of a judge, jury, and numerous court employees; and, ultimately, incarceration and supervised release. According to the investigation, these services cost the public $100,646.57.[194] Incredibly, for every dollar stolen, the public paid $.25.

As in the Wilkinson case, the social costs of casinos often fall hard on innocent parties that do not gamble. Laura Iserloth of Sheboygan, Wisconsin, was a sixty-four-year-old grandmother of seven who stole $298 thousand from her employer, Kettle Moraine Employees Credit Union, over a ten-year period, driving it out of business.[195] In this chapter, we provide numerous examples of gambling-related crime, ranging all the way to murder, to make the connection between casinos and externalities.

SOCIAL COST TAXONOMY

SUMMARY. The social costs caused by casinos are classified as externalities because they represent direct harm to others that does not operate through the price system, are not borne by the agents that create them, and, therefore, are not included in the decision-making process of the externality-causing agents. The social costs of casinos include crime, business and employment costs such as lost time on the job, bankruptcy, suicide, illness, direct regulatory costs, family costs such as child neglect and abuse, and abused dollars. Ideally, these mutually exclusive categories of costs should fully identify the types of social costs attributable to casinos. Taxes raised to pay publicly borne social costs entail additional burden to society in the form of **deadweight**

losses. The public-finance literature has estimated that an additional dollar of taxes costs the private sector $1.17 to $1.57. The upward scaling of publicly borne costs could be counted as social costs as well.

It does not take many cases of the Riva Wilkinson type to account for a tremendous amount of social costs. For example, consider a community of 100 adults without casinos who decide to introduce them. Further assume that the availability of casinos each year causes just one tenth of 1 percent of the population to commit crimes as costly as Wilkinson's. Those 100 adults would have to divide $10,064.66 in costs among them each year.

In Chapter 5, we explained the use of cost–benefit analysis as a tool to identify the framework for evaluating the social impact of casino gambling in the United States. Chapter 6 discussed the benefit side; we now look at the cost side.

According to Equation 5.12, casinos could create conditions that cause resources to be removed from the productive stream of the rest of the economy, as the Wilkinson case did, but they also could interfere with market operation. For example, the failure of a stolen art object to be retained in the hands of the individual who valued it most represents a social cost due to interference with market operation – in this case, the destruction of distributive efficiency.[196] To make the concept of social costs operational, in this chapter we separate them into nine categories and then examine cost estimates for those components for which numbers are available. The nine categories are crime, business and employment costs, bankruptcy, suicide, illness, social service costs, direct regulatory costs, family costs, and abused dollars. We briefly explain each category before discussing what is known about its size.

Crime

Gambling has been linked to a variety of crimes, including FBI Index I violent crimes (i.e., aggravated assault, robbery, rape, and murder) and Index I property crimes (i.e., larceny, burglary, and auto theft). Non-Index I crimes that have been tied to casinos include fraud, forgery (including check forgery), tax evasion, tax fraud, confidence games (e.g., swindling, hustling cards, dice, or other games), bookmaking, working in an illegal game, pimping, prostitution, selling drugs, and fencing stolen goods. Representative coverage reads as follows:

> A decade ago police and prosecutors in Louisville saw very few criminal cases for embezzlement and fraud linked to gambling debts. But that has changed in the past five years.[197]

Smith et al. (2003) examined police records in Edmonton from January 2001 to July 2002 to assess gambling-related crime. They found 680 criminal offenses related to gambling such as fraud and employee theft. The most common were fraud, theft, forgery, and embezzlement to cover gambling losses. According to police records, casino transactions also accounted for 27 percent of counterfeit money seized during the eighteen months of the study. They found three suicides caused by gambling problems during this time.

Organized crime also has been associated with gambling. Although the connections are more difficult to monitor and denials by the industry are common, the connections are referenced frequently in the newspapers and courtrooms of America.

To be counted as a social cost, economists generally would assert that a crime must lead to real resources being used in policing, apprehension, adjudication, incarceration, and rehabilitation of criminals. It is a sometimes little understood fact that economists do not treat a stolen $100 in property as a social cost because the thief is better off by the $100 when the victim is made $100 worse off. That is, an economist might assert that after a sixty-one-year-old resident of Jefferson County, Kentucky, pleaded guilty to embezzling $493,180 from the U.S. Postal Service (USPS),[198] we must assume that the value to him of gambling and losing the stolen dollars at the nearby Caesar's casino matched one for one the value of the dollars to the USPS and, therefore, they represent no social cost. This conclusion is false if the value of gambling to the thief is less than the amount stolen. Moreover, if we drop the assumption in Chapter 5 that the benefits to all citizens are treated equally, we can report the real resources stolen *as social costs to the victimized public.*

The mental anguish suffered by a crime victim – imagine a woman robbed in her home at night by an intruder – also would count as social cost (a negative amenity in the terminology of Chapter 5), but in practice would not be measured in any study of social costs because of the obvious difficulties. If a survey somehow were able to elicit truthful and accurate answers to the question: "Given the true probability of your being robbed in your home by an intruder, how much would you be willing to pay each year if it guaranteed that no episode of this type of crime would take place?," such answers could be used to establish the social cost of this type of crime to the average citizen.

In summary, stolen resources are costs to the victimized public, and even when we count the gains of the thief as a social benefit and do not count mental anguish as a social cost, there frequently remains an associated social cost because the value of the property was greater to the victim.

Examples of crime drawn from news accounts over the three-year period 1998–2001 are provided in the examples section.

Business and Employment Costs

Business and employment costs borne by the employer, the employee, and society are as follows:

- lost productivity on the job because of reduced performance
- lost time and unemployment that includes sick days off for gambling, extended lunch hours, leaving early and returning late due to gambling, and firing because of gambling problems such as employee embezzlement

Problem and pathological gamblers frequently impose costs on their employers in the form of unreliable presence on the job and increased search and training costs to replace workers. These costs are greater for firms with higher requirements for their employees to have firm-specific training and knowledge. Between 21 and 36 percent of problem gamblers in treatment reported losing a job because of their gambling (Lesieur, 1998b).

One often-misunderstood form of business and employment cost is *directly unproductive profitseeking* (DUP).[199] DUP refers to activities that remove resources from productive use and, although they may be personally rewarding to the agent, lower national income because they produce nothing of social value. A former colleague related that in Las Vegas, people were hired to watch selected slot machines to report how long they had gone without paying out. The watchers were paid $10 an hour; presumably, those hiring them were able to make money by the knowledge they gained – or at least believed they did. Neither the watchers nor their employers were seeking entertainment from their activity. The time spent watching was time that could have been used in some other productive way. The activity would classify as socially unproductive profitseeking. In a political context, DUP might refer to an industry in a small country that devotes lobbying resources to pass protective legislation. Protection might lead to increased profits for the industry, but the resources used for lobbying are wasted from society's point of view because they produce nothing of direct economic value. In fact, in the case of a small country, a tariff harms the welfare of the country as a whole. One author describes DUP as "ways of making a profit (i.e., income) by undertaking activities which are directly unproductive; that is, they yield pecuniary returns but produce neither goods nor services that enter a conventional utility function directly nor intermediate inputs into such goods and services."[200] A professional poker player who does not gamble for enjoyment and gives up working to gamble for his living engages in DUP activity that reduces national income by the amount of his lost output. An individual who gambles for entertainment, on the other hand, purchases a service – entertainment – much like any other service, and does not engage in DUP.

The fact of business and employment costs to society related to gambling has been recognized for centuries in societies that have had experience with gamblers. In 1638, a Massachusetts statute based on the Idleness

Organized Crime

The federal government generally regulates the gambling industry very little, except when organized crime is involved (Frey, 1998). According to Lee and Chelius (1989), the New Jersey Casino Control Commission kept New Jersey casino ownership and management free from organized crime, but organized crime played a large role in the casino labor unions. Despite industry denials, reports of organized crime connections to casinos are common. A sampling from 1998–2001 includes the following:

- "The Illinois Gaming Board on Tuesday rejected a planned Rosemont casino, concluding that top officials of the would-be riverboat had misled the board and that some investors had links to mob figures. 'The investigation record establishes the insidious presence of organized crime elements associated with this proposed project that cannot be ignored,' Gaming Board Administrator Sergio Acosta said in a statement to the board." (*Chicago Tribune, January 31, 2001*)

- "Tribes across the country consistently say there's no proof of any organized crime infiltration," said (Assistant Florida Attorney General John) Glogau. "But law enforcement people say that's nonsense." (*St. Petersburg Times*, February 19, 1999)

- Lacking the resources to start and run casinos, many tribes turn to outsiders. In the process, some have welcomed individuals with histories of illegal gambling and suspected ties to organized crime because they brought money to finance casinos or to ensure players have ready access to cash. FBI officials quoted by The Tribune acknowledged that there are crooks and con artists in the Indian gaming industry. (*Associated Press*, 18 January 1999)

- Angelini was sentenced to three years of imprisonment in 1993 for conspiring with other Chicago organized-crime figures to use mob money to gain control of an Indian reservation casino in San Diego County, California. (*Chicago Tribune*, October 24, 1999)

- With the sentencing of a former tribal councilwoman, the case of the Pittsburgh mob's failed attempt to set up shop on the Rincon Indian Reservation (near San Diego) has come to an end.... The tribe's contract with a consortium called the Columbia Group ... later was exposed as a mob front. (*Sacramento Bee*, April 21, 1998)

- The leading advocate for an Indian casino for New Buffalo, Michigan, a lakeside resort community about 90 minutes from Chicago, is identified by law enforcement officials as an associate of several Chicago organized-crime figures, the *Chicago Sun Times* has learned. (*Chicago Sun Times*, December 13, 1998)
- Federal court documents and South Carolina corporate records show a link between South Carolina's video gambling industry and a Pittsburgh organized-crime ring. ([Charleston, SC] *Post and Courier*, February 15, 1998)
- Three loan-sharking arrests in California casinos.... Police link to Asian organized-crime groups... (*Arizona Republic*, September 11, 1998)
- (T)he presence of organized crime remains strong through covert ties to seemingly legitimate casino operators, according to Tom Fuentes, chief of the FBI's Organized Crime Section in Washington, D.C. (14 December 1998)
- Chinese organized crime may be pocketing more than $500,000 in [Las Vegas] Strip casino money each month, say Metro Police detectives.... (*Las Vegas Review-Journal*, January 21, 1999)
- (Dune Lop) Moy [an inveterate gambler who owed a Chinatown bookie] was tapped out. Two months ago, authorities found his beaten body folded and stuffed into a large green suitcase that had been tossed in the weeds in Weymouth. Now, as the investigation continues, sources familiar with the Chinatown underworld believe that Moy was marked for murder by Asian organized-crime figures, or their mob associates, intent on sending a chilling message to their customers: Pay your debts or die. (*Boston Globe*, June 3, 1999)
- Offshore Internet gambling sites are proving a safe bet for organized-crime groups looking to launder money.... British officals are warning that dirty money is flooding through the sites. (*Agence France-Presse*, November 25, 2000)

Statute of 1633, which outlawed the possession of gambling devices such as cards and dice, was passed to prevent unproductive time and idleness associated with gambling.[201] In 1847, Pennsylvania law incorporated the observation that gamblers were "parasites and thieves." In the twentieth century, Nobel-prize–winning economist, Paul Samuelson, connected DUP to gambling as follows:

> There is, however, a substantial economic case to be made against gambling . . . . It involves simply sterile transfers of money or goods between individuals, creating no new money or goods. Although it creates no output, gambling does nevertheless absorb time and resources. When pursued beyond the limits of recreation, where the main purpose after all is to "kill" time, gambling subtracts from the national income.[202]

Bankruptcy

Bankruptcy imposes social costs by diverting resources to lawsuits, legal costs, and bill-collection costs. Never-paid debts of gamblers are a social cost to the rest of society.

From 1980 to 1998, personal bankruptcies in the United States rose more than four times.[203] In 1998, 1.3 million Americans defaulted on their debts by declaring bankruptcy. The changing legal environment, the intense marketing of credit cards by banks with less regard for creditworthiness, and the diminished social stigma of bankruptcy are among the reasons for the secular increase in bankruptcy filings.[204] Since the mid-1990s, the increase in casinos has been another cause for rising bankruptcy. Federal bankruptcy forms require listing "all losses from fire, theft, other casualty, or gambling within one year immediately preceding" the commencement of the case.[205] Casino-industry sources report that 40 to 60 percent of the cash wagered in casinos is not carried onto the property; this means that credit cards and cash machines are supplying the difference.[206]

Research on the connection between casinos and bankruptcy is ongoing. Because there are many causes of bankruptcy, the connection to gambling has been challenged by the casino industry, as have the estimates of other social costs. The connection is supported by information from a wide variety of geographical areas and a number of formal studies. Casinos opened in Baton Rouge in 1994. The Baton Rouge Crisis

Intervention Center subsequently reported that gambling-related calls jumped from 39 in 1993 to 1,375 in 1995. Consumer Credit Counseling Services (CCCS) of the same city also reported a significant increase in the number of people with gambling-related problems calling for assistance. At the same time, the personal bankruptcy rate rose 53 percent for the first half of 1996 compared to the year earlier; bankrutpcy lawyers stated that gambling was a factor.[207]

Kansas City's casinos opened in 1994. By 1996, bankruptcies were on the rise in Kansas City. The Kansas City offices of CCCS reported, "Before the [casino river] boats, we saw maybe one person a year because of a gambling problem. Now about twenty people a month come in because of gambling-related issues."[208]

Michelle Clark Neely, writing for the the St. Louis Federal Reserve, concluded that "Compulsive gambling is increasingly being blamed for the rising tide of bankruptcy, especially in the states that have casinos."[209]

Wisconsin opened its first casino in 1991. In 1996, the AP reported from Wisconsin, "People in eastern Wisconsin are seeking bankruptcy protection at a pace 25 percent greater than last year, and gambling is often a factor, bankruptcy lawyers and financial counselors said. According to them, one in ten bankruptcies is linked to gambling debts – more than double the rate of years past."[210]

The connection between casinos and bankruptcy is corroborated by the testimony of attorneys who specialize in bankruptcy and credit-counseling services.[211] A 1995 study in Minneapolis of 105 bankruptcy filers found that 52 percent had gambling losses; the average gambling loss was $22 thousand.[212]

A study conducted by Iowa State University also found a connection between casinos and bankruptcy.[213] SMR Research Corporation of Hackettstown, New Jersey, reported in 1998 that information from experts on the financial impact of gambling has been consistent that more than 20 percent of compulsive gamblers have filed for bankruptcy as a result of their gambling losses.[214] "The 298 U.S. counties which have legalized gambling within their borders had a 1996 bankruptcy filing rate

18 percent higher than the filings in counties with no gambling, and the bankruptcy rate was 35 percent higher than the average in counties with five or more gambling establishments."[215]   In areas near major casinos, "gambling-related bankruptcies account for 10 to 20 percent of the filings." Follow-up studies three years later "confirm a finding that SMR made in 1997: Some of the rise in personal bankruptcy has been related to the dramatic 1990s spread of casino and other legal gambling in the U.S."[216]   According to SMR, their work

> elicited an angry response from the American Gaming Association (AGA), the casino industry trade group. The AGA published an article suggesting that our entire study was about nothing but gambling, and was entirely without merit. . . . Their analysts must have misplaced the other 226 pages. . . .

According to SMR, 2.5 to 10 percent of annual bankruptcy filings in the United States have a gambling component. "Virtually all studies (other than commentary or sponsored work by the gaming industry) show a relationship between compulsive gambling and insolvency."[217]

Suicide

Studies of problem and pathological gamblers report that they both contemplate and commit suicide at a rate higher than the general public (Lesieur, 1992, 1998c; and Frank, Lester, and Wexler, 1991). Nationally, deaths by suicide number about twelve per 100 thousand population per year, or 0.012 percent. Studies report that 15 to 24 percent of Gamblers Anonymous gamblers and hospitalized pathological gamblers have attempted suicide, rates that are five to ten times the average for the general population.[218]   Of these gamblers, 12 to 18 percent have made potentially lethal suicide attempts; 45 to 49 percent have made plans to kill themselves; and 48 to 70 percent have seriously contemplated suicide (Lesieur and Anderson, 1995).

Such information is invaluable, but leaves questions unanswered. That is, we know that suicide and suicide attempts are elevated among pathological gamblers. We also know that gambling causes suicide, but we do not know precisely how large the phenomenon is because of information limitations. Moreover, the suicide of a pathological gambler who was also a drug addict and alcoholic could have been caused by a combination of his or her addiction, alcoholism, and gambling pathology. Thus, examples of individuals with no known problems prior to gambling who develop gambling problems and kill themselves are particularly important.

Recent years have witnessed the growing phenomenon of gamblers killing themselves on-site at a casino. For example, in an August 1999 episode, a Florida "gambler who had lost $87,000 jumped to his death off a ten-story casino parking garage Wednesday in the third such suicide in Atlantic City in eight days."[219] Eight similar suicides were reported by January 18, 2001.[220] In Detroit in January 2000, an off-duty police officer lost $15,000 to $20,000 playing high stakes blackjack at the newly opened MGM Grand Casino. After losing $4,000 in his soon-to-be last hand, he rose and, using his concealed gun, fired a bullet into his own head, killing himself instantly. In Rhode Island,

> Police sources said that Carvalho, who had no history of addictions and lived a quiet, middle-class life, had developed a gambling habit over the past few months that began on a trip to Las Vegas this summer. Police believe he was driving home from Foxwoods Resort Casino when, in desperation, he killed himself.[221]

The victim had a 14-year-old-daughter whom he had dropped off on the Sunday before his body was found hanging from a piece of twine tied to a tree branch in a densely wooded area. Police who investigated the bank employee's background reported, "He was squeaky clean."[222] The same article reported other suicides, including one in the Foxwoods parking lot where the victim ingested a mixture of drugs and cut his arms; a thirty-eight-year-old woman who drowned herself in the Thames River after losing at Foxwoods and gambling the maximum amount allowed on her credit cards; and a number of attempts, including a man who shot himself in the head in a Foxwoods parking garage.

Not all gambling suicides are so public. Like the Rhode Island bank employee, a former Hillsdale, Illinois, fire chief embezzled more than $150 thousand from the department's account over four years to pay gambling debts. The police investigation found that he had lost $104,873 between April 1996 and May 1999 at the Lady Luck Casino, compared to winnings of only $14,823 for the same period. His body was found in his truck, dead of carbon-monoxide poisoning, at a nearby rural cemetery in May 1999.[223]

Government data make the study of suicides difficult because not all suicides are reported or recorded as suicides, nor are the reasons for suicide always known or recorded. Phillips, Welty, and Smith (1997) studied the relationship between gambling meccas and suicide. Their research found that deaths in Las Vegas were 2.5 times more likely to be a result of suicide than deaths in other comparably sized metropolitan areas.[224] Stronger evidence of a connection, however, was that Atlantic City and Reno visitors were 1.75 and 1.50 times more likely to die in suicides than tourists in other nongambling areas. In Atlantic City, which introduced casinos in 1978, the suicide rates did not become elevated until after casinos were introduced.[225] McCleary et al. (1998), in a study funded by the AGA, the lobbying arm of the gambling industry, contested the Phillips, Welty, and Smith findings. Although gambling clearly has been the cause of many suicides, the full extent of the influence and when it will be identified in the aggregate statistics of regions with a prominent casino industry remains a question for further research.

Illness

Gambling has been tied to a number of forms of illness, including depression, stress-related illnesses, chronic or severe headaches, anxiety, moodiness, irritability, intestinal disorders, asthma, cognitive distortions, and cardiovascular disorders. Many of the costs of sickness are borne by the gambler, but they also can lead to real resource costs to society as a whole, usually in the form of treatment costs.

The Maryland Department of Health (1990) noted that problem and pathological gamblers are prone to more automobile accidents than the population at large.[226] The connection between casinos and elevated alcohol consumption, drug use, and other potentially harmful activities has been an often-observed aspect of gambling.[227] Statistical procedures applied to samples that include individuals who have gambling problems only, in addition to individuals who engage in multiple potentially harmful activities, can sort out the contributions from different sources. Economists using econometric techniques routinely deal with the problem of multiple causes in their studies. To produce good numbers, however, requires good samples and sufficiently large numbers of observations to identify the size of the effects that are present. In the absence of firm estimates of the strength and extent of a connection between casino gamblers and impaired driving habits, for example, such costs other than the measurable illness costs must be treated as zero.

Social Service Costs

The extreme financial stress and employment difficulties associated with problem and pathological gambling can lead to unemployment and require periods in which government assistance is needed. Social service costs include therapy and treatment costs, as well as unemployment insurance costs, Medicaid, energy assistance costs in some states, and the cost of other social services, such as welfare and food stamps.

Direct Regulatory Costs

As discussed in Chapter 3, gambling has been regulated by government because it historically has been subject to fraud and abuse. Direct regulatory costs are paid primarily by government through taxes on society as a whole. A carefully done 1999 study in Louisiana found that the costs to the state of regulating gambling were $50.02 million per year. Dividing this by 3,026,372 – the estimated number of adults twenty years and older in the state in 1999 – implies that the direct regulatory cost per adult was $16.53.

Family Costs

The family costs related to gambling include the costs of divorce, separation, spousal abuse, and child neglect and abuse. Children of pathological gamblers report reactions of depression, anger, and sadness. Many of the spouses and children of pathological gamblers are physically and verbally abused.[228] Research conducted for the National Gambling Impact Study Commission found that 53.5 percent of pathological gamblers reported having been divorced, whereas only 18.2 percent of the nongamblers were divorced.[229] Again, we make the obligatory observation that there are other causes of divorce that may interact with pathological gambling. Many of these costs are nonmonetary, but others imply real resource costs to society. Most are rarely measured or quantified. Those that do enter into social computations typically arise when social intervention becomes necessary, as in the case of divorce. These costs represent resources lost to other uses and can be measured by the cost of the services provided.

Abused Dollars

Abused dollars is the term applied to lost gambling money acquired from family, employers, or friends under false pretenses. Stealing from an employer that is never reported out of concern for the employee, stealing that is never reported because the thief is a relative or friend, and money "loaned" under duress that is never repaid are examples of abused dollars.

We have discussed the issue of social accounting that applies to recording social costs in the case of theft. A similar situation applies to abused dollars. It is often wrongly asserted that abused dollars do not represent social costs because "the thief gets the money." This view fails to recognize that if $1 thousand is abused, the rest of society loses $1 thousand of real goods and services that it represents and that – even treating the thief's gain as part of the social calculation – there remains a social cost connected to abused dollars. For example, if the abuser does not receive equal value from his or her use of the money – say, he or she sells the $1 thousand stolen electronic good to someone who is only willing to pay $500 – then society as a whole has a social cost of $500.

EXAMPLES

SUMMARY. It is important to put a face on the social costs of casinos because many of the social costs are hidden. Among the more visible consequences is crime. Examples of crimes caused by gambling are not difficult to find; a search of the Internet and America's newspapers and magazines is all that is required. Many involve individuals without a record of previous criminal activity or evidence of other social problems. The number of examples presented here could easily have been greater. Also included are a few examples involving other social issues. The following examples are dated mostly between 1998 and 2000.

"A woman who lost more than $30,000 at Joliet [Illinois] casinos was sentenced to twenty-one years in prison Wednesday after a judge determined she suffocated her seven-week-old child to collect insurance money to continue her gambling habit." (*Copley News Service*, 10/23/99)

"A South Bend [Indiana] man convicted of murdering a man for his casino winnings was sentenced to sixty-five years in prison. The prosecution charged that (Abdullah) Alkhalidi was having financial problems and killed Claude Purdiman, Jr., 29, for the approximately $2,000 he won while the two were together early May 3 at the Blue Chip Casino in Michigan City." (*Las Vegas Sun*, 3/14/00)

"A Hancock County [Mississippi] woman says she killed her mother and husband last year as part of a suicide pact made in despair over large gambling debts the trio had run up at Gulf Coast casinos. Julie Winborn pleaded guilty in the death of her husband, Grady Winborn, 57, and her mother, Inez Bouis, 66. She was sentenced Thursday to two life sentences. She had testified that the three lost $50,000 at casinos and decided to end their lives because they could not repay bank and credit union loans." (*Associated Press*, 9/10/99)

"Clay County [Missouri] Judge Larry Harman on Monday sentenced an Overland Park (Kansas) woman to fifteen years in prison for killing her husband in a Northland church parking lot. Bonnie Knapp, 50, spoke barely above a whisper Monday when she admitted stabbing 85-year-old Joseph Knapp in the parking lot of Avondale Baptist Church in Kansas City, North, on August 22, 1997.

Knapp was accused of stabbing her husband more than seventy-five times because he would not give her more gambling money. Prosecutors said the crime occurred after the couple and a friend left Harrah's North Kansas City Casino & Hotel about midnight." (*Kansas City Star*, 12/21/99)

"Two former employees at a Westport [Missouri] bank facility pleaded guilty Thursday to a decade-long embezzlement of about $1.58 million that, among other things, financed gambling sprees and vacations in exotic locales." (*Kansas City Star*, 3/16/00)

"Prison sentences have been ordered for two men, including a former loan officer who admitted having a gambling addiction, for defrauding a Morgan City [Louisiana] bank of $250,000 through false loans." (*Associated Press*, 11/4/99)

"The abuse of gambling has led to many 'social evils' and any government that encouraged gambling has a lot to answer for, [Australian] Prime Minister John Howard said today. Mr. Howard was commenting after a Melbourne woman was charged with manslaughter yesterday over the death of her nineteen-month-old baby after leaving it in extreme heat inside a car as she gambled at a hotel." (*AAP Newsfeed*, 2/24/00)

"After sixteen months of study, the Governor's Task Force on Illegal Gambling says the problem has increased as Texas has embraced legal gambling.

'The proponents of gambling have largely succeeded in persuading the broader culture to accept gambling as a legitimate form of entertainment rather than a vice,' the task force concluded. 'The impact, from a fiscal perspective, has been enormous.'

Without quantifying it, the task force said the downside also has a large bottom line, especially at the state's multibillion-dollar lottery. 'Its substantial social costs, however, while actual and acknowledged, have yet to be accurately measured,' the report says about the lottery." ([Austin] *American-Statesman*, 1/27/99)

"A fifty-six-year-old [Southern California] compulsive gambler pleaded guilty Tuesday to several bank robberies and the attempted murder of a police officer.... Ball has been battling a severe gambling addiction since at least 1971, when he received the first of his four state and federal robbery convictions, [his attorney] said. His struggle was highlighted in the past year when he won $250,000 from a casino bet on horseraces ... and lost the entire amount within three weeks, [his attorney] said." (*Los Angeles Daily News*, 10/27/99)

"A worker at Harvey's casino [Omaha, Nebraska] ran out of luck after stealing money from his employer to gamble at Ameristar [casino]. Andrew Beam, 34, of 1910 Jones Saint, who earlier pleaded guilty to stealing more than $10,000 while a slot machine technician at Harvey's, has been granted a deferred judgment and ordered to repay the loss." (*Omaha World-Herald*, 10/26/99)

"[Mississippi] Gulf Coast banking officials are looking for the best combination of security measures to deal with an increase in bank robberies that has accompanied the growth in casinos and other businesses since 1992. Harrison, Hancock, Jackson, and Stone counties reported only two bank robberies in each of 1990 and 1991. Robberies have climbed from that time, reaching a high of thirty holdups in 1997." (*Associated Press*, 10/11/99)

"Anthony Czamara, who is serving a jail term for stealing from a Hamburg (New York) bistro, Friday was ordered to serve a prison term of two to five years for embezzling more than $77,000 from a Buffalo restaurant. The judge said Czamara's 'troublesome' history of criminal 'shortcomings' seemed linked to both his admitted alcoholism and his addiction to gambling." (*Buffalo News*, 10/10/99)

"Compulsive gambling within the Southeast Asian community in the Twin Cities has increased so much that some families have been left homeless, said Diane Dovenberg, who works with Southeast Asians.

'I'm hearing more and more about gambling with Southeast Asian refugees,' she said. 'They have experienced horrendous trauma from war, escaping their own countries, spending years in refugee camps in Thailand, and then experiencing the trauma of coming to this country and having it be so different from the lives they were leading over there. The hopelessness is relieved at the casinos.'" (*Minneapolis Star Tribune*, 10/12/99)

"Before casino gambling, [Atlantic City] was home to numerous thriving churches of various denominations. But in recent years, churches and synagogues have begun to close. The Rev. Patrick J. Hunt, pastor at [the Church of the Ascension], said the casino industry is helping society gradually erode. 'We want anybody to come to church,' Hunt said. 'But gambling is a vice and the casinos do their darndest to make sure we don't exist and that every other church doesn't exist.'" (*Atlantic City Press*, 10/11/99)

"Of the forty-two armed robberies investigated by the York County Sheriff's Office this year, twenty-three have been video-poker–related. Additionally, there have been at least seventeen property crimes directly connected with video gambling machines, including burglaries, larcenies, and fraud. But Cauthen, Fortson, York County Sheriff Bruce Bryant and other law enforcement officials throughout the region say those numbers don't begin to paint the whole picture. Many domestic cases that officers respond to involve arguments that stemmed from one spouse's gambling habit. Deputies are responsible for serving civil court papers, such as divorce decrees, and Bryant said a growing number of those appear to be tied to gambling. Police also say they spend more and more time responding to false reports filed by gamblers who don't want a spouse to learn they lost money to the video machines." (*Charlotte Observer*, 10/3/99)

"A Denham Springs [Louisiana] man was sentenced Monday to thirty-seven months in prison and ordered to repay $933,845 to victims of his investment scam. U.S. District Judge Frank Polozola told Mike D. Nolan he was responsible for 'a very big case of fraud' that hurt lots of people, including a widow who lost her nest egg and couples whose marriages fell apart because of failed investment schemes. . . .

The judge said Nolan's gambling problem fueled the fraud scheme." ([Baton Rouge, Louisiana] *Advocate*, 9/28/99)

"There is a trail of broken homes, bankruptcies, crime and suicides, say those who work with problem gamblers in that state. 'We've treated some people who have lost their life savings on the lottery,' said Jack Gronewald, chief operating officer of Ridgeview Institute, a mental-health treatment center near Atlanta. . . .

[T]here were four groups of Gamblers Anonymous meeting in Georgia when the lottery was instituted there in 1992, but today there are ten or more groups, indicating that the number of problem gamblers increased, and some play only the lottery." (*Birmingham News*, 9/24/99)

"A [Las Vegas] woman who embezzled more than $1 million during her eighteen-year career as a paralegal with the U.S. attorney's office was sentenced to thirty months in prison Friday. Elizabeth 'Becki' Simmons, who has admitted having a gambling problem, pleaded guilty in March to embezzlement, making false statements, and filing a false income tax return." (*Las Vegas Review-Journal*, 9/18/99)

"Former (Mississippi) state worker, Deidre Marshall, has been sentenced to five years of probation for embezzling $100,000 from a state program for the disabled. Marshall said she stole the money to pay for her compulsive gambling habit." ([Baton Rouge, Louisiana] *Advocate*, 9/12/99)

"It is a hard-edged reality that happens – at casinos, at racetracks, at church bingos, at state lottery outlets. The Mississippi Coast has seen a twenty-six-fold increase in the number of Gamblers Anonymous meetings – to thirteen a week – since the first casino opened in 1992." (Lexington [Kentucky] *Herald-Leader*, 9/12/99)

"A three-month investigation by the *Pittsburgh Tribune-Review* found Pennsylvania Lottery sales come disproportionately from the poor and working class. In Allegheny County, the most recent lottery records available show stores in neighborhoods with per capita incomes lower than $20,000 sold more than twice as many tickets per resident as those in neighborhoods where average incomes exceeded $30,000.

The lottery's 1997 study found 39 percent of 'heavy' players – those who bet at least once a week – report household incomes below $25,000 a year." (*Pittsburgh Tribune-Review*, 8/22/99)

"A German tourist jumped to his death off a ten-story casino parking garage Wednesday in the third such suicide in Atlantic City in eight days. On August 17, a gambler who had lost $87,000 jumped to his death off a Trump Plaza roof. On Monday, a dealer at Caesar's Atlantic City Hotel Casino committed suicide by leaping off the casino's parking garage. (*Associated Press*, 8/25/99)

"An Edgefield County [South Carolina] man was killed in a shootout at a casino he apparently was attempting to rob. Dexter Wooden, 25, went to Bryant's Discount Beverage Center Wednesday night and tried to hold up four customers who were gambling." (*Associated Press*, 8/26/99)

"–Tourism. City officials insist the Milwaukee casino draws few tourists and say most gamblers are lower income residents of the city and Milwaukee County.

–Crime. Prosecutors have not broken cases directly related to casinos, but the district attorney reports his staff has seen more burglaries, larcenies, and crimes of opportunity related to gambling. The most celebrated local case involved a woman who stole nearly $100,000 from her grandmother to gamble in Milwaukee and other Wisconsin casinos." ([Milwaukee] *Journal Sentinel*, 12/27/98)

"Debts of more than $100,000 prompted a woman's botched bank-robbery attempt that led to an eight-hour hostage situation on New Year's Eve [in Olathe, Kansas], her attorney said. [The suspect's attorney] told [U.S. Magistrate David] Waxse that [Pheng] Siriboury was 'addicted to gambling' and had run up debts – 'maybe as high as $150,000.'" (*St. Louis Post-Dispatch*, 1/6/00)

"Bankruptcies citing gambling debts as a contributing factor have jumped since the riverboats entered the Kansas City market in mid-1994. The first Kansas City area riverboat casino opened in mid-1994. In that year, only 13 of the 3,501 bankruptcy filings in Kansas City – 0.37 percent – listed gambling losses. . . .

By 1998, 194 of the 5,618 persons who filed – 3.5 percent – said gambling was a contributing factor in their bankruptcies. They listed unsecured debts of more than $7.5 million, much of it to credit-card companies. Bankruptcy lawyers and gambling counselors say actual figures might be higher because people are reluctant to admit they have a gambling problem." (*Kansas City Star*, 1/9/00)

"The battle against domestic violence is gaining ground, and work by University of Nebraska Medical Center researcher, Dr. Robert Muelleman, is helping. 'It looks as if problem gambling in the partner is going to be as much a risk factor as problem alcohol, and that's really new information,' he said." (*Daily Nebraskan*, 1/13/00)

A former [New Bedford, Massachusetts] elementary school principal has admitted stealing $20,000 in student funds she used to support a gambling habit, prosecutors said." (*Associated Press*, 1/13/00)

Terry Twist, a former supervisor at a Naperville (Illinois) bank whose cooperation helped lead to federal charges against two bank supervisors, pleaded guilty Thursday to his role in the theft of nearly $90,000 from the bank vault in a staged holdup. Twist, 26, had sizable gambling debts." (*Chicago Tribune*, 1/14/00)

"A gambler losing big dollars in the high-roller area of the MotorCity Casino in Detroit pulled out a gun Wednesday, shot himself in the head, and died, police said. Terrified gamblers fled from the blackjack table where off-duty Oak Park Police Sgt. Solomon Bell had been consistently losing large bets, witnesses said." (*Detroit Free Press*, 1/27/00)

"A thirty-seven-year Detroit Fire Department veteran threatened to kill himself while gambling at the MGM Grand Detroit Casino on

Thursday, police said. 'I guess he lost all the money he had, and he made a statement to the dealer saying he was going to do the same thing as the gentlemen yesterday did,' [a police spokesman] said." (*Associated Press*, 1/27/00)

"Two multinational lottery operators spent more than $135,000 in 1999 in their efforts to win access to South Carolina lawmakers and put a lottery on the ballot." (*Augusta Georgia Chronicle*, 1/22/00)

"A man known as the 'Groucho Marx' bandit was sentenced Friday to more than four years in prison for a pair of bank robberies in Southcentral Alaska. Federal public defender, Richard Curtner, said [Scott] Morgan was deep in debt because of gambling and alcohol addictions." (*Associated Press*, 1/22/00)

"A former [Memphis] Service Merchandise store manager who admitted stealing more than $150,000 in deposits and gambling much of it away in Tunica casinos was sentenced to six years in prison Tuesday." ([Memphis] *Commercial Appeal*, 2/2/00)

"Rosemont (Illinois) Mayor Donald E. Stephens is getting a hefty reward for his role in convincing state lawmakers to approve sweeping gambling law changes last year. Campaign finance records obtained Wednesday show Stephens received $96,000 in contributions from gambling interests in the six months after Governor George Ryan signed legislation that opened Cook County to a casino, created lucrative subsidies for the horseracing industry, and allowed casinos to stay dockside rather than cruise." (*Chicago Daily Herald*, 2/3/00)

"Sixteen employees or owners of 'cash for gold' shops that line Atlantic City's casino strip were accused Thursday of preying on the desperate by charging up to 500 percent interest on hocked jewelry." (*Associated Press*, 2/10/00)

"An admitted thief and pathological gambler has six months to pay almost $155,000 back to the Pierre (South Dakota) Area Chamber of Commerce or face time in the women's prison. Former chamber financial

manager, Linda K. Thomsen, 55, was sentenced Tuesday afternoon."
(*Pierre [South Dakota] Capital Journal,* 2/16/00)

"The death of a [Frederick, Maryland] debt-ridden accountant who bad-gered a colleague into shooting her was a homicide, not a suicide, so her life insurance company must pay out $1.5 million, a judge ruled. Circuit Judge Mary Ann Stepler ruled last week against Allstate Life Insurance Co. in a dispute over the 1996 death of Mary Gaye Fister. Fister, a forty-five-year-old high-rolling gambler, died on a country road where she had gone with fellow accountant Lawrence H. Gold-man. He said they planned to make the death look like a mob hit so that Fister's creditors could collect in insurance money the $800,000 she owed....

Investigators said Fister persuaded friends and clients to lend her money to support a lifestyle that included driving her turbocharged red sports car to Atlantic City casinos, where she sometimes lost as much as $30,000 per trip." (*Las Vegas Sun,* 2/14/00)

"A former casino consultant fought back tears as he told a federal jury Thursday that he funneled hundreds of thousands of dollars in payoffs to former [Louisiana] Governor Edwin Edwards and his son Stephen – before and after Edwards left office in 1996. Ricky Shetler's testimony was backed by Shetler's own ledgers and conversations secretly recorded by the FBI.

It was the most damaging to date in the six-week-old trial and, per-haps, in the forty-year public life of the often scandal-plagued four-term governor who was acquitted of federal racketeering charges in 1986. Federal prosecutors say Edwin and Stephen Edwards and five other men took part in a years-long series of schemes to manipulate the licensing of riverboat casinos." (*Associated Press,* 2/24/00)

"A notorious Chinatown gang has expanded its loansharking operation to legal card clubs in the Bay Area, particularly the Lucky Chances Casino in Colma, according to an FBI affidavit made public yesterday." (*San Francisco Chronicle,* 3/4/00)

"By the time former Placerville [California] police officer, Jerry Olson, was arrested for bank robbery last month, he had hit 'rock bottom,' his father said. Battling drug addiction and crushed under gambling debt, the thirty-nine-year-old already had lost his job. FBI agents say he may have robbed ten banks in Northern California and Nevada." (*Associated Press*, 3/8/00)

"Casino Rama, one of Canada's most lucrative gambling palaces, was supposed to be a financial saviour to Ontario's impoverished First Nations. For two members of the Rama Chippewa band that hosts the casino, it's meant something quite different: personal downfall, criminal records, and a humiliating admission of guilt before their tight-knit community. The pair were quietly convicted recently of stealing more than $100,000 from the Mnjikaning band to fuel out-of-control gambling habits." (*Ottawa Citizen*, 11/15/99)

"The number of gambling-related suicides in Quebec has more than doubled this year from last. According to reports provided by the Quebec coroner's office, fifteen people, all men, have killed themselves so far this year because of their gambling problems. That's up from six in all of 1998, and two in 1994, when the provincial government first legalized casinos and video lottery terminals." ([Montreal] *Gazette*, 11/25/99)

"Gambling debts led former Hillsdale (Illinois) Fire Chief Bill Phillips to siphon more than $150,000 out of the department's bank account, investigators have concluded. Phillips, 56, was found dead in his truck at a rural Hillsdale cemetery May 19, the victim of carbon monoxide poisoning." (*Associated Press*, 11/24/99)

"Nearly five months have passed since the MGM Grand Detroit Casino opened its doors near the Salvation Army's Bagley Center, and since then, the stream of penniless gamblers looking for a helping hand has been steady....

As casinos, lotteries, and other recreational gambling spread throughout Michigan, workers at social service agencies say the number of people reaching out for help is growing. Five years ago, metro Detroit had about six Gamblers Anonymous groups; today there are about twenty, said Warren Biller, director of the Michigan Council on Problem Gambling." (*Detroit Free Press*, 12/7/99)

"The sentencing of a [Greensboro, North Carolina] life insurance agent who cheated his clients out of at least $1.6 million was postponed on Wednesday for the third time. [Paul] Blackburn said he embezzled the money to feed a gambling addiction. He fantasized about gambling, fell asleep to dreams of gambling, and could spend twenty-six hours playing craps in a casino without rest." ([Greensboro, North Carolina] *News & Record*, 12/16/99)

"Households earning less than $25,000 accounted for 35 percent of the California Lottery's ticket sales last year, its newly released review shows."The 32 percent of Californians with incomes below $25,000 account for less than one in every five dollars earned by state residents, [David Rogosa, a statistician and associate professor at Stanford] said in a telephone interview. Based on that, their 35 percent share of lottery purchases 'is far, far greater than their proportion of (the) income,' Rogosa said." (*Sacramento Bee*, 12/15/99)

"Authorities say they have linked a woman arrested in Bradenton [Florida] to what might be the largest and most profitable burglary ring in the country. Barbara Dolinska is a member of a roving group of bandits who travel the country committing burglaries, Baton Rouge, Louisiana, police detective Jonny Dunham said Wednesday. 'Dolinska and her cohorts like to gamble,' authorities said. 'They committed many of the crimes in areas that either had riverboat gambling operations or other kinds of gaming,' Dunham said." (*Sarasota* [Florida] *Herald-Tribune*, 12/23/99)

"A Florida man who lost about $50,000 while gambling [in Atlantic City] during the past two days died Tuesday after he jumped seven floors from a Trump Plaza Hotel and Casino roof onto Columbia Place, officials said." (*Atlantic City Press*, 8/18/99)

"A former Brown County [Wisconsin] deputy treasurer convicted of embezzling $197,000 was sentenced Friday to twelve years in prison. Prosecutors contend Barbara Berger, 47, stole the money over three years to support a gambling habit." (*Associated Press*, 8/20/99)

"An addiction to riverboat gambling led Boone County's [Kentucky] property valuation administrator to plead guilty to a theft charge Friday. David Turner admitted to authorities he used as much as $45,000 in office funds to feed his habit." (*Cincinnati Enquirer*, 8/14/99)

"Four days after [Illinois] Governor [George] Ryan signed gambling legislation, the Empress River Casino deposited $10,000 into the governor's campaign fund. On the same day of the Empress contribution, Hollywood Casino gave $10,000 to a Senate Republican campaign fund controlled by Senate President James 'Pate' Philip (R-Wood Dale), who favored last spring's gambling deal. In fact, more that 40 percent of the $272,405 that gambling interests gave last spring to Ryan and members of the General Assembly came during May and June, a critical period when the measure passed the Legislature and the governor signed it." (*Chicago Sun-Times*, 8/11/99)

"Tribal leaders declared victory in July when the House defeated a measure that would have forced tribes opening casinos to continue to hammer out agreements with state governments first. Before the vote, fifty of the American Indian leaders met with top House Republicans – a landmark day that reflected the growing political clout of tribes bolstered by a newly vigorous self-determination movement and financial gains from casino gambling. Since the 1991–92 campaign cycle, Indian tribes have shelled out more that $3.3 million in soft-money contributions to the Republican and Democratic national committees." (*Detroit News*, 8/11/99)

"The number of Wisconsin communities holding Gamblers Anonymous meetings has mushroomed from six to twenty-nine since 1992, the year Indian tribes began agreements with the state to open casinos, and half of today's meetings are within 30 miles of a casino, an Associated Press review found. During a typical week, nearly 250 people attend Gamblers Anonymous meetings statewide seeking help with gambling problems, compared with about 100 in 1992. . . . 'Eleven people who contacted the group in 1997 committed suicide because of gambling,' John W. said." (*Chicago Tribune*, 8/2/99)

"In the first six months of 1999, Attorney General Bill Lockyer received at least $32,500 in campaign contributions from California card clubs he licenses and regulates, according to campaign reports filed yesterday with the state." (*San Francisco Chronicle*, 8/3/99)

"The gaming industry increased its financial contributions to federal candidates and political parties by about 400 percent from 1992 through 1998. The General Accounting Office, the investigative arm of Congress, found that total gaming donations rose from $1.1 million in 1992 to $5.7 million in 1998." (*Las Vegas Review-Journal*, 7/28/99)

"Tuesday in Ridgeland, a woman whose ten-day-old baby died in a sweltering car while she played video poker, was given a suspended sentence and five years' probation."York County [South Carolina] Sheriff Bruce Bryant said many of the social problems brought on by video poker are not recorded in police reports. 'Arguing over video poker is the reason for many domestic-abuse cases,' Bryant said. 'We've had murders in York County because of video poker.'" (*The State* [Columbia, South Carolina], 7/23/99)

"The conviction of [a Louisiana] ex-legislator imprisoned for a bribery scheme to protect video poker was upheld Thursday by a federal appeals court. Former state Senator Larry Bankston was found guilty in June 1997 of taking $1,500 from one-time video-poker operator Fred Goodson." (*Associated Press*, 7/22/99)

"Gambling problems led a former Columbus [Ohio] police officer to steal about $20,000 in diamonds from a Northland Mall jewelry store where he was providing security." (*Columbus Dispatch*, 7/17/99)

"A military judge ordered a compulsive gambler locked up for sixty days after she admitted she wrote about $14,000 in bad checks to feed slot machines at Air Force clubs. Testimony at her court-martial yesterday at

Davis-Monthan Air Force Base showed that [Tech. Sgt. Gloria] Calhoun, a seventeen-year-veteran with a previously exemplary record, got hooked on slot machines last year at Osan Air Base in South Korea. (*Arizona Daily Star*, 7/15/99)

"Reno [Nevada] ministers said they have seen too many people who've lost rent money and more at slot machines, craps, and blackjack tables. 'My appointment schedule is full with marriages that have been destroyed by gambling,' said the Rev. Joe Taylor of the South Reno Baptist Church in southwest Reno near Meadowood Mall. He said his church receives ten to twenty calls a day from gamblers asking for bus tickets. "The Rev. Carey Anderson, pastor of the Bethel AME Church in Sparks... said he hears from abusive gamblers each week. 'They're calling us wanting money because they blew their rent on gambling,' he said. 'They can't feed their children, and they can't pay their rent. And they need food, and they can't pay their power bills.' The pastor said his phone log for Tuesday was typical: it showed thirteen gambling-related calls by 3 p.m." (*Reno Gazette-Journal*, 6/30/99)

"Some of Illinois' prosecutors are lending credence to a nationwide study that concludes gambling increases crime. Prosecutors in Tazewell and Peoria counties, near one of the state's oldest riverboats, have seen a definite rise in gambling-related crime. Kevin W. Lyons, Peoria County state's attorney, rattles off a list of cases where problem gamblers got in trouble. Just the other day, he said, his office won a conviction against a teacher who stole money to support a gambling habit. 'I've convicted some lawyers and taken away their law licenses for stealing client money' for gambling.... Stewart Umholtz, state's attorney for Tazewell County, has seen embezzlement, theft, and burglary cases arising from problem gamblers. In fact, he asked state Rep. Michael K. Smith of Canton to sponsor a bill that would have provided state aid to prosecutors to help pay for increased caseloads resulting from gambling." (*Copley News Service*, 6/28/99)

"Proponents of riverboat gambling and horseracing pumped $1 million during the last two years into the campaign funds of [Illinois] legislators who voted for the sweeping legislative package that squeaked through the General Assembly last month, a new study shows. The money is more than ten times the $83,460 that progambling interests gave to lawmakers who later voted against the gambling package." (*Chicago Tribune*, 6/14/99)

"A man arrested in the armed robbery of a [New Orleans] bar told deputies of his motive for the holdup: he wanted to recover the several hundred dollars he lost playing the lounge's video poker machines." (*Las Vegas Sun*, 6/14/99)

"New Jersey casino regulators have agreed to look further into payments totaling $240,000 that a gaming company made to former Florida House Speaker Bo Johnson at a time when Florida was considering legalization of casinos." (*Las Vegas Sun*, 6/9/99)

"A former employee for the Chicago Transit Authority was sentenced to twelve months in prison Wednesday in federal court for embezzling more than $187,000 from the agency in less than one year. Sheila Short, 36, of Richton Park, admitted she blew the money gambling on the state lottery and riverboats." (*Chicago Tribune*, 5/20/99)

"A veteran employee of the Lehigh and Northampton [Pennsylvania] Transportation Authority, who said compulsive gambling led her to steal $17,765, has been put on three years' probation. Margaret Hansen, who will be 65 next month, was fined $2,000 and ordered to make restitution to the authority.... Authority lawyer, Kent Herman, and Executive Director, Armand Greco, said the restitution agreement was appropriate because Hansen was an exemplary employee for many years who fell victim to a gambling addiction in the latter part of her career." ([Allentown, Pennsylvania] *The Morning Call*, 5/20/99)

"A 37-year-old Little Silver [New Jersey] man who a judge said compulsively fleeced people was sentenced yesterday to seven years in state prison for stealing more than $150,000 from several banks through a check-kiting scheme. Joshua Roslin told Superior Court Judge John A. Ricciardi that he suffers from a gambling problem." ([Neptune, New Jersey] *Asbury Park Press*, 5/15/99)

"The families of two politically connected lawyers who helped bring the Showboat Mardi Gras riverboat casino to East Chicago made more than $20 million selling their interest in the riverboat after putting up essentially no money for the shares, a newspaper reports." (*Associated Press*, 5/11/99)

"Former DeSoto County Supervisor James D. 'Jake' Person pleaded guilty Friday to embezzling $50,000 from the DeSoto Shrine Club and gambling the money away in casinos in Tunica County." ([Memphis] *Commercial Appeal*, 5/8/99)

"Before taking his life last November, Central Falls [Rhode Island] Police Chief Thomas Moffatt had misappropriated departmental funds and borrowed heavily from his officers to pay gambling debts, a state police investigation has concluded. Moffatt owed more than $60,000 to his officers and possibly thousands more to several accounts within the department that were under his control, Col. Edmond Culhane, state police superintendent, said yesterday. Culhane declined to answer a question about a report that Moffatt owed $40,000 to the Foxwoods and Mohegan Sun casinos. 'The message from the whole thing is the dangers of gambling, quite frankly,' said Culhane. 'Tom Moffatt was a truly honorable guy. He had a superb career as a state trooper. He was a great family man and a terrific policeman. This was his one weakness and it took him down.'" (*Providence Journal*, 5/2/99)

"Fueled by profitable casinos at a handful of reservations, Native American leaders are planning to spend $1 million to $5 million in the 2000 election to try to defeat Republican Sen. Slade Gorton, whom they regard as their primary political enemy in the United States." (*Seattle Times*, 4/5/99)

"Problem gambler Scott A. Correia gave a lesson Thursday in how not to commit a bank robbery. Police say the thirty-three-year-old Dartmouth [Massachusetts] man, who lives at 10 Sol-E-Mar Road, made several mistakes when he robbed $1,300 from the Fall River Five Cents Savings Bank. 'He used his parents' car and parked near the bank, didn't switch license plates, dropped his baseball cap outside, and abandoned the vehicle a short distance from the bank,' according to police. Correia took the cash with him to the Foxwoods Resort and Casino, Ledyard, Connecticut, police said." ([Fall River, Massachusetts] *Herald News*, 4/3/99)

"Though casinos can now be found throughout the country, the gambling industry continues to lavish campaign contributions on its original allies, lawmakers from New Jersey and Nevada. New Jersey's two senators and the representative whose district includes Atlantic City are among the biggest beneficiaries of campaign cash from the industry, according to a report by the Center for Responsive Politics. From 1993 through 1998, Sen. Robert Torricelli, a Democrat, received $86,600 from political action committees and individuals in the gambling business. That put him third among senators, behind only Nevada Sens. Harry Reid and Richard Bryan, also Democrats.... Among House members, New Jersey Rep. Frank LoBiondo, R-Vineland, received $64,750 from gambling interests in 1997 and 1998, ranking him third nationally behind Nevada Reps. Shelley Berkley, a Democrat, and Jim Gibbons, a Republican. LoBiondo's district includes Atlantic City. 'With Congress taking more of an interest in issues related to gambling, the $50-billion-a-year gambling industry has increased its giving to lawmakers.' The center reported that the gambling industry donated more than $6.2 million to federal candidates and parties in the 1997–98 election cycle, twice what it gave during the last mid-term elections." (*Associated Press*, 4/6/99)

"After cleaning out her bank account, selling her possessions, and stealing from her employer to support her video poker habit, Jann knew she had hit bottom. 'I had used up all of my resources and abused the trust of everybody around me,' she said. 'You get very suicidal.' (*Associated Press*, 3/29/99)

"Citing severe losses from a gambling addiction, a prominent Plaquemines Parish [Louisiana] developer admits he forged documents and tried to sell residential lots he no longer had clear title to, his attorney said. But gambling losses to casinos in Louisiana and Mississippi pressured him to raise cash, [his attorney] said. Sercovich mortgaged as many as forty-six

Pleasant Ridge lots to raise money. Lots in the subdivision range from $70,000 to $127,000. George Ruppenicker, an attorney for Southern Title, Inc., which conducted the title search on the lots, said its insurance carrier has paid out more than $1 million in claims related to Pleasant Ridge and Sercovich.'" ([New Orleans] *Times-Picayune*, 3/31/99)

"[Michael Belletire, administrator of the Illinois Gaming Board] is resigning effective April 15 and will become chief operating officer of Specialty Events, an affiliate of Sportsman's Park horseracing track in Cicero. Charles Bidwill III, the president of Sportsman's, is a part owner of the Casino Queen riverboat in East St. Louis. Ed Duffy, the president of Specialty Events, is a consultant for Sportsman's and the Casino Queen. Belletire and Gaming Board Chairman, J. Thomas Johnson, said the new job does not conflict with the board's code of conduct, which prohibits members or employees from working for or representing a riverboat licensee or applicant within a year of leaving the board." (*Associated Press*, 4/1/99)

"This is a tale of two counties. One is Hancock County, Georgia, a rural spot northeast of Macon where most residents are black, half the adults never graduated from high school, and more than a third of the children are poor. The other is Fayette County, a thriving Atlanta suburb where most residents are white, a fourth of adults have college degrees, and less than one percent of families receive welfare. Hancock doesn't outdo Fayette on much. But it does beat its well-heeled neighbor in state lottery sales. Hancock's lottery sales in 1997 translated to $554 for every county resident from age 18 to 64. The same figure in Fayette came to $139....

A *Birmingham News* review of lottery sales in Georgia counties showed some trends. Generally, the lottery has weak sales in rich counties and strong sales in poor counties." (*Birmingham News*, 3/23/99)

"A former federal paralegal [in Las Vegas] with a reported gambling habit embezzled as much as $1.5 million over ten years by betraying the trust of her colleagues, U.S. Attorney Kathryn Landreth said Tuesday." (*Las Vegas Sun*, 3/17/99)

"Gambling interests gave more to [West Virginia] legislative candidates in 1998 than ever before, according to the latest figures from the People's Election Reform Coalition. 'Gambling donations to members of the Legislature totaled $63,125 in the 1996 elections,' [according to the coalition]. 'Although the 1998 data is still being audited, PERC has already documented $164,500 in gambling donations – an increase of more than 2.5 times.'" (*West Virginia Gazette*, 3/10/99)

"If Minnesotans have a reputation for generosity, this may be the reason: fifty of the state's eighty-seven counties are above the national average in their disposition toward charitable giving, according to a recent study. Only sixteen counties are ranked below average. "Generosity generally flourishes in counties with average to relatively low pulltab and lottery gambling. Counties with high per-capita gambling include all but three of those labeled least likely to give by the national study." ([Minneapolis] *Star Tribune*, 2/5/99)

"Florida officials say the Halloran saga shows how the tribe's largely unregulated casinos are a powerful lure for organized crime. 'Tribes across the country consistently say there's no proof of any organized crime infiltration,' said [Assistant Florida Attorney General John] Glogau. 'But law enforcement people say that's nonsense.'" (*St. Petersburg Times*, 2/19/99)

"[A]n Omaha woman [pled] guilty to charges that she took thousands of dollars from mentally retarded adults under her care. Police said the woman took $21,000 from fourteen mentally retarded adults and used the money to play blackjack 'at nearby casinos.'" (*Omaha World-Herald*, 2/21/99)

"A former San Jose police officer sentenced yesterday to fourteen years in prison for burglaries will continue to receive $27,000 a year in disability benefits for his gambling addiction. Johnny Venzon, Jr., 48, had been accused of stealing from people on his own beat while in uniform. Venzon, who blamed his actions on a gambling addiction, often burglarized homes and then investigated the crimes." (*San Francisco Chronicle*, 2/25/99)

"The former bookkeeper for a chain of Midas Muffler shops [in Wisconsin] pleaded guilty Friday to stealing a little more than $306,000 from the stores to pay off gambling debts incurred first at Potawatomi Bingo Casino and later in Las Vegas." (*Milwaukee Journal Sentinel*, 2/14/99)

"A federal jury convicted a suburban [Chicago] mother Thursday of insurance fraud in the death of her infant daughter, rejecting defense claims the baby died of Sudden Infant Death Syndrome. [Dina] Abdelhaq, an admitted gambling addict, had taken out a $200,000 insurance policy on newborn daughter Tara fifteen months after another infant daughter died of unexplained causes. "Records from one riverboat casino showed that Abdelhaq had gambled there the day after the death of her first daughter, Lena, in 1994. On public aid and denied credit at a riverboat casino after she bounced checks, Abdelhaq took out the $200,000 life insurance policy on Tara." (*Chicago Tribune*, 2/13/99)

"A ring of Gaston County residents has stolen more than half a million dollars from video poker machines across South Carolina over the past year by unlocking the machines with copies of master keys, police said Monday. Police say about two dozen thieves took turns emptying video poker machines while partners distracted clerks and communicated across stores with an elaborate system of hand signals." (*Charlotte Observer*, 2/16/99)

"A former East Fork [Nevada] Justice Court clerk pleaded guilty to one count of unlawful use of public funds in the theft of more than $17,000 from the court. A gambling problem led to the embezzlement, according to court records." (*Las Vegas Sun*, 1/2/99)

"Son Tram never talked about her husband. How the beatings had gotten worse in recent months since her husband began gambling and frequenting bars. But relatives knew. They tried to persuade her to leave. The last plea came from her younger brother, who stayed with her in her Olney rowhouse for the last couple of months. He told her to come and live with him and his family in Florida. She refused. Last Friday, her husband kicked the brother out of the house. Saturday morning, she was dead.

Trung Hieu Tram, 32, had bludgeoned his thirty-five-year-old wife in the back of the head with a hammer. . . . Recently, [Vin Thach's] niece had been struggling to feed the kids, telling Thach she had no money. Trung Hieu had been spending the family money betting on football and going to casinos, and he was going into debt." (*Philadelphia Daily News*, 2/2/99)

"In a string of murders that shocked the rural [Louisiana] River Parishes, six wealthy, mostly elderly residents were bludgeoned and stabbed to death in their homes, their safes stolen and pockets emptied. After six hours of denials in a stark white room in the courthouse, [Daniel] Blank broke down and wept, then confessed to a killing spree that went from October 1996 to July 1997, tapes and transcripts show. In only one brief statement does Blank even hint at his motivation for the brutality, although investigators said it is clear that he was in pursuit of cash to support almost daily trips to video poker halls and casinos. The chronic gambler's combined take from seven break-ins was about $101,120, the records show, and he sometimes headed for casinos right after committing the crimes." ([New Orleans] *Times-Picayune*, 1/28/99)

"As Jim Hodges celebrated his startling victory on election night, a man stepped out of the raucous crowd to slap the Democratic governor-elect on the back and shout, 'Marvelous, governor!' The smiling man was Fred Collins, a multimillionaire and the biggest operator in South Carolina's fast-growing $2.3-billion-a-year video-poker business. Hodges and his allies spent at least $6 million to boost his candidacy. About half of that money came from video-poker operators." (*USA Today*, 1/7/99)

"The Mashantucket Pequots – who have given more than $1 million to national political parties – now have a way to donate directly to candidates' campaigns. The Pequots, owners of the highly lucrative Foxwoods Resort Casino in Mashantucket, Connecticut, formed a political action committee, or PAC, last year, according to Federal Election Commission records." ([Hartford] *Courant*, 1/11/99)

"Nereida 'Nettie' Benitez saved for thirty years for her dream home. But now, her dream home is just a weed-filled hole in a lot next to her son-in-law's parents' house. Her life savings are gone, gambled away by the builder, who stole her money. Benitez hired [Thomas] James to build her house and gave him her life savings, $65,000." (*Kansas City Star*, 1/14/99)

"After a night of drinking at a Kenner [Louisiana] casino Saturday night, a Ponchatoula man apparently shot himself to death in his car outside the gambling boat, police said." ([New Orleans] *Times-Picayune*, 11/8/99)

"One man was shot to death and another critically injured following an argument outside the Mohegan Sun casino [Montville, Connecticut], police said." (*Las Vegas Sun*, 11/8/99)

THE NUMBERS

SUMMARY. There are two ways to identify social costs: the first is through the study of problem and pathological gamblers, and the second is through direct statistical analysis. In 2003 dollars, the cost to society of an additional pathological gambler is $10,330 based on studies performed in the mid-1990s, whereas the cost to society of an additional problem gambler is $2,945. Accounting for the cost of raising tax dollars to cover some of these costs (see Chapter 8), raises the totals to $11,304 and $3,222, respectively.

Pathological gambling is a recognized impulse control disorder in the DSM-IV of the American Psychiatric Association. Pathological gamblers (often referred to as "addicted" or "compulsive" gamblers) are identified by a number of characteristics, including repeated failures to resist the urge to gamble; loss of control over their gambling, personal lives, and employment; reliance on others to relieve a desperate financial situation caused by gambling; and the committing of illegal acts to finance gambling. Problem gamblers have similar problems, but to a lesser degree. Often the two groups are combined and referred to as *problem and pathological gamblers.*

Medical research suggests that gambling may affect the brain in ways similar to addictive drugs and that a portion of the population may be more susceptible to the addiction response.[230] With respect to gambling, the latent propensity to problem and pathological gambling becomes overt when the opportunity to gamble is available and sufficient time has elapsed for the problem to manifest. Pathological gamblers are generally found to constitute 1 or 2 percent of the population; problem gamblers are another 2 to 3 percent in gambling areas where casino gambling is available.[231] One study of gamblers in treatment found that 62 percent committed illegal acts as a result of their gambling: 80 percent had committed civil offenses, and 23 percent were charged with criminal offenses, according to a 1990 Maryland Department of Health and Mental Hygiene survey. A similar survey of nearly four hundred members of Gambler's Anonymous showed that 57 percent admitted stealing to finance their gambling. Moreover, the amounts are not small. On average, they stole $135,000, and total theft was more than $30 million, according to Henry Lesieur, of the Institute of Problem Gambling, before the National Gambling Impact Study Commission, Atlantic City, New Jersey, January 22, 1998. The National Gambling Impact Study Commission's final report, issued in June 1999, reported that among those who did not gamble (i.e., had not gambled in the past year), only 7 percent had ever been incarcerated. In contrast, more than three times this number (i.e., 21.4 percent) of individuals who had been pathological gamblers at any point during their lifetime had been incarcerated.

By studying the social costs connected with the activities of pathological gamblers, we can determine the average cost to society of an additional pathological gambler. The same procedure can be applied to problem gamblers. Combining what is learned with information about the number of problem and pathological gamblers provides cost figures for the entire society. The advantage of this procedure is that problem gamblers are an available object of investigation and have been increasingly studied; the disadvantage is that it overlooks social costs that do not derive from problem and pathological gamblers.

The second route to social cost looks directly at the levels of cost-creating activities such as crime, suicide, and bankruptcy. If areas with casinos have higher crime rates due to the casino, for example, this can be identified statistically. The direct route has the advantage that it considers more costs than just those caused by problem and pathological gamblers. On the other hand, the direct route is often difficult because it requires a sufficiently good sample of social statistics. It is often difficult to separate the effects of casinos from all the other contributory causes of crime. Econometricians talk of "the Iron Law of Econometrics," which says that estimated coefficients tend to be too low when the underlying data is measured imperfectly, a problem that is nearly always present to some degree. In many cases, such as suicide, the cause of the suicide may not be recorded at all. Relatively few studies of the effect of casinos on crime exist, and there is one national study on the effects of gambling on bankruptcy. For many other social costs, no direct studies exist.

In this chapter, we report social cost estimates derived from the study of problem and pathological gamblers. In most studies, problem and pathological gamblers were studied as a group. Because the social costs associated with a pathological gambler normally exceed those of a problem gambler, combining the two groups produces an estimate of social costs that lies between the costs of each. In the remainder of this chapter, we will continue to distinguish between problem and pathological gamblers when possible. In summarizing the literature, we will assign to pathological gamblers the results of studies that combined groups, which probably understates the social cost of a pathological gambler. In addition, many studies report that they consciously chose to understate the costs of social problems they found when choices had to be made, and that their numbers should be treated as conservative. For this reason, too, the social costs that are available may understate the true average cost to society of an additional pathological gambler. Lastly, not all social costs were estimated by some studies, and some social costs were not estimated by any studies. To the extent that social costs are omitted, the totals represented in this chapter also tend to be understated.

Social science rarely gets to study a situation where all variables can be treated in a controlled experiment the way they frequently can be in hard science. If not handled well, there are two issues that can cause the estimates of social costs to be inaccurate: the presence of multiple causality and sampling error. We have already discussed the problem of multiple causes of bankruptcy and the need to identify the separate contribution of casino gambling, for example. The issue sometimes appears under other names. In the medical profession, *co-morbidity* refers to situations where individuals suffering from one disease also suffer from others as well. Which disease killed the patient? In the present context,

are the problems of an alcoholic, drug-using gambler due to gambling
or to substance abuse?

Research has found that many of the problems associated with gambling rise with the degree of pathology, but that other causal factors are
also present. For example, the problem of job loss was reported by only
4 percent of low-risk, nonproblem gamblers who had been employed
during the previous year, but was reported by 10.8 percent of problem
gamblers and 13.8 percent of pathological gamblers.[232] After allowing
for other factors that would lead to job loss that also were evident in the
problem and pathological groups, it was predicted that the prevalence
of job loss would have been 5.5 percent among problem gamblers and
5.8 percent among pathological gamblers. The role of pathological gambling, therefore, was to raise the rate of job loss from 5.8 to 13.8 percent,
not from 4.0 (observed in nonproblem gamblers) to 13.8 percent that a
less careful study might have inferred.

Many individuals suffering from gambling-related problems have no
history of other problems, others do. With a representative sample of
both types of individuals, it is possible in principle to identify the (possibly different) consequences of gambling on *both* groups. Schwer et al.
(2003), for example, reported per individual average annual social costs
of $19,324 for their sample of 93 individuals with gambling problems,
whereas the thirty-nine saying that they did not have other addictions
had costs only eighty-eight percent as high, at $17,056. The only co-
morbidity statistics currently available on the connection between pathological video-poker playing and other disorders from a South Carolina
study show that although there is overlap, it is far from complete. The
study found, for example, that 30 percent of pathological gamblers suffered from alcohol abuse, 70 percent did not; 18.75 percent suffered
from drug abuse, 81.25 percent did not; 57.5 percent suffered from depression, 42.5 percent did not. Also reported were the figures for eating
disorders (23.75 and 76.25 percent), compulsive shopping (22.5 and
77.5 percent), and bipolar depression (12.75 and 87.25 percent). In
contrast, the percentages of pathological gamblers who engaged in
behavior that was found to be "due to gambling" were as follows:
wrote bad checks, 54.4 percent; stolen from work, 37.1 percent; arrested,

41 percent; filed for bankruptcy, 25.7 percent; missed work, 71.4 percent; lost or quit job, 27.1 percent; suicidal ideation, 77.5 percent; and suicide attempts, 18.75 percent.[233]

A second problem that researchers must be careful to account for is the problem that their sample of problem and pathological gamblers may be unrepresentative of other problem and pathological gamblers. For example, if pathological gamblers who seek treatment are systematically different than pathological gamblers in general, then an uncritical extrapolation of their social costs would not be representative of social costs that apply to all pathological gamblers. For example, if pathological gamblers who commit the more damaging types of crime do not respond to surveys, crime costs based on sampled pathological gamblers would likely understate the true costs. If pathological gamblers in treatment are more likely to suffer from other disorders than those who do not seek treatment, assigning some of their costs to other disorders will again understate the share of costs due to pathological gambling in the general population. Most studies are aware of these problems and acknowledge the need to take them into account where they apply.

Table 7.1 lists the findings of nine studies that provide original research on the gambling social costs discussed in this chapter.[234] The first row lists the location studied, the authors, and year of publication. Costs are distributed down the column according to type. All dollar figures are converted into common year 2003 dollars using the Consumer Price Index for urban consumers (CPI-U).[235] Of the studies, Gerstein et al. (1999) study the fewest number of costs,[236] estimating only lost time and unemployment, illness, and social service costs. On the other hand, it is the only study to provide data on illness. The right-hand column contains row averages for those studies with entries. The sum across averages, representing the estimate of the annual cost to society of one *pathological* gambler, is $10,330.[237]

Table 7.2 replicates for problem gamblers the information in Table 7.1. As the table shows, the annual cost to society of a single problem gambler is $2,945 in 2003 dollars. This figure represents only a partial cost estimate. Estimates for four of nine categories of social costs are not available.

In Chapter 8, we consider the implications of the social-cost figures.

TABLE 7.1. Social Costs per Pathological Gambler: 2003 $

	MD Politzer et al., 1981	FL Exec. Office of Gov., 1994	WI Thompson et al., 1996	CT Thompson et al., 1998	SD SD Leg. Research Council, 1998–99	LA Ryan et al., 1999	US Gerstein et al., 1999	SC Thompson, Quinn, 1999	NV Schwer et al., 2003	Adjusted Row Averages for Studies 1994–2003
CRIME										
Apprehension and Increased Police Costs			$26	$41	$1,129	$34		$65	$51	$224
Adjudication (Criminal and Civil Justice Costs)	$3,619		$733	$568	$31	$420		$266	$46	$344
Incarceration and Supervision Costs	$5,724	$18,898	$450	$508	$431	$447		$252	$173	$3,023
BUSINESS AND	$22,803									
EMPLOYMENT COSTS										
Lost Productivity on Job						$82	$353	$605	$1,457	$715
Lost Time and Unemployment			$1,506	$1,833		$3,511		$1,125	$1,529	$1,643
BANKRUPTCY			$306					$66	$381	$251
SUICIDE										

| | MD | FL | WI | CT | SD | LA | US | SC | NV | Adjusted Row |
	Politzer et al., 1981	Exec. Office of Gov., 1994	Thompson et al., 1996	Thompson et al., 1998	SD Leg. Research Council, 1998–99	Ryan et al., 1999	Gerstein et al., 1999	Thompson, Quinn, 1999	Schwer et al., 2003	Averages for Studies 1994–2003
ILLNESS							$773			$773
SOCIAL SERVICE COSTS										
Therapy/Treatment Costs			$260	$65	$85	$256	$33	$46	$148	$128
Unemployment and Other Social Service (Including Welfare and Food Stamps)			$360	$555	$620	$39	$160	$178	$99	$287
GOV'T DIRECT										
REGULATORY COSTS										
FAMILY COSTS										
Divorce, Separation								$62		$62
ABUSED DOLLARS	$29,055		$2,258	$5,442	$271	$2,056		$1,362	$5,892	$2,880
										$10,330

WI, CT, SC, and NV figures were adjusted by the author to correct for multi-causality according to Schwer et al. (2003) findings. WI, CT, LA, SC, and NV figures were adjusted by the author for sample selection bias according to Ryan et al. (1999) findings.

Table 7.2. Social Costs per Problem Gambler: 2003 $

	LA Ryan et al., 1999	US Gerstein et al., 1999	SD SD Leg. Research Council, 1998–99	Adjusted Row Averages, 1998–99
CRIME				
Apprehension and Increased Police Costs	$16			$16
Adjudication (Criminal and Civil Justice Costs)	$198			$198
Incarceration and Supervision Costs	$210			$210
BUSINESS				
Lost Productivity on Job	$39			$39
Lost Time and Unemployment	$1,747	$221		$984
BANKRUPTCY				
SUICIDE				
ILLNESS				
SOCIAL SERVICE COSTS				
Therapy/Treatment Costs	$121	$398		$259
Unemployment and Other Social Services (Including Welfare and Food Stamps)	$18	$171	$620	$270
GOV'T DIRECT REGULATORY COSTS				
FAMILY COSTS				
Divorce, Separation				
ABUSED DOLLARS	$968			$968
	$3,318	$790	$620	$2,945
	48.5%		59.8%	

Percent of corresponding study's pathological gambler cost.
LA figures were adjusted by the author for sample selection bias according to Ryan et al. (1999) findings.

8 The Present and The Future

> Facts are stubborn things; and whatever may be our wishes, our inclinations, or the dictates of our passion, they cannot alter the state of facts and evidence.
>
> *John Adams (1770)*

CHAPTER SUMMARY. Applying estimates of the prevalence of problem and pathological gamblers to the cost estimates of Chapter 7 produces social cost totals. A citizen or local government official also might be interested in knowing the additional social cost of introducing casinos. In this chapter, we report three numbers: first, the implied social cost of problem and pathological gambling on the national level; second, the cost–benefit ratio for the casino industry based on per-adult numbers adjusted to a common base; and third, an estimate of the long-term social costs from introduction of casinos into an economy or region that did not have them previously. On a national basis, the social costs of problem and pathological gambling are between $32.4 billion and $53.8 billion. On a per-adult basis, these translate to $165 to $274 per year, or $219 on average. Comparing the costs of Chapter 7 to the benefits of Chapter 6, adjusted to a common base and including regulatory costs, implies that costs outweigh benefits by a factor between 3.9:1 and 6.3:1. The long-term cost-to-benefit ratio from introducing casinos to a region that did not have them previously is greater than 3:1. As a device for raising taxes, casinos are more socially costly than a conventional tax. Even assuming that cost numbers are overstated by a factor of three and correcting them, casinos still barely fail a cost–benefit test.

The social-cost estimates in Tables 7.1 and 7.2 were derived by averaging over the available studies for each category of social cost, adjusting to 2003 dollars, and summing over cost types. Roughly half of the social costs are publicly borne[238] and 37.5 percent require tax dollars.[239] Assuming that an additional tax dollar costs the public $1.25[240] and applying this multiplier to 37.5 percent of the social costs in Tables 7.1 and 7.2 implies that a pathological gambler generates social costs of $11,304 and a problem gambler generates $3,222. What do these numbers imply at the national level? To answer, we need an estimate of the number of problem and pathological gamblers. For this, we turn to information about the country as of the mid-1990s. To the extent that the percentage of problem and pathological gamblers has changed since then, the figures in Table 8.1 would have to be adjusted.

Shaffer, Hall, and Vander Bilt (1997) reviewed 120 studies of the prevalence of problem and pathological gambling. They estimated that

Table 8.1. National Costs of Problem and Pathological Gamblers, Adjusted by Prevalence Estimates Confidence Bounds (National Cost in $ Billion)

National Cost: Billions of Dollars				Per Adult Cost			
Problem	High	$43.10	$53.80	Problem	High	$219	$274
Rate	Low	$32.40	$43.00	Rate	Low	$165	$219
		Low	High			Low	High
		Pathological Rate				Pathological Rate	

Pathological 95% Confidence Bound:	LOWER	0.90%
Pathological 95% Confidence Bound:	UPPER	1.38%
Problem 95% Confidence Bound:	LOWER	1.95%
Problem 95% Confidence Bound:	UPPER	3.65%

1.14 percent of the adult population were past-year pathological gamblers with 95 percent confidence bounds of 0.9 and 1.38 percent.[241] The equivalent figures for problem gamblers were 2.8 and 1.95 to 3.65 percent.

Applying the lowest and the highest percentages to the number of adults (196,649,000) and multiplying by cost implies that problem and pathological gambling costs the United States between $32.4 billion and $53.8 billion annually, or $165 to $274 on a per-adult basis. The average figures are $43.1 billion and $219 per adult. Adding representative direct regulatory costs for gambling of $15 per adult (see the discussion of direct regulatory costs in Chapter 7) raises the average per adult social costs to $234. For comparison, the GAO reported annual costs of $110 billion for drug abuse.[242] Thus, problem and pathological gamblers are about 40 percent as costly to the nation as the drug problem. Lost output of the 1991–92 recession was approximately $164 billion in 2003 dollars. The costs of problem and pathological gambling are comparable to the value of the lost output of an additional recession in the economy every four years.

Chapter 6 explained that the long-term benefits of casinos took the form of distance benefits, estimated to be $34 per adult based on the highest estimate of three procedures. We used economic theory to construct a bound for measuring benefits based on information on how much consumers gamble when they are different distances from the casino. The bound was applied to data on distance and demand reported in industry studies and to a rule of thumb about how casino demand drops off with distance. The highest estimate was derived from simulating the gambling choices of a representative consumer that incorporated 1991–93 information on the amount gambled by adults living near casinos.

Social costs were reported in 2003 dollars in Chapter 7. Thus, to compare benefits and costs, we adjust benefits to a 2003 base. Making this change, we find that the long-term benefit of casino expansion (e.g., having them within 5 miles of every adult), compared to the alternative in which casinos are absent from the economy, is approximately $46 per adult. The costs reported in Tables 7.1 and 7.2 range from $180 to $289 per adult, after including direct regulatory costs. The costs of problem and pathological gambling versus the benefits of casino expansion, therefore, range from 3.9:1 to 6.3:1.

The rate of problem and pathological gambling might be expected to be positive, even with no casinos present anywhere in the United States. Therefore, what is the additional social cost incurred by a region that introduces casinos for the first time? We do not know what the long-term rate of problem and pathological gambling would be without casinos anywhere, even in Nevada. However, some evidence about the effect of casinos comes from the State of Iowa, which performed a before-and-after study of problem and pathological gambling.

In 1985, dogracing began in Iowa followed in 1989 by horseracing. In 1991, Iowa became the first state to introduce riverboat casinos. American Indian casinos were established the following year. Slot machines at racetracks were approved in 1994. The legislature removed betting limits in 1994. By 1995, gambling activities in the state included – in addition to games like bingo and the lottery – nine casinos, three dogtracks, and one racetrack. In 1995, the Iowa Department of Human Services commissioned a replication study to see what changes had occurred in the number of problem and pathological gamblers in the state since 1989, when an earlier study was completed.[243] Table 8.2 summarizes the main findings. Lifetime problem gamblers are individuals who have satisfied the conditions for problem gambling at some time during their lifetime as indicated by their answers to a questionnaire screen, while current problem gamblers are those who satisfy the criteria in the immediate past

Table 8.2. Iowa Replication Study: Problem and Pathological Gamblers (Percent)

	1989	1995	Change
Current Pathological Gamblers	0.05*	1.0	0.95
Current Problem Gamblers	1.05*	2.3	1.25
Lifetime Pathological Gamblers	0.1	1.9	1.8
Lifetime Problem Gamblers	1.6	3.5	1.9

*Calculated as a proportion of the 1989 lifetime rate.

year.[244] The same distinction applies to current and lifetime pathological gamblers. Although lifetime pathological gamblers may have exhibited pathologies in the past, they need not be pathological today.[245] Based on Tables 7.1 and 7.2, the social cost to Iowa of additional problem and pathological gamblers after the advent of casinos was $148 per adult per year, rounded to the nearest dollar.[246]

The 1995 replication study concluded that "there has been a significant increase in the prevalence of problem gambling in Iowa since 1989."[247] Although the increase in problem and pathological gamblers might have occurred for reasons other than the increased availability of casinos and racetracks in Iowa, if one is willing to assign the change to casinos, then the estimated costs can be used. Multiplying cost per adult by the adult population of Iowa (estimated by the U.S. Census Bureau as 2,058,627 on July 1, 1999) determines that casinos are costing the state $304 million annually in social costs. Added to these would be the direct regulatory costs of casinos in the state.

The final report of the National Gambling Impact Study Commission includes less direct evidence that may be used as a confirmation of the Iowa data. The Commission provides data on the percentages of the population that are problem and pathological gamblers by their distance from the nearest casino. This research indicates that the share of the population that are problem gamblers rises from 0.3 to 1.1 percent when the distance to the nearest casino falls from more than 250 to less than 50 miles.[248] The figures are given in Table 8.3 along with the corresponding numbers for pathological gamblers.

It is unfortunate that no figures were given for distances of less than 50 miles, which would have provided a better benchmark for the effect of

Table 8.3. Share of Problem and Pathological Gamblers in the Population by Distance from the Nearest Casino

Distance	Problem	Pathological	Total
0–50 miles	1.1%	1.3%	2.4%
51–250 miles	0.6%	0.3%	0.9%
250+ miles	0.3%	0.4%	0.7%

introducing casinos to an area that did not have them before. The share of the population that is problem and pathological gamblers might be expected to continue to rise for certain distances below 50 miles. Also, the drop in the number of pathological gamblers, from 0.4 percent of the population to 0.3 percent as one moves *closer* to the nearest casino (i.e., 51 to 250 miles versus 250+ miles), seems to indicate a sampling problem. The reported percentages may not be representative. Nevertheless, taking the figures as they are and presuming that the difference between the 250+ and below 50 miles numbers approximates the increase in the share of problem and pathological gamblers to be expected from the introduction of casinos, the number of problem gamblers rises by 0.8 percentage points and the number of pathological gamblers rises 0.9 percentage points. The increase in social costs per adult based on Tables 7.1 and 7.2 is $143; [249] adjusting the social benefits to 2003 dollars produces $45.93. The extra cost of casinos exceeds the extra benefits to the region by a ratio of more than 3:1. Thus, even if the social costs are cut by two thirds, casinos still fail a cost–benefit test.

Regional governments continue to consider casino-expansion proposals, often appearing in related guises such as providing EGDs at racetracks. The reason is that casinos can be taxed and the money raised appears to be "free," or at least voluntarily paid. Once a proposal is considered in these terms, it should be evaluated for what it is: a tax mechanism. Because government always has the option of levying conventional taxes, such proposals should be compared to conventional taxes in terms of their efficiency. Conventional taxes cost the private sector between $1.17 and $1.57 per additional dollar collected (see Chapter 7 and footnote 240); the cost per dollar of "tax by casino" is generally higher.

To show this, let C be the social cost per adult of introducing casinos. Based on Iowa, let us set $C = \$163 (= \$148 + \$15)$. Let L be the average loss for adults in the region to be served by the casino. For purposes of discussion, let $L = \$400$. Finally, let t be the tax rate on casino revenues. We will assume that $t = 0.2$, a not unrepresentative rate. Then the tax dollars collected (a cost to the private sector) plus the direct social costs are $tL + C$ per adult for tL dollars collected. The social cost per tax dollar raised is, therefore, $1 + C/tL = \$3.04$. Even with a higher tax rate, the cost per tax dollar of "tax by casino" remains above \$1.57 until the tax rate exceeds 71 percent. By a wide margin, tax by casino is inferior to levying a conventional tax.

CONCLUSION

This book was written out of the growing realization that those who most needed to understand the economic effects of casinos were receiving neither balanced nor conceptually valid information. It is not surprising that a straightforward activity, which nevertheless earns its promoters huge amounts of money, should be the focus of intense lobbying, misrepresentations, and overstatements. Chapter 3 addressed this issue. What *is* surprising is the extent of misunderstanding that exists regarding the theoretical and conceptual underpinnings of the evaluation of the social desirability of adding an industry to the economy. The casino industry is simply a case in point. Nevertheless, it is a fascinating study because it is the only available example of an industry that was criminalized and intentionally eradicated in one century and then reintroduced from zero in the next. Most areas of America had no legal casino gambling before 1990; therefore, we should be able to compare two extremes: one where the industry is totally absent from society, and the other where it is permitted laissez faire free entry. The question is whether society is better off with or without casino gambling. We showed in Chapters 4 and 5 that the analysis of this question is quite different from applying a net export multiplier model; that jobs are not the measure of economic development nor of the economic benefits of casinos; and that to evaluate the economic impact of casinos requires the use and understanding of cost–benefit analysis grounded on individual well-being and utility.

Although the primary purpose for this book was to establish the conceptual basis for the evaluation of casinos, this particular theoretical contribution is general and also would apply to other industries. The application to casinos involves estimating a number of externality costs that are specific to casinos. Chapter 5 provides the first explicit theoretical justification of what should be included as costs and benefits and how they should be computed. This justification is based on individual utility and distinguishes business and social profitability for industries with externalities. The heretofore lack of a clear theoretical basis has impaired the entire research agenda on this issue. Much research has examined relatively minor issues or issues that are not even part of a properly defined cost–benefit analysis. Conversely, there are relatively few estimates of some of the key components of social costs and benefits. Consequently, a well-grounded theoretical framework of costs and benefits makes future research more productive.

Using the theoretically laid foundation, Chapters 4 and 5 corrected common conceptual mistakes prevalent in the casino and gambling literature. One example of a common error is the focus on local rather than total social costs or benefits. On the benefits side, increases in local profits and taxes are often weighted heavily, whereas losses in profits and taxes from geographically distant areas are weighted less or not at all. Similarly on the cost side, local crime is often weighted heavily, whereas there is little discussion about whether crime was simply moved from other areas. Another error is the frequent use of the net export multiplier modeling of jobs with no investigation of the social value of additional jobs on existing residents, an inappropriate method to determine social costs and benefits. Clearly, identifying these errors is the first step to reducing them in the future.

The second objective of the book was to fill as much as possible the unfilled gaps of a complete cost–benefit analysis of the casino industry. Chapters 6 and 7 applied the theory to construct a taxonomy of benefits and costs as applied to the casino industry. To estimate costs, the original research on this topic was treated and organized.

The evidence indicates that casino gambling fails a cost–benefit test by a wide margin. Chapter 6 found that social benefits were $34 per adult based on simulations representative of the early 1990s, or $46 if adjusted to 2003 dollars; Chapter 8 found that social costs were between $180 and 289 per adult in 2003 dollars, adjusted for direct regulatory costs and the tax deadweight loss involved in covering 37.5 percent of the social costs. Even if these numbers are not known with complete accuracy, adjustments to them are unlikely to overturn the conclusion that casinos create more costs than benefits.

Standard public-finance corrective theory for an industry with externalities is that it should be taxed by an amount equal to the costs that it imposes on society. By internalizing the externalities, corrective taxes would cause casinos to adjust their operations or go out of business. Only those that could pass a cost–benefit test by compensating society for the damage they cause would continue to operate. How big would corrective taxes be? In 2000, the average adult in the United States lost $181 at casinos. If casinos were more readily available in all locations, this figure would undoubtedly be higher; it is not unreasonable that it could rise to $400 per year. Social costs between $180 and 289, therefore, suggest that Pigouvian corrective taxes should be in the vicinity of 45 to 70 percent of casino revenues. If casinos paid 45 to 70 percent of their gross revenues in taxes, according to the theory, those that continued to operate would have internalized the social damage they cause, and the casino industry as whole would be induced to operate at a socially desirable level. Once taxes have been imposed that induce the right level of gambling – whatever that may be – it is immaterial to legislators, from an economic standpoint, whether the activity survives or not; gambling can be removed from the list of problems requiring ongoing legislative attention.

With respect to the future, it is evident that there is the need for more quality research on both the benefit and cost sides. Chapter 6 estimated the social benefits of casinos, but there remains the need for more and better research. The simulations of Chapter 6 indicate social benefits to casinos that are relatively small. This is due partly to the fact that the American economy is large and diverse, offering many forms of entertainment. The absence of one form of recreation – casino gambling – is, therefore, overshadowed by the wide range of others.

There is a need for greater uniformity in the manner in which costs and benefits are classified and treated. Focusing future research questions and methodologies on a clearly formulated theoretical foundation will allow us to make our estimates of both the costs and benefits of casino gaming more precise. Chapter 7 is the first attempt to construct exhaustive and mutually exclusive cost categories into which the results of research from different sources can be placed and compared. Peer-review-quality studies not funded by the casino industry or by progambling or antigambling groups are especially needed to refine and improve the cost–benefit numbers.[250]

Finally, it is important to keep in mind the alternatives. Citizens of the nineteenth century chose to ban casino-style gambling, and by 1900 it was not allowed in any state. Another choice is to freely license casinos, letting as many operate as choose to do so and the market will bear, as was done in Nevada in the 1930s, in Atlantic City in 1978, and in some other parts of the United States in the 1990s. Not unmindful of the fact that casinos can – in principle and under the right conditions – generate true economic development, the research presented in this book suggests that the social costs from widespread expansion of casinos are more than three times the benefits and that the second option should be rejected. What is not known is whether there is a third option: Can casino gambling be offered in such a way that it does not create high social costs and could pass a cost–benefit test in its altered form? For example, can gambling be provided in a manner that does not generate problem and pathological gamblers, and thereby lead to fewer crimes?

To answer this question, as well as to further refine the cost–benefit analysis of casino gambling, the following questions would have to be addressed:

- **What is the effect of the presence of casinos on the number, life cycle, gambling patterns, and social costs of problem and pathological gamblers?** Because the social costs of the casino industry are heavily although not exclusively related to problem and pathological gamblers, it is essential to know how casinos affect problem and pathological gamblers. There is abundant evidence that increased gambling opportunities increase problem and pathological gambling. As discussed in Chapter 7, the National Gambling Impact Study Commission reported that the presence of a casino within 50 miles roughly doubled the prevalence of problem and pathological gambling.[251] Other indicators include the tremendous increase in the numbers of gamblers seeking help when casinos enter a market, the increase in gamblers-anonymous groups when gambling enters a state, and the evidence from survey data on the number of problem and pathological gamblers before and after casino expansion.

How much an additional problem or pathological gambler costs society is best addressed by studying problem and pathological gamblers directly. However, estimates derived from this sample may be biased because only a small fraction of problem and pathological gamblers seek formal treatment. If those who seek help impose the greatest costs on society, our cost estimates of problem and pathological gamblers would be overstated; of course, the reverse is also true.

Casinos benefit from the gambling habits of problem and pathological gamblers. Whereas an average adult might lose several hundred dollars each year in casinos if they are nearby, a typical pathological gambler often loses ten to twenty times that amount. Therefore, a small number of pathological gamblers accounts for a significant portion of casino revenues. A related issue is to determine the share of casino revenues that derive from problem and pathological gamblers. Does this share differ by type of gambling? For example, lotteries receive a smaller portion of their revenues from problem and pathological gamblers because lottery play attracts a larger portion of the population.

When casino gambling becomes available for the first time, what is the behavioral time profile for individuals who enter and leave the states of problem and pathological gambling? Do individuals begin with a period of increasing gambling dependence, move through a period of problem gambling, progress to pathological gambling, seek treatment (or withdraw unilaterally from the problem), and abstain thereafter? Or are there relapses and continued problems if treatment is not sought? This information could be used to predict how many currently active problem and pathological gamblers to expect for a given population as a function of the availability of casino gambling.

- **What effect do different types of treatment have on problem and pathological gamblers?** Such information would help knowing how to efficiently allocate funding resources for treatment interventions.
- **How can casino gambling be offered to minimize its social costs?** Quinn (2001) discusses many possible ways of offering casino gambling to reduce social costs. To evaluate the effectiveness of these interventions and their impact on casino benefits, one would need to estimate the response of both problem and pathological and non-problem and nonpathological gamblers to such actions.
- **What are the distance benefits of increasing casino gambling?** To date, only the present study has attempted to answer this important question. Testing the strength of the result will provide more insight into this understudied area.

The numbers and theory presented in this book indicate that casino-style gambling is associated with social consequences whose nature and magnitude make it one of a small family of activities, including drug abuse and alcoholism, that cause significant negative externalities. The size of the social costs – 40 percent of the costs of drug abuse – are not so great that the economy cannot sustain them. The economy could almost surely sustain the costs of three, four, or more social problems of this size. The question, however, is why should the economy accept an unnecessary social cost? Unlike American prohibition of alcohol, which most regard as a failure, criminalization and prohibition of casino gambling was successfully practiced for most of the twentieth century. Perhaps we can learn ways to offer gambling that do not lead to harmful consequences. However, if not, the logical implication is to ask whether the experiment in the present generation should be allowed to continue or should be reversed. In South Carolina, slot machines were banned by court action beginning July 1, 2000. At that time, the state had thirty-two active gamblers-anonymous groups with a typical meeting size of almost 40. Six months later, there were 11 groups and the size had dropped to as few as one or two in many of those remaining. During the same time, the number of help-line calls in Horry County, South Carolina (Myrtle Beach) dropped from two hundred per month to zero.[252]

APPENDIX A

Cost-Benefit to the Locality: A Scenario

Many considerations relevant to the cost–benefit and impact analysis of one region are common to the analysis of others. This appendix constructs an example that considers the cost–benefit analysis of a regional casino, where the focus is the economic impact and cost–benefit relevant to the county containing the casino. The county is a subset of the area that would be affected by the presence of the casino; therefore, its costs and benefits are a portion of the totals.

The innermost shaded circle in Figure A.1 represents a city of approximately 200 square miles (8-mile radius) with population density of 1,800 per square mile, which is not untypical for cities in the United States.[253] This implies a city population of 361,911. The next circle, with a 25-mile radius, represents the county. Its population density is fifty people per square mile, which is also representative.[254] We assume that there is a city 150 miles away in a neighboring state that has a population of 300 thousand. The solid vertical line in Figure A.1 represents the border and the dashed vertical line is the midpoint line between the two cities. The outermost circle has a radius of 250 miles. It represents the effective limit of demand for the casino located in the center. Individuals farther away have more attractive opportunities elsewhere. We assume that the population density outside the county is forty people per square mile, not counting the neighboring city.

We now proceed to ask three questions about the impact of placing a casino in the center city. First, what will casino revenues and profits be, and what taxes will the city receive from the casino? Second, will the

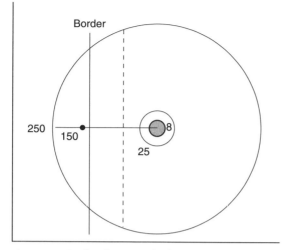

Figure A.1. Regional Geography for the New Casino

casino have an effect on county income? Third, what will be the costs and benefits to the county of the casino? In answering these questions, we will see that the casino can be profitable, lead to a net increase in regional income, and yet worsen the well-being of county residents – that is, fail a cost–benefit test.

REVENUE, PROFITS, TAXES

According to research conducted for the National Gambling Impact Study Commission, people who live near a casino typically spend $400 to $600 per adult per year on casino gambling.[255] Chapter 6 also reported that, as a rule of thumb, gambling demand falls 30 to 35 percent for each doubling of distance from the casino, at least for distances not too close or too far from the casino. We assume for this example that adults living within 3 miles of the casino lose $500 per year and that demand for those living from 3 to 100 miles drops 32.5 percent – the average of 30 and 35 percent – for each doubling of distance.[256]

The rule that demand falls 30 to 35 percent for each doubling of distance overpredicts demand for gamblers greater distances away from the casino. Studies of Wisconsin and Illinois casinos found that they received 18.9 percent and fewer than 2 percent, respectively, of their revenues from gamblers 100 miles or farther from the casinos.[257] In Chapter 6, we nevertheless used this rule of thumb to produce figures in Tables 6.3 and 6.4 because we wanted to give the benefit of the doubt to casinos and overstate consumer distance benefits. In the present context, we assume that demand for consumers more than 100 miles away falls exponentially at a rate that implies that 14.4 percent of casino revenues derive from gamblers living 100 to 250 miles from the casino.[258]

In the United States, approximately 71 percent of the population consists of adults ages twenty or older. In our example, therefore, we use this figure to compute the number of adults. Calculating demand per adult for each distance and adding over all areas displayed in Figure A.1 reveal that the gross revenue of the casino is $211.5 million. This is a successful casino. For comparison, Illinois casinos in 2001 averaged about $200 million in revenues.[259]

We assume that the casino has the financial structure described in Table 4.1. Profits are $42.3 million and taxes paid are $25.1 million, of which the local share is $8.4 million.[260]

REGIONAL INCOME

We now turn to the second question: the impact of the casino on county income. Casino revenues, profits, and taxes are not the measure of impact because some of the casino revenues would have been earned by other county businesses – these are the *cannibalized dollars* described in Chapter 6. Some income earned by the casino is spent outside the county and not retained by the county – *leakages*. On the other side of the ledger, some of the casino revenues from local citizens represent new local money because it would have been spent outside the county if not for the casino – *recaptured dollars*. Adjusting casino revenues by adding recaptured dollars and substracting cannibalized dollars and leakages generates net exports, to which the regional multiplier can be applied.

Much of the discussion of how to compute net exports – that is, *Revenues* – *Cannibalized* + *Recaptured* – *Leakage* – replicates the discussion in Chapter 4. In the present scenario, 49.2 percent of the casino's revenues come from adults living outside the county. Because 30 percent of their spending would have been spent in the county anyway, cannibalized dollars are $1 - \theta + s_O\theta$ times revenue, where $\theta = 0.492$ and $s_O = 0.3$. Similarly, of the money spent at the casino by county residents, 10 percent would have been spent outside the county. Perhaps these residents would have taken an occasional trip to visit a restaurant in the neighboring city 150 miles to the west, but with the casino they go less often. Recaptured dollars are, therefore, $s_R(1 - \theta)$ times revenue. In our example, cannibalized dollars = \$138.6 million and recaptured dollars = \$10.7 million.

Leakages are dollars that are not retained by the county after they are acquired by the casino. Many times casino owners are not residents, have business dealings and personal interests elsewhere, and for various reasons spend little of their profits in the community where it was acquired. In this example, we assume that only 20 percent of profits are spent outside the county, suggesting that ownership and use of funds are predominantly local.

In addition to leakage through profits, leakages can occur through taxes and government expenditures. We have already indicated that the state is the recipient of the noncounty portion of casino taxes. One third of income taxes paid by the casino are retained locally. We assume that amounts equal to 10 percent of the local share of taxes and 1 percent of casino revenues are spent outside.[261]

Some leakages occur through the casino wage bill. Some employees may not be residents and for other reasons have spending patterns that do not cause them to spend 100 percent of wages earned in the county. In this example, 90 percent of wages are retained locally, of which the marginal propensity to spend 0.7 percent is applied to determine local spending.

Finally, the casino itself must devote a portion of its revenues to the purchase of materials and inputs. In this case, the casino spends

14 percent of its revenues on purchases outside the county. The discussion in Chapter 4 indicated that this was representative of the amount spent out of state for casinos in Iowa. Using the out-of-state number for the out-of-county spending shows that the casino in this example is a particularly good local citizen, in the sense of devoting a sizable portion of its purchases to the county. Its out-of-state purchases would be far lower than 14 percent.

Overall, leakages as a percent of revenues are 14 percent for inputs, 4 percent for profits, 11.8 percent for wages, and 9.4 percent for taxes. Applying a multiplier of 2.2 to *Revenues − Cannibalized + Recaptured − Leakage*, a multiplier that would apply to a city of this size and situation, implies that postcasino income in the county will be higher by $1.13 million. The number of additional jobs that would be needed to produce this level of increased output is approximately thirty-eight.

This number of jobs is far smaller than might be anticipated, given casino revenues of $211.5 million and taxes to the city of $8.4 million. The explanation is that most of the casino revenues come from the nearby population and represents reshuffling rather than attraction of new demand.

COST-BENEFIT

The major advantage of the casino to county residents whose only connection to it occurs when they choose to gamble in it is the amenity value of having this additional form of recreation more accessible. In addition, a small advantage may accrue to residents from other beneficial effects, such as price effects. For example, as explained in Chapter 5, there could be an increase in housing values due to the demand of thirty eight new adults in the area. In addition, to the extent that the county receives more casino taxes and casino profits than are lost in taxes and profits of competing local businesses hurt by the casino, there could be net benefits from this source.

In the initial situation, we assumed that the nearest casinos were 500 miles away from the city center. This means that residents living within 25 miles of the city center gain distance benefits averaging $37.27 per adult.[262] The implied benefit to county residents is $11.9 million.

A net change in productive activity generates a portion of the total as profits for county residents. In our example, we assume that profit is 8.4 percent of output and that the local area retains two thirds of the total once federal and state taxes are paid.[263] Part of the increased local output occurs in the casino sector. Locally retained profits, therefore, are adjusted for this portion of the total for the different locally retained profits of casinos. If casinos provide profit as a percent of sales higher than 8.4 percent, this adjustment is positive; if lower, the adjustment is negative. A similar procedure is applied to taxes. Increased economic acitivity is assumed to generate 6 percent of the total as additional taxes to the county. This could represent additional local sales taxes, for example. Part of the total increased activity is in the casino sector; therefore, taxes again are adjusted for the different tax rate that applies to casinos compared to 6 percent. The local net change in profits and taxes in the present example is a positive $24.2 million.

Finally, Chapter 6 indicated that benefits to residents of increased economic activity accrued in other forms such as consumer surplus and capital gains. The literature on major-league sports stadiums estimated that these gains varied from $0 to $1,500 per job. In this example, this value is $750 per job (the average value) leading to gains of $28,142, a relatively small number compared to the other benefits. Total benefit to residents, therefore, is $36.2 million.

Table 8.3 indicated that the population share of pathological gamblers rises from 0.3 or 0.4 percent to 1.3 percent when the nearest casino drops to fewer than 50 miles from farther away. We assume in the present case that the share of pathological gamblers rises by 0.95 percent of the population within 25 miles of the casino; the share of problem gamblers rises from 0.3 to 1.1 percent. From Chapter 8, the social costs of an additional pathological and problem gambler are $11,304 and $3,222 respectively, after adjusting for tax deadweight loss on the portion covered by public expenditures. This implies that the social costs to the county will be $42.5 million; adding to this the government's direct expenditures for regulation and infrastructure brings the total to $46.6 million.[264] Thus, costs exceed benefits by $10.4 million.

LESSONS

We have answered our three questions to find that the casino would be profitable to its owners, would increase economic activity in the county, and would simultaneously fail a cost–benefit test. This means that the casino reduces the well-being of county residents even though an uncritical listing of the associated financials might seem to suggest otherwise. The need for a cost–benefit study, therefore, cannot be dismissed.

Two other observations are in order. First, the neighboring city 150 miles to the west and its surrounding region lose several million dollars of income due to the casino. The experience of the 1990s tells us that to reclaim this loss, its leaders will want to place a casino of their own in the city or near the state border. If they do, residents who are closer to the neighboring city will shift their gambling to the closer location. This removes all of the revenue to the west (see the dashed line in Figure A.1), making benefits to the county even smaller.

Second, in this appendix, we computed the costs and benefits to the county only, consisting of the area 25 miles or closer to the casino. Because the casino was a regional monopoly, it concentrated monopoly profits in this area at the expense of the surrounding area. Costs outside the county, on the other hand, would be significant, based on the substantial amount of gambling by this group of residents[265] and the creation of problem and pathological gamblers there. A cost–benefit calculation for a larger area would show a far less favorable balance. Were casinos introduced everywhere in the county, the balance of costs to benefits would approach the ratio of more than 3:1 (discussed in Chapter 8).

Glossary

Abused dollars   Dollars improperly obtained – for example, stolen from a relative or friend, such as balances improperly placed on another's credit card – but not reported as a crime.

Amenity benefit   A feature of the economic environment that increases well-being and/or confers utility on consumers. The terms *distance benefit* and *distance consumer surplus* refer to the amenity benefit that is the value to consumers of having casinos geographically closer.

Cannibalization   Demand for the products of a business taken from the demand of other local businesses. *Demand substitution* – a more formal term for cannibalization – refers to the substitution of the products of one local business for another by consumers to meet their demand. See also **Leakage** and **Recapture.**

Capital gains (losses)   The increase (decrease) in value of an asset due to price changes or changes in perception about its worth.

Casino   A firm offering Class III gambling, generally including EGDs or VLTs and table games such as roulette and blackjack.

Citizen   See **Household.**

Class III gambling   The IGRA of 1988 defines Class III gambling in reference to Classes I and II. Class I gambling consists of "social games solely for prizes of minimal value." Included in Class I gambling are traditional Indian games identified with tribal ceremonies and celebrations. Class II gambling includes bingo and "games similar to bingo." Class III gambling includes all forms of gambling that are not Class I or Class II gambling, such as blackjack, baccarat, slot machines, roulette, electronic games like video poker, and other casino-style games.

Consumer surplus   The amount of money a consumer would be willing to pay to cause a specified price to be changed in a favorable direction, or the amount he or she would have to be paid to hold utility constant if the price is adjusted in an unfavorable direction.

Cost–benefit analysis   A process for measuring the increase or decrease in household utility attendant upon a change in economic circumstances. Cost–benefit analysis identifies and separates the components of utility change, measured in common units, so that they are exhaustive and mutually exclusive.

Deadweight loss   See **Tax deadweight loss.**

Directly Unproductive Profitseeking   Making an income by activities that yield a pecuniary return to the undertaker, but do not produce goods or services that enter utility directly or indirectly. Directly unproductive profit-seeking reduces economy income by removing real resources from the productive economy. An extreme example might be quitting one's job for a life of begging: though one does not enjoy begging, and it produces no goods or services entering utility, one might nevertheless make a living at it.

Distance benefit   See **Amenity benefit.**

Distance consumer surplus   The amount of money a consumer would be willing to give up to have a casino located a specified distance closer.

Economic base   A region's initial income, net-export–induced changes to which a multiplier must be applied to calculate the change in total income of all economic activity in the region. See **Net export multiplier model.**

Economic development   The increase in the well-being of households from given resources; the creation of greater value by society from its available resources. Economic development is often associated with and connnotes the ability to better manage existing resources in response to conditions.

Economic growth   The increase in the well-being of households due to technological change – including the introduction of new industry – or increase in the availability and use of productive inputs.

Externality   An effect that a firm or household's choices have on other firms or households that does not operate through market prices. A helpful effect is referred to as a **positive externality**; a harmful effect is referred to as a **negative externality**. A firm whose production process pollutes the air creates a negative externality. It is the nature of externalities – because the positive or negative effects apply to others – that the agent causing them does not consider them properly when making the decisions that cause the externality.

Gambling   The risking of something of value on the outcome of chance.

Gross profit   Profit before a full accounting of costs, depreciation, and taxes; that is, revenues after subtracting a subset of costs, depreciation, and taxes.

Household   The consumer decision-making unit. A household may consist of a single individual, a family, or a group of individuals that makes decisions as a unit. **Citizens** are households that are the proper object of a political jurisdiction's attention. **Residents** are households living within a specified region.

Impact study   See **Net export multiplier model.**

Import substitution   Meeting demand with locally produced goods and services that might otherwise have been met by imports.

Job impact study   See **Net export muliplier model.**

Jobs multiplier model   See **Net export muliplier model.**

Laissez faire   A policy of "hands off" or noninterference by government in the affairs of markets.

Leakage   The share of revenues earned by a local firm in a geographical region of interest that is spent outside that region and so does not add to the region's economic base. See also **Cannibalization** and **Recapture.**

Lottery   Any game of chance or game in which chance predominates. The elements of a lottery are payment for play, a prize, and chance.

Multiplier   A multiplier quantifies how a change in one sector of the economy impacts the entire economy. The multiplier is the amount that the initial change must be multiplied by to calculate the change in the total income of the entire economy of the region of interest. See **Net export multiplier model.**

Net export multiplier model   Net export multiplier models conceptualize the regional economy as consisting of exporting and nonexporting sectors. Increased net exports by a sector cause that sector to spend some portion of the additional dollars in the regional economy, leading to increased income in the supplying sectors. These sectors, in turn, increase their regional purchases and the process continues. The ratio of the ultimate change in the region's total income to the initial change in the sector's net exports produces a multiplier. An increase in the net exports of a given sector is said to increase the economic base. Applying the multiplier to the increase in the economic base generates the increase in regional income due to the original change in net exports. More detailed models track the precise flows between a larger number of disaggregated sectors and use multipliers that reflect the greater degree of detail. Multipliers are larger if the portion of sectoral income spent regionally is larger.

Net exports   The excess of exports of a region to the outside and its imports from the outside; exports to the outside minus imports from the outside.

Pathological gambling   According to the DSM-IV of the American Psychiatric Association, pathological gambling is "Persistent and recurrent maladaptive gambling behavior as indicated by five (or more) of" ten items. Among the items are: needing to gamble with increasing amounts of money; repeated unsuccessful attempts to control, cut back, or stop gambling; after losing money gambling, often returning another day to get even ("chasing" one's losses); lying to family members or others to conceal the extent of gambling; committing illegal acts such as forgery, fraud, theft, or embezzlement to finance gambling; jeopardized or lost significant relationships, jobs, or career opportunities because of gambling; and relying on others to provide money to relieve a desperate financial situation caused by gambling. The gambling behavior must not be better accounted for by a manic episode.

Perfect competition   An idealized state of competition between firms characterized by a standardized product, costless entry and exit, perfect information, and nonstrategic price-taking behavior. An implication of perfect competition is zero economic profits; that is, profits at the average or normal business level. Perfect competition is often associated with the market presence of many competitors.

Prisoner's dilemma   The prisoner's dilemma is representative of a class of noncooperative games. A game is characterized by players, choices, and rules about how choices of players interact to produce payoffs to the players. In a noncooperative game, players cannot make agreements with other players about their choices. In the prisoner's dilemma, Prisoners A and B were apprehended and questioned in separate rooms by police who need evidence from them to convict. If one prisoner provides evidence against his partner, he will be given a more lenient sentence and his partner a stiffer sentence. Acting in isolation, each prisoner has an incentive to provide evidence, sending both to jail for long terms, even though acting cooperatively would allow both to do much better and get off with lesser sentences. The prisoner's dilemma has sometimes been characterized as a "race to the bottom" because both parties have an incentive to take action, even though the outcome is worse than mutually agreeing not to take action.

Private goods   Goods exhibiting rivalness: one's consumption of the good prevents another from consuming the same good. Food is a private good.

Problem gambling   Problem gambling is a nontechnical term that refers to gambling that exhibits similar persistent and recurrent maladaptive behavior as pathological gambling, except to a lesser extent. In some usages, it is any gambling behavior that causes disruptions in psychological, physical, social, or vocational areas of life and includes pathological gambling as a special case.

Propensity to spend   The share of an additional dollar spent on a designated activity. "The **propensity to spend** locally is 0.6" means that $.60 of each additional dollar is spent locally.

Public goods   A good having the property of nonrivalness. That is, the consumption of a public good by one individual does not diminish the ability of another to consume the same units. My listening to a radio broadcast does not limit your ability to listen to the same broadcast.

Recapture   Demand served by a local business that previously was met by providers outside the local geographical area of interest. See also **Cannibalization** and **Leakage.**

Social Cost   Components reflecting a decline in the utility of households. Social costs are the cost components of a cost–benefit analysis.

Tax deadweight loss   The amount by which lost consumer surplus and firm profits due to a tax exceeds the amount of tax collected; the extra loss incurred by the private sector, beyond the amount of tax collected.

Transactions constraint   An impediment that limits the ability of a firm or household to make choices in its own best interest. For example, an individual who wants to work at the going wage and is otherwise qualified for the work, but who remains unemployed, is encumbered in choosing how much labor to supply and, therefore, experiences a transactions constraint.

Utility   The numerical measure of a consumer's level of well-being; a measure of the consumer's satisfaction or level of welfare. **Well-being, welfare,** and **utility** are synonyms.

Value added   The value of a good or service minus the cost of the material inputs used to produce it.

Wealth   The claim to something of value.

Welfare   See **Utility.**

Well-being   See **Utility.**

Notes

1. Attichison, Diana, *Kansas City Star,* 1994.
2. Grinols, Earl L. (1995a). "Time for a National Policy," Congressional Testimony, Committee on Small Business, House of Representatives, One Hundred Third Congress, 1994 Hearing on the National Impact of Casino Gambling Proliferation, Washington, DC: U.S. Government Printing Office, Serial 103–104, pp. 8–11, 76.
3. Economists refer to the *prisoner's dilemma* as representative of a class of noncooperative games. Prisoners A and B were apprehended and questioned in separate rooms by police who need evidence from them to convict. If one prisoner provides evidence against his partner, he will be given a more lenient sentence and his partner a stiffer sentence. Acting in isolation, each prisoner has an incentive to provide evidence, sending both to jail for long terms, even though acting cooperatively would allow both to do much better and get off. The prisoner's dilemma has sometimes been characterized as a "race to the bottom" because both parties have an incentive to take action, even though the outcome is worse than mutually agreeing not to take action.
4. Committee to Study the Impact of Gambling in Ohio (2002), p. 8.
5. *The National Gambling Impact Study Commission: Final Report,* June 18, 1999, introductory page by the commission chair.
6. Berns, D. (1998), p. D1, reported in John Kindt (2001), p. 32.
7. Associated Press; Jackson, MS; September 26, 1999 (story on the annual meeting of the National Coalition Against Legalized Gambling).
8. On several occasions, I was told that government panel members asked to evaluate a casino proposal had been promised a board of director's position if the proposal were implemented.
9. Wheeler (1999).
10. Committee to Study the Impact of Gambling in Ohio, p. 6.
11. Ibid., p. 2.
12. Ibid., p. 30.
13. Richard Balkite, personal correspondence to the author, January 9, 2003.
14. Shaffer, et al. (1997), pp. 78–9.
15. Letter to Brian Nordahl, Deloitte & Touche LLP, from Terry C. Anderson, Director, South Dakota Legislative Research Council; December 17, 1998.

16. Abraham Lincoln (1809–65), U.S. president. Quoted in John Bartlett (1820–1905), *Familiar Quotations,* 10th ed., 1919.

17. For example, *State ex Inf. McKittrick v. Globe-Democrat Co.,* 110 S.W. 2d. 705 (S. Ct. Mo. 1937), p. 713.

18. See Pickett (1932).

19. Thompson (1997b), p. 12.

20. Debra Bennett (1998), *Randomness,* p. 18.

21. Ibid., p. 23–4.

22. Warren (1828), pp. 223, 247.

23. Smith (1776), p. 45.

24. *Encyclopedia Britannica* (2002), p. 104.

25. *Encyclopedia Britannica* (1970), p. 1116.

26. Fenich (1996), p. 70.

27. Ibid., p. 71.

28. Frank Kelley, Attorney General, Michigan; Testimony to the Governor's Committee on Gaming, State Legislature; Lansing, Michigan; March 3, 1995.

29. GLS Research (1994).

30. Tice (1995).

31. National Gambling Impact Study Commission (1999), pp. 7–10.

32. Gazel and Thompson (1996).

33. Thomas R. O'Brien (1984).

34. Dopamine is a bodily produced brain chemical that produces pleasurable sensations.

35. Sandra Blakeslee (2002).

36. Ibid.

37. Productivity Commission (1999), p. 2. This would translate into approximately $7,200 U.S. in 1999.

38. Gerstein, et al. (1999), p. 28. Pathological gamblers were 1.1 percent of the population and problem gamblers were 1.3 percent.

39. $2.4 \times 17 \times x = 40.8x$ is the amount lost by problem and pathological gamblers; $100 \times x$ is the loss by all adults.

40. op. cit., pp. 22, 2.

41. Australian Institute for Gambling Research (2001), p. 114.

42. See Grinols and Omorov (1996), Lesieur (1998c), Polzin et al. (1998), and Volberg et al. (2001).

43. *The Video Gambler* (2000), p. 1.

44. Newspoll Market Research (2002).

45. Michael Rose (1994), Chairman and CEO of the Promus Companies, Incorporated, p. 1.

46. William N. Thompson (1994), p. 398.

47. National Gambling Impact Study Commission, pp. 2–8.

48. Gazel and Thompson (1996).

49. Productivity Commission (1999), p. 13.

50. Ibid.

51. Norris (1993).

52. Drinkard, Jim, "Gambling Money Uses Big Money to Woo States," *News Tribune*; Jefferson City, MO; February 25, 1996.

53. Goodman (1994), p. 16.

54. Ibid.

55. Robert Sigman, "Assault on Law Enforcement," *Kansas City Star*, April 28, 1996, p. K2.

56. State v. Becker, 1996, Mo. App. LEXUS 628, at *5 (Mo. App. 1996), 938 S.W. 2d, at 268 (1997), "Under the plain language of the statute, the Attorney General's authority to prosecute is equivalent to that of the local prosecuting attorney. Both have such authority independent of any recommendation or referral by the Gaming Commission."

57. Goodman (1995b), p. 190.

58. Kevin Sack, "Gambling's New Winnings," *New York Times*, December 18, 1995, p. B12.

59. Kindt (1998), p. 87.

60. Sack, op. cit., p. B12.

61. New Orleans *Times-Picayune*, January 25, 2000.

62. Reported to the author with request of anonymity.

63. John Kindt (1998), *Annals*, p. 87.

64. A. Lynch (1997), cited by Harvard Medical School Division on Addictions and Massachusetts Council on Problem Gambling. *The Wager*, pp. 2 and 39.

65. Gannet News Service, May 3, 1996.

66. Zremski, Jerry, (2002).

67. Las Vegas, *Review Journal*, July 28, 1998.

68. Zremski, op. cit.

69. *Charlotte Observer*, January 8, 1999.

70. Goodman (1995b).

71. A boat that cruises to international waters for the purpose of gambling and returns to shore when gambling is over.

72. Zabilka (1994), p. 3.

73. *Des Moines Register*, December 5, 1996, p. 1M.

74. Las Vegas *Review-Journal*, February 28, 2000.

75. Earl L. Grinols (1995b), p. 9.

76. Committee to Study the Impact of Gambling in Ohio (2002), p. 44.

77. Jim Drinkard (1996), p. 7.

78. U.S. House, 1995, 19.

79. Associated Press, May 9, 2000.

80. Rick Alm (2000), p. A1. Wolfson was chairman of the Missouri Gaming Commission from its inception in 1993 to February 1999.

81. Ibid.

82. The reader is referred to Tyler Bridges, *Bad Bet on the Bayou*, for a history of the Edwards era.

83. See *The Day*, New London, Connecticut; April 30, 1995, A1.

84. Anders (1998), p. 104.

85. Pauline Randall, quoted in "Casino Boom a Bust for Most Members of Indian Tribe"; *News-Gazette*, September 2, 2000, pp. A-1, A-6.

86. Associated Press (2000), "Casino Boom a Bust for Most Members of Indian Tribes: analysis shows tribes gained little from profit growth," News-gazette, (Champaign-Urbana) Sept. 2, A1, A6.

87. Lawrence, Neal (1995), "Gambling on a New Life," *Midwest Today*, January. Reported in Gary C. Anders, (1998), p. 107.

88. See the chapter on economic development.

89. See 25 U.S.C. 2710 [Sec. 11]. According to the IGRA, Class I gambling consists of "social games solely for prizes of minimal value." Included in Class I gambling are traditional Indian games identified with tribal ceremonies and celebrations. Class II gambling includes bingo and "games similar to bingo." Class III gambling includes all forms of gambling that are not Class I or Class II gambling, such as blackjack, baccarat, slot machines, roulette, electronic games like video poker, and other casino-style games.

90. This has to do with use of net revenues, outside audits, contracts for outside supplies and services, protection of the environment, licenses and background investigations, per-capita distribution plans, nontribally owned gaming, federal commission approval of the license, and certificate of self-regulation.

91. Arizona, California, Colorado, Connecticut, Idaho, Iowa, Kansas, Louisiana, Michigan, Minnesota, Mississippi, Montana, Nebraska, Nevada, New Mexico, New York, North Carolina, North Dakota, Oklahoma, Oregon, Rhode Island, South Dakota, Washington, and Wisconsin.

92. *Federal Register*, 44, 26, February 6, 1979, 7235–7237, plus information supplied by the Bureau of Indian Affairs, "Federal Recognition of Indian Entities for Past 20 Years."

93. *Time*, "The Last Tribe?: a Connecticut Band seeks Federal Recognition as Indian – and Plan's the World's Biggest Casino," March 6, 2000, v155, 9, p. 66+.

94. Ibid.

95. *Time*, December 16, 2002, "Look Who's Cashing in at Indian Casinos; Hint: It's Not the People Who are Supposed to Benefit," pp. 44–58.

96. Associated Press (2001), p. A-3.

97. Brian M. Greene, (1996), "The Reservation Gambling Fury: Modern Indian Uprising or Unfair Restraint on Tribal Sovereignty," *BYU Journal of Public Law*, 10, 1, 93–6, p. 96.

98. Anders, p. 99.

99. *Clark County Residents Study: 1993, 1994*, Conducted by GLS Research, 1993–94, Las Vegas Convention and Visitors Authority.

100. Volberg, et al. (2001), Table 2, p. 82.

101. Charles Clotfelder and Charles Cook (1989), p. 93.

102. Ron Cease, *Governing* magazine, May 1966. Quoted in John Kindt, *Legal Gambling in Illinois: A Primer*, www.igpa.uillinois.edu/htm/policya/98pa_gambling/981008.htm, accessed March 1, 2001.

103. Ibid.

104. John Caher (2002).

105. Ibid.

106. Ibid.

107. R. Randall Bridwell and Frank L. Quinn (2002), p. 578.

108. Ibid.

109. Russ Pulliam (2002).

110. Ibid.

111. See Chapter 8.

112. Leven, et al. (1998), p. 75.

113. Noll and Zimbalist (1997), p. 1.

114. Rappaport and Wilkerson (2001), p. 64.

115. We have not yet introduced social costs in the form of externalities; see Figure 4.4.

116. Rappaport and Wilkerson (2001), pp. 64–5; Rosen (1979); Roback (1982); Gyourko and Tracy (1991); and Hamilton and Kahn (1997). Rappaport and Wilkerson use $750 as their baseline.

117. Mark S. Rosentraub (1999).

118. Joanna Cagan and Neil DeMause (1998).

119. Rappaport and Wilkerson (2001), p. 72.

120. Siegfried and Zimbalist (2000), p. 95.

121. John B. Shoven and John Whalley (1984), p. 1032; and A. Lans Bovenberg and Lawrence H. Goulder (1996), p. 994.

122. See Noll and Zimbalist (1997), p. 61.

123. Felsenstein and Freeman (1998), p. 146.

124. National Research Council (1999), pp. 5-5.

125. Goss & Associates (2002), p. 7.

126. Rosentraub (1999), p. 134.

127. Noll and Zimbalist (1997), p. 25.

128. Cagan and De Mause (1998), pp. 36–7.

129. Siegfried and Zimbalist (2000), p. 103.

130. Rappaport and Wilkerson (2001), pp. 60–1.

131. Noll and Zimbalist (1997), p. 496.

132. Cagan and DeMause (1998), p. 35.

133. Siegfried and Zimbalist (2000), p. 105.

134. Noll and Zimbalist, p. 69.

135. Siegfried and Zimbalist (2000), p. 105.

136. Rappaport and Wilkerson (2001), p. 62.

137. Rosentraub (1999), p. 132.

138. Papajohn and Reardon (1994), p. 8.

139. Rosentraub (1999), pp. 151–3.

140. Mike Whalen, head of Heart of America Restaurants and Inns and president of Iowa Hospitality Association, quoted in Bowers (1995).

141. Bowers (1995), p. 1.

142. Petton (1994).

143. Ibid., p. 8.

144. Bowers (1995), pp. 1M, 7M.

145. This section is based on Grinols and Omorov (1996).

146. Rappaport and Wilkerson, p. 63.

147. Siegfried and Zimbalist, p. 106.

148. Janove, Bill (1995),"Residents Find Careers at Casino: Overall Effect on Job Market Remains Unknown," *Daily Herald*, Elgin, Illinois, Section 1, p. 7.

149. Borden, Jeff (1996).

150. Petroski, William "Casinos Buy Too Much from Outside Iowa, Gaming Official Says," *Des Moines Register*, May 16, 1997.

151. Dorr (1999), p. 15.

152. Felsenstein and Freeman (1998), p. 145.

153. Noll and Zimbalist, p. 65, "The Dependence of Estimated Net Benefits on Arbitrary Line Drawing"; and Siegfried and Zimbalist, p. 107, Footnote 8.

154. Rappaport and Wilkerson, p. 63.

155. Noll and Zimbalist (1997), pp. 497–8.

156. Average receipts per admission were $87.19 in 2000 for Illinois casinos.

157. Taxes and savings generally account for more than 30 percent of income, leaving 70 percent or less for consumption. Noll and Zimbalist (1997), p. 75.

158. Petroski (1997), p. 2A.

159. Adam Rose and Associates (1998), p. 13.

160. *USA Today,* "Casinos Offer Losing Bet," November 2, 1994.

161. Felsenstein and Freeman (1998), p. 146.

162. Societe des Casinos Du Quebec (1994).

163. Goss & Associates (2002), p. 5.

164. Whereatt (1993), p. 16A.

165. Minnesota Gaming Commission, 1993. Cited in Adam Rose (1998), p. 12.

166. Borden (1996), p. 3.

167. Janov (1995), Section 1, p. 7.

168. Papajohn and Reardon (1994), Section 1, pp. 1, 9.

169. Adam Rose Associates (1998), p. 8.

170. Ibid., p. 3.

171. Goss & Associates (2002), p. 57.

172. Eadington (1999).

173. Ibid.

174. I show in the following discussion that it should be present.

175. The utility function is continuous, weakly convex, and locally nonsatiable. If consumption Bundle A is preferred or indifferent to Bundle B, then for $\lambda \epsilon [0, 1]$, bundle $\lambda A + (1 - \lambda)B$ is preferred or indifferent to Bundle B. For any consumption Bundle A, there exists another bundle with quantities close to A, which is strictly preferred by the household.

176. Let the term in square brackets in Equation 5.1 be written as E_i. Then $\Delta W = \sum_i E_i + \sum_i (w_i - 1)E_i$. Because the average value of w_i is 1, the second term on the right can be interpreted as being the covariance of the change in household utility E_i with the social weights w_i. (Actually, it is proportional to this covariance.) The closer the pattern of utility increases matches the desired pattern given by the weights (greater covariance), the larger the second term. Thus, cases in which weights differ from one differ from the text assumption by this covariance.

177. Public goods, such as a radio broadcast or the provision of national security, have the feature that the consumption of them by one individual does not limit the ability of others to consume the same good. For example, if national defense makes you safe in your home, then your neighbor is able to consume the same safety in his or her home.

178. One reviewer noted that it is not inconceivable that casinos might generate public goods. Whereas casinos might be associated with positive or negative externalities that share a characteristic of public goods (i.e., consumption by one does not limit consumption by another), the production by a casino is generally of private goods. We consider the externalities generated by casinos separately.

179. The i'th consumer sees prices $p_i = p + t_i$, where t_i is the list of applicable consumer taxes and p is domestic prices. Producers likewise see prices $p_j = p - \tau_j$. Noting that $\sum_i x_i = x$, $\sum_j y_j = y$, and $x = y + \omega + z - r$ gives $\sum_i p_i x_i = \sum_j p_j y_j + p \cdot \omega + \left[\sum_i t_i x_i + \sum_j \tau_j y_j + p \cdot z\right] - p \cdot r$. The first term is after-tax profits to firms, the third is tax revenues T, and the last is the cost of resources E.

180. Use the fact that $\sum_i \theta_{ij} = 1$.

181. Some readers may wonder where deadweight loss appears. When a tax causes the private sector to lose more in social value than the amount of taxes collected, the extra loss is called *deadweight loss*. It takes the form of lost consumer surplus and lost profits to firms that exceeds the tax collection of government. The change in profits in Equation 5.11 are after-tax profits to the firm. Equation 5.9 records the effect of the change on consumer surplus. Thus, deadweight loss is automatically included in the measure of change.

182. The expansion of nongambling services can be considered in their own right, but that is another topic.

183. This section draws on Grinols (1999a).

184. The emphasis in this section on distance benefits should not be misunderstood. The issue is not whether a popular and widely engaged-in activity has benefits, but rather what form they take. If expansion casinos offer gambling at lower prices, some of the benefits would assume the form of increased consumer surplus. If expansion casinos were to offer gambling in a form that is inferior (superior) to gambling offered in Las Vegas, free entry would still imply that profits would be competed down to ordinary business levels, but the amount of gambling we observed with distance would be less (more). This would be reflected in smaller (larger) distance benefits. Restricting casino expansion so that monopoly profits are earned would change some of the benefits into profit form, but would diminish the amount of benefits that appear as distance benefits. Other variations could be imagined. The point is that limiting the spread of an activity limits the total benefits created by the activity, as well as altering the form that the benefits take.

185. See Grinols and Omorov (1996).

186. Australia's Productivity Commission found one third of gambling revenues came from problem gamblers. Subtracting one third of $48 leaves $32; subtracting one fourth leaves $36. The average is $34.

187. Earl L. Grinols (1995a).

188. National Gambling Impact Study Commission (1999), p. 2.

189. See Economic Report of the President, February 1, 2000, Table B-91.

190. If casinos offer their services on the same terms as preexisting casinos, there are no consumer surplus benefits. If, on the contrary, distance is held fixed and new casinos offer identical service at a *lower* effective price than preexisting casinos, then there would be consumer surplus gains.

191. Variations that might produce price effects include the payback rate of slot machines, which determines the price of play. "Looser" machines have a lower price than "tighter" ones.

192. They were later divorced.

193. McGrath (1995), p. A18.

194. Minneapolis *Star Tribune*, December 4, 1995, p. A6.

195. *Milwaukee Journal Sentinel*, August 9, 2000.

196. Distributive efficiency requires that goods be distributed to individuals in such a way that no rearrangement of them across consumers could increase one consumer's utility without lowering another's utility.

197. Schneider (2002), Louisville, Kentucky, The *Courier-Journal*, December 23, 2002.

198. Ibid.

199. See Grinols and Mustard (2000) for a discussion.

200. Bhagwati (1984).

201. Fenich (1999).

202. Samuelson (1970), p. 402.

203. Melloan (1998), p. A23.

204. One bankruptcy researcher noted that many people reported being influenced to file for bankruptcy after seeing advertisements from lawyers specializing in bankruptcy. (Hira, 1998).

205. Form 7, Title 11, Appendix-Bankruptcy Rules, Question 8. The listing of casinos is notable, as well as the other causes with which it is grouped.

206. *International Wagering and Gaming Business*, Director of Casino Money Centers, September 1996.

207. *The Advocate*, Baton Rouge, Louisiana, October 28, 1996.

208. Reno (1997).

209. Neely (1998).

210. *Associated Press*, September 22, 1996.

211. "I have a number of clients in excess of $40,000 in gambling losses in the last year," said Joe Peiffer of Cedar Rapids, a specialist in bankruptcy cases. According to his records, debtors with gambling losses of more than $5,000 show up in about 15 percent of the 150 bankruptcies Peiffer handled in the past year. (*Cedar Rapids Gazette*, December 11, 1997.) Other forms of recreation have not been mentioned in the same way as gambling as a contributing or primary cause of bankruptcy.

212. Data compiled by Tom Coates, head of Consumer Credit Counseling Services of Des Moines.

213. "Yes, there is a connection [between gambling and bankruptcy]," according to the study's author, Tahira Hira. Of Hira's bankruptcy filers, 28 percent were gamblers; 19 percent said gambling debt was an important factor. Gamblers also had 19 percent more debt than nongamblers. The average reported debt of gamblers was $41,342.

214. SMR Research Corporation (1998), p. 118.

215. Ibid., p. 117.

216. SMR Research Corporation (2001), p. 196.

217. Ibid., p. 212.

218. Lesieur (1992).

219. Curran (1999).

220. "A man who killed himself by jumping off a casino parking garage has been identified as a 39-year-old Californian. [Eric] Wheeler's death was the eighth such suicide at an Atlantic City casino since August 1999." *The Record* (Bergen County, New Jersey.)

221. Gustin, London, Connecticut, *The Day*, September 9, 2000.

222. Ibid.

223. Thomas Geyer, *Quad-City Times*, November 24, 1999.

224. Of visitor deaths in Las Vegas, 4.28 percent were the result of suicides compared to 0.97 percent for the rest of the nation.

225. Blaszczynski and Farrell (1998) studied forty-four cases of suicide. They concluded that there are "sufficient indicators to provide strong support for the argument that gambling acted as a catalyst or played a relevant role in the suicide."

226. "About a quarter of them [Gamblers Anonymous members] admitted to having been involved in auto accidents during the worst of their gambling. To be sure, almost half (47.3 percent) of the GA members reported speeding while heavily gambling. Many of these individuals seem to become more hurried, more accident-prone, and more risk-taking during their heavier gambling activity," p. 61.

227. Feigelman, Wallish and Lesieur (1998); Kaplan and Davis (1997); Smart and Ferris (1996); and Steinberg, Kosten, and Rounsaville (1992), among others.

228. Bland et al. (1993); and Lorenz and Shuttlesworth (1983).

229. Government Accounting Office (2000), p. 27.

230. See the report of research in The *New York Times*, "Hijacking the Brain Circuits with a Nickel Slot Machine," Sandra Blakeslee (2002), pp. 1, 5, 19.

231. Shaffer, Hall, and Vander Bilt (1997).

232. See Gerstein, et al. (1999), Table 21, p. 58. A similar progression was observed for other problems. The incidence rate – moving from the percentage rate observed for low-risk (i.e., nonproblem) gamblers to problem gamblers to pathological gamblers – went from 4.0 to 10.9 to 15.0 percent for unemployment insurance use among the three groups; from 5.5 to 10.3 to 19.2 percent for bankruptcy; from 29.8 to 39.5 to 53.5 percent for divorced ever; and from 4.0 to 10.5 to 21.4 percent for ever incarcerated.

233. Research conducted for the study by Thompson and Quinn (1999), reported in Bridwell and Quinn (2002), p. 696–97.

234. Even though Nevada has had casinos since 1931 and Atlantic City since 1978, little or no academic research conducted in those states resulted in information about the social costs of casinos.

235. CPI-U figures used for 1994–2003 are 148.2, 152.4, 156.9, 160.5, 163.0, 166.6, 172.2, 177.1, 179.9, and 184, respectively.

236. The Florida study, Office of Planning and Budgeting, The Executive Office of the Governor (1994), was not intended to consider more than the incarceration and supervision costs of increased crime using state cost figures.

237. Ryan et al. (1999) found that pathological gamblers not in treatment had lost productivity costs that were 51.6 percent of the comparable costs of gamblers in treatment. In general, only 3 to 5 percent of gamblers with problems seek treatment. Thus, using the midpoint of this range, $(0.96 \times 0.516 + .04) \times C$, is the lost productivity cost of one average additional pathological gambler, where C is the cost of a gambler in treatment. The corresponding correction for problem gamblers was 23.585 percent. For the remaining types of gambling costs, the correction factors were 55.6 and 23.98 percent. The cost figures in the columns for Wisconsin, Connecticut, Louisiana, South Carolina, and Nevada were adjusted downward from the orginal studies by these factors before entering into Tables 7.1 and 7.2.

238. Crime; lost productivity on the job; and a significant portion of lost time and

unemployment costs, bankruptcy, social service costs, and direct regulatory costs are burdens on the public.

239. Crime costs and social service costs are tax-supported.

240. See Ballard et al. (1985), p. 21. This is the low end of the range estimated in the public-finance literature for sales tax, and below the preferred range of 1.318 to 1.469 of Browning (1987). A lower choice lowers the estimated social costs of casinos.

241. In any estimation, we are not sure what the true number is. With 95 percent probability, however, we can say that the true number is between the 95 percent confidence bounds; in this case, 0.9 and 1.38.

242. GAO (2000), p. 28.

243. Volberg and Steadman (1989); and Volberg (1995).

244. Lifetime problem gamblers would be respondents who scored 3 or 4 points on the lifetime South Oaks Gambling Screen questionnaire. Current problem gamblers would be those respondents who scored 3 or 4 points on the past year South Oaks Gambling Screen items.

245. To calculate current (ongoing) costs, we use current problem and pathological gamblers to be consistent with the numbers in Tables 7.1 and 7.2. The 1989 Iowa study did not calculate current problem and pathological gamblers. Because lifetime problem gamblers grew by 119 percent, Table 8.2 applies the same proportion to current problem gamblers. A similar procedure was applied to pathological gamblers.

246. From Tables 7.1 and 7.2, the change in social costs per year, adjusted for tax dead-weight loss applicable to 37 percent of expenditures ($0.375 \times 1.251 + 0.625 = 1.09424$), for 100 average adults adds the costs of additional pathological gamblers and additional problem gamblers,

$$\frac{\$10,330 \times 1.09424}{year} \times 0.95 + \frac{\$2,945 \times 1.09424}{year} \times 1.25 = \qquad \text{(A.1)}$$

$$\$14,767 \text{ per year} \qquad \text{(A.2)}$$

On a per-adult basis, therefore, spread over everyone, the cost is approximately $148.

247. Ibid.

248. Gerstein et al. (1999), p. 28.

249. For 100 adults, $\frac{\$10,330 \times 1.09424}{year} \times 0.9 + \frac{\$2,945 \times 1.09424}{year} \times 0.8 = \$12,751.28$ per year. On a per-adult basis, therefore, the cost is approximately $128. To this we add direct regulatory costs of $15 per adult.

250. The research in this book was conducted in an independent manner. No funds were received from progambling or antigambling organizations or lobbying groups.

251. National Gambling Impact Study Commission (1996), p. 4-4.

252. Bridwell and Quinn (2002), p. 718.

253. More than thirty cities in the United States and Canada with populations greater than 250 thousand have population densities between 1,600 and 2,000. For example, Colorado, Springs, Colorado, is 185.8 square miles, has a 2000 population of 360,890, and 1,943 people per square mile.

254. In the United States in 2000, cities with populations of 50 thousand or more occupied 34,094 square miles and had a combined population of 99,596,972, leaving 3,502,200 square miles of land area for the remaining 180,965,517 residents. This implies a population density of 51.7 people per square mile.

255. Gerstein, et al. (1999), p. 81.

256. Losses to the casino by an adult living s miles from the casino would be $\frac{\$606.921}{3^k} s^k$, where s is between 3 and 100 miles and $k = \frac{Ln[1-0.325]}{Ln[2]}$.

257. Data supplied to the author by Dr. Ricardo Gazel, formerly of the University of Nevada, Las Vegas.

258. Losses to the casino by an adult living s miles from the casino would be $\frac{\$606.921}{3^k} 100^k e^{-0.05(s-100)}$, where s is between 100 and 250 miles and $k = \frac{Ln[1-0.325]}{Ln[2]}$.

259. Adjusted gross receipts for nine Illinois casino locations totalled $1,783,958,166. Illinois Gaming Board, *2001 Annual Report*, p. 9.

260. Many states share some of the casino tax with the local jurisdiction. A typical local share might be 25 percent. The state in our example is more generous; here, we used 33 percent.

261. Most governments must purchase many items from outside the community, some of which may vary with the size of the casino operation. Police cars and equipment, for example, are likely to be purchased from outside the area, as are many infrastructure-related purchases.

262. This involves a tedious calculation, forming values similar to those in Table 6.4, and integrating over resident location. We know how residents' gambling expenditures change by distance to the nearest casino, and how their number of visits changes by distance – the latter is assumed to follow the relation of Table 6.3. Calculating the integral in Figure 6.2 produces for each resident an upper bound for the value of reducing the distance to the nearest casino to 5 miles. Reducing by one third for the share of revenues due to problem and pathological gamblers and averaging over county residents gives the figure in the text.

263. Profit per unit of real output in dollars in 2002 was 8.4 percent. (See *Economic Report of the President*, February 2003, Table B-15, p. 295.)

264. Chapter 7 reported that annual direct regulatory costs in Louisiana were more than $16 per adult. The implied overhead figure here – $12.62 – is less than this.

265. The revenues from gamblers who live 25 to 250 miles from the casino are $104 million.

References

Adam Rose and Associates (1998). "The Regional Economic Impacts of Casino Gambling: Assessment of the Literature and Establishment of a Reasearch Agenda." Report prepared for the National Gambling Impact Study Commission (August).

Albanese, Jay S. (1985). "The Effect of Casino Gambling on Crime." *Federal Probation*, 49, 2 (June), 39–44.

Albanese, Jay S. (1999). "Casino Gambling and White Collar Crime: An Examination of the Empirical Evidence." Presented at the conference "Gambling and Gaming: Winners or Losers?," Omaha, NE (April).

Alm, Rick (2000). "KC Casino Faces Loss of License: Missouri Regulators Move to Oust Station." *Kansas City Star* (August 31), A1.

Anders, Gary C. (1998). "Indian Gaming: Financial and Regulatory Issues," *Annals*, American Academy of Political and Social Science, 556, March, 98–108.

Arthur Anderson & Co. (1996). *Economic Impacts of Casino Gaming in the United States, Volume 1: Macro Study*. Washington, DC: American Gaming Association.

Associated Press (2001). "Indian Tribe Gets Clause to Facilitate Casino Plan." *News Gazette* (Urbana-Champaign, IL), (February 5), A-3.

Australian Institute for Gambling Research (2001). "Survey of the Nature and Extent of Gambling and Problem Gambling in the ACT." University of Western Sydney (July), 114.

Ayres, Ian, and Steven D. Levitt (1998). "Measuring Positive Externalities from Unobservable Victim Precaution: An Empirical Analysis of Lojack." *Quarterly Journal of Economics*, 113 (February), 43–77.

Ballard, Charles L., John B Shoven, and John Whalley (1985). "General Equilibrium Computations of the Marginal Welfare Costs of Taxes in the United States," *American Economic Review*, 75, 128–38.

Bennett, Deborah J. (1998). *Randomness*. Cambridge, MA: Harvard University Press.

Berns, D. (1998). "Gambling Survey Approved." *Las Vegas Review-Journal* (October 10), D1.

Bhagwati, Jagdish (1984). "Directly Unproductive Profit-Seeking Activities and Economic Theory." *European Economic Review*, 24, 3, 291–2.

Blair, Benjamin F., R. Keith Schwer, and C. Jeffrey Waddoups (1998). "Gambling as an Economic Development Strategy: The Neglected Issue of Job Satisfaction and Nonpecuniary Income." *The Review of Regional Studies*, 28, 1, 47–62.

Blakeslee, Sandra (2002). "Hijacking the Brain Circuits with a Nickel Slot Machine." The *New York Times* (February 19), Sec. F, 1.

Bland, R. C., S. C. Newman, H. Orn, and G. Stebelsky (1993). "Epidemiology of Pathological Gambling in Edmonton." *Canadian Journal of Psychology*, 38, 108–12.

Blaszczynski, A., and E. Farrell (1998). "A Case Series of 44 Completed Gambling-Related Suicides." *Journal of Gambling Studies*, 14, 2, 93–109.

Bockstael, N. E., and K. E. McConnell (1993). "Public Goods as Characteristics of Non-Market Commodities." *Economic Journal*, 103 (September), 1244–57.

Borden, Jeff (1996). "Casino Wins Challenged; Riverboats Are a Wash, Study Claims." *Crain's Chicago Business*, Crain Communications, Inc. (June 10), 3.

Bovenberg, A. Lans, and Lawrence H. Goulder (1996). "Optimal Environmental Taxation in the Presence of Other Taxes: General Equilibrium Analysis." *American Economic Review*, 86 (September), 994.

Bowers, Frank (1995). "Business Can Suffer in Shadow of Casino." *Des Moines Register* (July 23), 1B, 5B.

Bridges, Tyler (2001). *Bad Bet on the Bayou*. New York: Farrar, Strauss, and Giroux.

Bridwell, R. Randall, and Frank L. Quinn (2002). "From Mad Joy to Misfortune: The Merger of Law and Politics in the World of Gambling." *Mississippi Law Journal*, 72, 2, 565–729.

Browning, Edgar K. (1987). "On the Marginal Welfare Cost of Taxation," *American Economic Review*, 77, 11–23.

Buck, Andrew J., Simon Hakim, and Uriel Spiegel (1991). "Casinos, Crime, and Real Estate Values: Do They Relate?" *Journal of Research in Crime and Delinquency*, 28 (August), 288–303.

Cagan, Joanna, and Neil DeMause (1998). *Field of Schemes: How the Great Stadium Swindle Turns Public Money into Private Profit*. Monroe, ME: Common Courage Press.

Caher, John (2002). "New York State Gambling Bill Attacked." *The New York Law Journal*, 2002 Law.com, http://www.law.com (January 29).

Chesney-Lind, Meda, and Ian Y. Lind (1986). "Visitors Against Victims: Crimes Against Tourists in Hawaii." *Annals of Tourism Research*, 13, 167–91.

Chiricos, Ted (1994). "Casinos and Crime: An Assessment of the Evidence." University of Nevada, Las Vegas, Special Collections.

Christiansen Capital Advisors, LLC (2000). "An Assessment of the Potential Demand for the Proposed Narragansett Tribal Casino and its Impacts on the State Lottery," Presentation to The Rhode Island House of Representatives Finance Committee, April 6, 2000.

Clotfelder, Charles T., and Philip J. Cook (1989). *Selling Hope: State Lotteries in America*. Cambridge, MA: Harvard University Press.

Committee to Study the Impact of Gambling in Ohio (2002). "Final Report to the General Assembly of Ohio," July 9.

Curran, John (1999). "Scary Streak: Third Suicide in Eight Days at Atlantic City Casino." Associated Press & Local Wire; Atlantic City, NJ (August 25).

Deloitte and Touche (1992). "Economic and Other Impacts of a Proposed Gaming,

Entertainment, and Hotel Facility." Prepared for the City of Chicago Gaming Commission.

Dorr, Robert "Casinos Urged to Spend More in Iowa," *Omaha World Herald*, September 24, 1999, p. 15.

Drinkard, Jim (1996). "Gambling Money Uses Big Money to Woo States." *New Tribune* (Jefferson City, MO), (February 25), 7.

Eadington, William R. (1999). "The Economics of Casino Gambling." *Journal of Economic Perspectives*, 13, 3 (Summer), 173–92.

Economic Report of the President (2000). Washington, D.C.: United States Government Printing Office, February.

Encyclopedia Britannica (1970). Chicago: Encyclopedia Britannica.

Encyclopedia Britannica (2002). Chicago: Encyclopedia Britannica.

The Evans Group (1996). "A Study of the Economic Impact of the Gambling Industry Through 2005." Study commissioned by International Game Technology (September), iii and 105.

The Executive Office of the Governor (1994). "Casinos in Florida." Office of Planning and Budgeting, The Capitol, Tallahassee, iii and 118.

Feigelman, W., L. S. Wallisch, and H. R. Lesieur (1998). "Problem Gamblers, Problem Substance Users, and Dual-Problem Individuals: An Epidemiological Study." *American Journal of Public Health*, 88, 3, 467–70.

Felsenstein, Daniel, and Daniel Freeman (1998). "Simulating the Impacts of Gambling in a Tourist Location: Some Evidence from Israel." *Journal of Travel Research*, 37 (November), 145–55.

Fenich, George G. (1996). "A Chronology of (Legal) Gaming in the U.S." *Gaming Research & Review Journal*, 3, 2, 65–78.

Finance and Administrative Cabinet Commonwealth of Kentucky (1999). "Assessment of the Economic and Social Impact of Expanded Gaming in the Commonwealth and Neighboring Region." (December) iii and 182.

Florida Department of Law Enforcement (1994). "The Question of Casinos in Florida: Increased Crime: Is It Worth the Gamble?" Tallahassee, FL: State of Florida.

Florida Sheriffs Association (1994). "Casinos and Crime: Is It Worth the Gamble? A Summary Report and Position Paper." Tallahassee, FL: Florida Sheriffs Association.

Frank, M. L., D. Lester, and A. Wexler (1991). "Suicidal Behavior Among Members of Gamblers Anonymous." *Journal of Gambling Studies*, 7, 249–54.

Frey, James H. (1998). "Federal Involvement in U.S. Gaming Regulation." *Annals of the American Academy of Political and Social Science*, 556 (March), 136–52.

Friedman, Joseph, Simon Hakim, and J. Weinblatt (1989). "Casino Gambling as a 'Growth Pole' Strategy and Its Effect on Crime." *Journal of Regional Science*, 29 (November), 615–23.

"Gaming Conference" (1999). Sponsored by the Federal Bureau of Investigation, The U.S. Attorney's Office, the Kentucky Association of Chiefs of Police, and the Kentucky Association of Commonwealth Attorneys; Louisville, KY (August 10).

Gazel, Ricardo, and William Thompson (1996). "Casino Gamblers in Illinois: Who Are They?" Report for The Better Government Association of Chicago (June), 1–25. (Plus data supplied by the authors.)

General Accounting Office (2000). "Impact of Gambling: Economic Effects More Measurable Than Social Effects." Washington: USGAO (April).

Gerstein, Dean, John Hofmann, Cindy Larison, Laszlo Engelman, Sally Murphy, Amanda Palmer, Lucian Chuchro, Marianna Toce, Robert Johnson, Tracy Buie, Mary Ann Hill, Rachel Volberg, Henrick Harwood and Adam Tucker, Eugene Christiansen, Will Cummings, and Sebastian Sinclair (1999). "Gambling Impact and Behavior Study: Report to the National Gambling Impact Study Commission." National Gambling Impact Study Commission (April 1).

Geyer, Thomas (1999). *The Quad-City Times*. Devenport, Iowa, November 24.

Glaeser, Edward L., Bruce Sacerdote, and Jose A. Scheinkman (1996). "Crime and Social Interactions." *Quarterly Journal of Economics*, 111 (May), 507–48.

GLS Research (1994). *Clark County Residents Study: 1993–94*. Las Vegas: Las Vegas Convention and Visitor's Authority.

Goodman, Robert (1994). *Legalized Gambling as a Strategy for Economic Development*. Aspen Insitute and Ford Foundation (March), 222 pages.

Goodman, Robert (1995a). *The Luck Business*. New York: Free Press.

Goodman, Robert (1995b). Presentation at the Annual Conference of the National Coalition Against Legalized Gambling (October 27–29), Orlando, FL; cited in Kindt (1998), p. 96.

Goss & Associates – Economic Solutions (2002). *The Economic Impact of an Omaha, Nebraska, Casino*. Prepared for the Greater Omaha Chamber of Commerce (August 12), 1–68.

Gould, Eric, David B. Mustard, and Bruce Weinberg (1998). "Crime Rates and Local Labor Market Opportunities in the United States: 1977–1995." University of Georgia Working Paper.

Government Accounting Office (GAO) (2000). "Impact of Gambling." GAO/GGD-00-78 (April), 1–68.

Grinols, Earl L. (1995a). "Time for a National Policy." Congressional Testimony, Committee on Small Business, House of Representatives, One Hundred Third Congress, 1994 Hearing on the National Impact of Casino Gambling Proliferation, Washington, DC: U.S. Government Printing Office, Serial 103–104, 8–11, 76.

Grinols, Earl L. (1995b). "Gambling as Economic Policy: Enumerating Why Losses Exceed Gains." *Illinois Business Review* (Spring), 6–9.

Grinols, Earl L. (1996). "Incentives Explain Gambling's Growth." *Forum for Applied Research and Public Policy*, 11, 2, 119–24.

Grinols, Earl L. (1999a). "Distance Effects in Consumption." *Review of Regional Studies*, 29, 1, 63–76.

Grinols, Earl L. (1999b). "Casino Gambling Causes Crime." *Policy Forum*, 13, 2, 1–4.

Grinols, Earl L., and David B. Mustard (2000). "The Economics of Casino Gambling." *Journal of Economic Perspectives*, 14, 1 (Winter), 223–5.

Grinols, Earl L., and David B. Mustard (2001). "Business Profitability versus Social Profitability: Evaluating the Social Contribution of Industries with Externalities and the Case of the Casino Industry." *Managerial and Decision Economics*, 22, 1–3 (January–May), 143–62.

Grinols, Earl L., and David B. Mustard (2002). "Measuring Industry Externalities: The Curious Case of Casinos and Crime." University of Illinois, University of Georgia (unpublished paper), 1–36.

Grinols, Earl L., and J. D. Omorov (1996). "Who Loses When Casinos Win?" *Illinois Business Review*, 53, 1 (Spring), 7–11, 19.

Grinols, Earl L., and J. D. Omorov (1997). "Development or Dreamfield Delusions?: Assessing Casino Gambling's Costs and Benefits." *Journal of Law and Commerce*, 16, 1, 49–87.

Grogger, Jeff (1997). "Market Wages and Youth Crime." NBER Working Paper #5983.

Gyourko, Joseph, and Joseph Tracy (1991). "The Structure of Local Public Finance and the Quality of Life." *Journal of Political Economy*, 99, 4 (August), 774–806.

Gustin, Georgina (2000). "Gambling Seen as Possible Motive in R.I. Man's Suicide," *The Day*. London, Connecticut, September 9.

Hamilton, Bruce W., and Peter Kahn (1997). "Baltimore's Camden Yards Ballparks." In Roger G. Noll and Andrew Zimbalist (eds.), *Sports, Jobs, and Taxes: The Economic Impact of Sports Teams and Stadiums*. Washington: Brookings Institution Press.

Hawthorne, Michael "Report on Casino's Fortunes Shows Why Others Seek Boat of Their Own," The *News Gazette*, Champaign-Urbana, IL, May 1, 1994.

Henriksson, L. E. (1996). "Hardly a Quick Fix: Casino Gambling in Canada." *Canadian Public Policy*, XXII, 2, 116–28.

Hira, Tahira K. (1998). "Bankruptcy and Gambling: Is There a Connection?" Iowa State University. Study also reported by Associated Press, "ISU Study Links Gambling, Bankruptcy" (August 5).

Hsing, Yu (1996). "An Analysis of Arrests Regarding Illegal Drugs: The Determinants and Policy Implications." *American Journal of Economics and Sociology*, 55 (January), 53–60.

International Gaming and Wagering Business (1999). 20, 8 (August).

Iowa Racing and Gaming Commission (1995). *Des Moines Register* (October 13), Christiansen/Cummings Associates of Arlington, MA.

Janov, Jill (1995). "Residents Find Careers at Casino: Overall Effect on Job Market Remains Unknown." *Daily Herald* (Elgin, Illinois), Sec. 1, 7.

Kaplan, G., and B. Davis (1997). *Gambling, Alcohol, and Other Drugs: Prevalence and Implications of Dual-Problem Clients*. Winnepeg: The Addictions Foundation of Manitoba.

Kindt, John W. (1994). "Increased Crime and Legalized Gambling Operations: The Impact on the Socioeconomics of Business and Government." *Criminal Law Bulletin*, 43, 538–9.

Kindt, John W. (1998). "Follow the Money: Gambling, Ethics, and Subpoenas." *The Annals of The American Academy of Political and Social Science*, 556 (March), 85–97.

Kindt, John W. (2001). "The Costs of Addicted Gamblers: Should the States Initiate Mega-Lawsuits Similar to the Tobacco Cases?" *Managerial and Decision Economics*, 22, 1–3, 17–64.

Lee, Barbara A., and James Chelius (1989). "Government Regulation of Labor-Management Corruption: The Casino Industry Experience in New Jersey." *Industrial and Labor Relations Review*, 42 (July), 536–48.

Lesieur, Henry R. (1990). "Compulsive Gambling: Documenting the Social and Economic Costs." Revision of paper presented at *Gambling in Minnesota: An Issue for Policy Makers*, Humphrey Institute of Public Affairs, University of Minnesota (December 1991).

Lesieur, Henry R. (1992). "Compulsive Gambling." *Society*, 29, 4, 43–50.

Lesieur, Henry R. (1998a). Testimony before the National Gambling Impact Study Commission; Atlantic City, New Jersey; Institute of Problem Gambling (January 22).

Lesieur, Henry R. (1998b). "Pathological Gambling Is a Psychiatric Disorder." In *Legalized Gambling: For and Against*, R. L. Evans and M. Hance (eds.), Chicago: Open Court Publishing, 37–63.

Lesieur, Henry R. (1998c). "Costs and Treatment of Pathological Gambling." *The Annals of the American Academy of Political and Social Science* (Gambling: Socioeconomic Impacts and Public Policy, J. H. Frey, special editor), 556 (March), 153–71.

Lesieur, Henry R. (2002). "Pathological and Problem Gambling: Costs and Social Policy." Testimony to Special House Committee to Study Gambling, State of Rhode Island, 15 October. Accessed www.rilin.state.ri.us/gen_assembly/gaming/ accessed December 2002.

Lesieur, Henry R., and Christopher Anderson (1995). "Results of a Survey of Gamblers Anonymous Members in Illinois." Park Ridge, IL: Illinois Council on Problem and Compulsive Gambling, manuscript.

Leven, Charles, Don Phares, and Claude Louishomme (1998). "The Economic Impact of Gaming in Missouri." Report to Civic Progress, St. Louis (April).

Levitt, Steven D. (1998). "Why Do Increased Arrest Rates Appear to Reduce Crime: Deterrence, Incapacitation, or Measurement Error?" *Economic Inquiry*, 36 (July), 353–72.

Lorenz, Valerie D., and D. E. Shuttlesworth (1983). "The Impact of Pathological Gambling on the Spouse of the Gambler." *Journal of Community Psychology*, 11, 67–76.

Lott, John R., and David B. Mustard (1997). "The Right to Carry Concealed Handguns and the Importance of Deterrence." *Journal of Legal Studies*, 26, 1, 1–68.

Louisiana Compulsive Gambling Study Committee (1996). "Report to the State Legislature of the State of Louisiana."

Maryland Department of Health and Mental Hygiene, Alcohol, and Drug Abuse Administration (1990). *Final Report: Task Force on Gambling Addiction in Maryland*, Baltimore: Author.

McCleary, Richard, Kenneth Chew, Wang Feng, Vincent Merrill, Carol Napolitano, Michael Males, and Brenda Graffeo (1998). "Suicide and Gambling: An Analysis of Suicide Rates in U.S. Counties and Metropolitan Areas: Report to the American Gaming Association." Manuscript (September).

McGrath, Dennis J. (1995). "Gambling-Related Crime Is Costly to Taxpayer." *Minneapolis Star Tribune* (December 4), A18.

Melloan, George (1998). "Politics Aside, Let's Look at Economic Dysfunction." *Wall Street Journal* (November 10), A23.

Miller, Ted R., Mark A. Cohen, and Brian Wiersema (1996). *Victim Costs and Consequences: A New Look*. Washington, DC: National Institute of Justice.

Miller, William J., and Martin D. Schwartz (1998). "Casino Gambling and Street Crime." *Annals of the American Academy of Political and Social Science*, 556 (March), 124–37.

Mirage Hotel (1993). "Response of the Developers of the Proposed Fox River Resort to the West Dundee Riverboat Project Task Force."

Mustard, David B. (2000). "Reexamining Criminal Behavior: The Importance of Omitted Variable Bias." University of Georgia Working Paper.

National Gambling Impact Study Commission (1999). *National Gambling Impact Study Commission Final Report* (June 18), www.ngisc.gov.

National Opinion Research Center (1999). "Overview of National Survey and Community Database Research on Gambling Behavior." University of Chicago.

National Research Council (1999). "Pathological Gambling: A Critical Review." (1 April), Study Conducted for the National Gambling Impact Study Commission.

Neely, Michelle Clark (1998). "Personal Bankruptcy: The New American Pastime?" *The Regional Economist* (October), 12–13.

Nelson, Dennis J., Howard L. Erickson, and Robert J. Langan (1996). "Indian Gaming and Its Impact on Law Enforcement in Wisconsin." API Consulting Services (October).

Newspoll Market Research (2002). "Victorians' Attitudes to Poker Machines." Survey Conducted for the Inter-Church Gambling Taskforce (November 15–17).

Noll, Roger, and Andrew Zimbalist (1997). *Sports, Jobs, and Taxes.* Washington: Brookings Institution.

Norris, Floyd, "Insiders Didn't Take Much of a Gamble with Argosy Gaming," *New York Times*, February 25, 1993.

O'Brien, Thomas R. (1984). Quoted in William N. Thompson, "Gambling: A Controlled Substance." *Pittsburgh Post-Gazette* (August 14, 1994), E-1, E-4.

Papajohn, George, and Patrick J. Reardon (1994). "City Hoping to Attract Tourists, But Odds Are Most Patrons Would Be From Area." *Chicago Tribune* (May 13), Sec. 1, 1, 9.

Petroski, William (1997). "Casinos Say 86 Percent of Spending Done in Iowa." *Des Moines Register*, (August 23).

Petton, Tom (1994). "Aurora Casino Boom Fails to Register with Merchants." *Chicago Tribune* (28 June), Sec. 1, 1, 8.

Phillips, David P., W. R. Welty, and M. M. Smith (1997). "Elevated Suicide Levels Associated with Legalized Gambling." *Suicide and Life-Threatening Behavior*, 27, 373–8.

Pickett (1932). "Contests and Lottery Laws." *Harvard Law Review*, 45, 1196.

Politzer, Robert M., James S. Morrow, and Sandra B. Leavey (1981). "Report on the Societal Cost of Pathological Gambling and the Cost-Benefit/Effectiveness of Treatment." The Johns Hopkins Compulsive Gambling Counseling Center, presented at Fifth National Conference on Gambling and Risk-taking, 1–48.

Polzin, P. E., J. Baldridge, D. Doyle, J. T. Sylvester. Bureau of Business and Economic Research (University of Montana-Missoula), R. Volberg, W. L. Moore (1998). *Final Report.* Presented to the Montana Gambling Study Commission (September 30).

Productivity Commission (1999). "Australia's Gambling Industries: Final Report." Summary (November 26), Rep. No. 10.

Pulliam, Russ (2002). "A State History of Poor Best on Gambling." *The Indianapolis Star* (February 17).

Quinn, Frank (2001). "First Do No Harm: What Could Be Done by Casinos to Limit Pathological Gambling?" *Managerial and Decision Economics*, 22, 1–3, 133–42.

Rappaport, Jordan, and Chad Wilkerson (2001). "What Are the Benefits of Hosting a Major League Sports Franchise?" *Economic Review* (Federal Reserve Bank of Kansas City), 86, 1, 55–86.

Reno, Ronald A. (1997). "False Hope." *Citizen*, 6, 6, 10–13.

Roback, Jennifer (1982). "Wages, Rents, and the Quality of Life." *Journal of Political Economy*, 90, 6 (December), 1257–78.

Rose, Michael (1994). "The Gaming Industry and Economic Growth." *Alec Forum*, 4, 1 (May), 1–4.

Rosen, Sherwin (1979). "Wage-Based Indexes of Urban Quality of Life." In Miezkowski and Straszheim (eds.), *Current Issues in Urban Economics*. Baltimore: Johns Hopkins University Press.

Rosentraub, Mark (1999). *Major League Losers: The Real Cost of Sports and Who's Paying for It*. New York: Basic Books.

Ryan, Timothy P., J. F. Speyrer, with S. T. Beal, D. V. Burckel, B. R. Cunningham, M. M. Kurth, L. C. Scott, J. L. Wall, and James R. Westphal (1999). *Gambling in Louisiana: A Benefit/Cost Analysis*. Prepared for the Louisiana Gaming Control Board, Louisiana State University Medical Center (April).

Sack, Kevin (1995). "Gambling's New Winnings." *New York Times* (18 December), B12.

Samuelson, Paul A. (1970). *Economics*, 6th edition.

Schneider, Grace (2002). "Gambling Blamed in More Embezzlement Cases." *The Courier-Journal* (Louisville, KY), (23 December), accessed on www.courier-journal.com/localnews/2002/12/23/ke122303s336023.htm, January 9, 2003.

Schwer, R. Keith, William N. Thompson, and Daryl Nakamuro (2003). "Beyond the Limits of Recreation: Social Costs of Gambling in Southern Nevada." Paper presented at the Far West and American Popular Culture Association Annual Meeting; Las Vegas, Nevada; February 1, 2003.

Shaffer, Howard J., Matthew N. Hall, and Joni Vander Bilt (1997). "Estimating the Prevalence of Disordered Gambling Behavior in the United States and Canada: A Meta-Analysis." Boston: Harvard Medical School.

Shoven, John B., and John Whalley (1984). "Applied General Equilibrium Models of Taxation and International Trade: An Introductory Survey." *Journal of Economic Literature*, 22 (September), 1032.

Siegfried, John, and Andrew Zimbalist (2000). "The Economics of Sports Facilities and Their Communities." *Journal of Economic Perspectives*, 14, 3, 95–114.

Sigman, Robert (1996). "Assault on Law Enforcement." *Kansas City Star* (April 28), K2.

Smart, R. G., and J. Ferris (1996). "Alcohol, Drugs, and Gambling in the Ontario Adult Population, 1994." *Canadian Journal of Psychiatry*, 41, 36–45.

Smith, Adam (1776). *An Inquiry into the Nature and Causes of the Wealth of Nations*. Chicago: Encyclopedia Britannica; William Benton, Publisher; 1952.

Smith, Frederick, and William J. Craig (1992). "Who's in for How Much?" CURA Reporter, Center for Urban and Regional Affairs, 22, 1, 11–14, 16. (Plus data supplied to the authors.)

Smith, Gary, Harold Wynne, and Tim Hartnagel (2003). *Examining Police Records to Assess Gambling Impacts: A Study of Gambling-Related Crime in the City of Edmonton*, A Study Prepared for the Alberta Gaming Research Institute. March, 1–111.

SMR Research Corporation (1998). "The Personal Bankruptcy Crisis, 1997: Demographics, Causes, Implications & Solutions." Hackettstown, NJ: Author.

SMR Research Corporation (2001). "Bankruptcy & Gambling." (August), Hackettstown, NJ: Author.

Societe des Casinos Du Quebec (1994). "Casino de Montreal Announces Profile of Its Clientele." Montreal: Author.

South Dakota Legislative Research Council (1998). "Economic and Fiscal Impacts of the South Dakota Gaming Industry." (December 8), 1–145.

South Dakota Legislative Research Council (1998). "Economic and Fiscal Impacts of the South Dakota Gaming Industry." 1–146, + Attachment: Letter of January 7, 1999, to Terry Anderson, Director, S.D. Legislative Research Council. Table "South Dakota Total Estimated Incremental Social Costs."

State ex Inf. McKittrick v. Globe-Democrat Co., 110 S.W. 2d. 705 (S. Ct. Mo. 1937), 713.

Steinberg, M. A., T. A. Kosten, and B. J. Rounsaville (1992). "Cocaine Abuse and Pathological Gambling," *The American Journal on Addictions*, 1, 2, 121–32.

Thompson, William N. (1994). "The States Bet on Legalized Gambling." *World Book Encyclopedia: 1994 Year Book*, Chicago: World Book, Inc.

Thompson, William N., Ricardo Gazel, and Dan Rickman (1997a). "Social and Legal Costs of Compulsive Gambling." *Gaming Law Review*, 1, 1:81–9.

Thompson, William N., Ricardo Gazel, and Dan Rickman (1997a). "The Social Costs of Gambling in Wisconsin," *Wisconsin Policy Research Institute Report*, 9, 6 (July), 1–44.

Thompson, William N. (1997b). *Legalized Gambling*. Santa Barbara, CA: ABC-ClIO, 2nd. ed.

Thompson, William N., Ricardo Gazel, and Dan Rickman (1996a). "Casinos and Crime in Wisconsin: Is There a Connection?" Milwaukee: Wisconsin Policy Research Institute, 9, 8 (October).

Thompson, William N., Ricardo Gazel, and Dan Rickman (1998). "Social Costs of Gambling: A Comparative Study of Nutmeg and Cheese State Gamblers." Twelfth National Conference on Problem Gambling, NV, published in *Gaming Research & Review Journal*, 5, 1, 1–15.

Thompson, William N., and Frank L. Quinn (1999). "An Economic Analysis of Machine Gambling in South Carolina." The Education Foundation of the South Carolina Policy Council (May).

Tice, Douglas L. (1995). "Why the Press Hates Gaming." *Casino Executive* (August), 57–8.

U.S. House. (1995). Committee on the Judiciary. National Gambling Impact and Policy Commission Act: Hearing on H.R. 497 Before the House Committee on the Jucidiary. 104th Congress, 1st Session.

Video Gambler, The (2000). 2, 8, 1–2.

Volberg, Rachel (1995). "Gambling and Problem Gambling in Iowa: A Replication Study," Report to the Iowa Department of Human Services (July 28), ii and 55.

Volberg, Rachel, D. R. Gerstein, and E. M. Christiansen (2001). "Assessing Self-Reported Expenditures on Gambling." *Managerial and Decision Economics*, 22, 1–3 (January–May), 77–96.

Volberg, R., and H. J. Steadman (1989). "Problem Gambling in Iowa." Report to the Iowa Department of Human Services.

Walker, Mabel L. (1934). "American City." 49:57–8 (October), cited in Helen M. Muller, *Lotteries*. New York: The H. W. Wilson Company, 1935, 108–9.

Warren, Caroline M. (1828). *The Gamesters; or Ruins of Innocence. An Original Novel, Founded in Truth*. Boston: J. Shaw.

WEFA Group, ICR Survey Research Group, H. Lesieur & W. Thompson (1997). A Study

Concerning the Effects of Legalized Gambling on the Citizens of Connecticut. State of Connecticut Department of Revenue Services, Division of Special Revenue.

Westphal, J. R., L. J. Johnson, and L. Stevens (1999). "Estimating the Social Costs of Gambling Disorders in Louisiana for 1998." Louisiana State University Medical Center. Study performed under subcontract from University of New Orleans, UNO #313-20-4124 (March 23).

Wheeler, David L. (1999). "A Surge of Research on Gambling Is Financed in Part by the Industry Itself." *The Chronicle of Higher Education*, 60, 26, 17–18.

Whereatt, Robert (1993). "The True Take: Legal Gaming in State Smaller than It Appears." Star Tribune, (March 7).

Zabilka, Ivan L. (1994). Editorial. Gambling Economics, 2 (November), 3.

Zremski, Jerry, "A Gambling Boom Beckons," *Buffalo News*, August 5, 2002, Internet http://www.buffalonews.com/editorial/20020825/1027267.asp, accessed September 3, 2002.

Index

Note: An "*f*" after a page number indicates a figure on that page; an "*n*" after a page number indicates a note on that page; a "*t*" after a page number indicates a table on that page.

A
abused dollars, 66, 145–46, 197
Adam Rose and Associates, 88
AGA, *see* American Gambling Association
alcoholism, 186
amenity benefits
   definition of, 98, 197
   vs. costs, 58–59
   see also consumer surplus; distance
      benefit; distance consumer surplus
American Gaming Association (AGA), 32,
   33, 141, 143
American Indian bingo, 44
American Indian casino
   acquiring land for, 42–43
   allowed/banned, 15*t*, 16*t*, 17*t*
   campaign spending for, 35
   effect on local economy, 37–38, 39
   employment impact of, 37
   Indian Gaming Regulatory Act, 30,
      39–40, 41, 42, 44–45
   lack of benefit to local tribe, 38–39
   organized crime and, 137–38, 164
   profitability of, 37, 38
   see also American Indian tribe
American Indian tribe,
   campaign contribution by, 157, 161, 166
   difficulty in defining, 41–42
   IGRA definition of, 41
   increase in federally recognized, 40–41*f*
   see also American Indian casino
Apache Gold Casino, 38–39

Argosy Gaming Company, 28
Australian Productivity Commission, 22, 25
Australia's Gambling Industries (Australian
   Productivity Commission), 22

B
Bad Bet on the Bayou (Bridges), 20
bankruptcy, 139–41, 152, 210 (*nn 211,*
   213)
bathtub model, of determining job creation,
   70
Baton Rouge Intervention Center, 139–40
Beasley, David, 33–34
BIA, *see* Bureau of Indian Affairs
bingo, 15*t*, 16*t*, 17*t*, 44, 197, 206 (*n 89*)
Blaszczynski, A., 211 (*n 225*)
"boat-to-nowhere", 15*t*, 34, 45, 205 (*n 71*)
Bockstael, N. E., 116
Bridges, Tyler, 20
Bureau of Indian Affairs (BIA), 40, 42
business *vs.* social profitability, 108

C
*California v. Cabazon Band of Mission
   Indians*, 44
campaign/official contribution
   see social costs taxonomy, campaign/
      official contribution example
cannibalization
   definition of, 197
   effect on restaurant industry, 74
   and major league sports, 73, 74

cannibalization (*contd.*)
  tax receipt evidence of casino, 74–78, 75*f*,
      77*f*
  see also leakage; net export multiplier
      model, representative casino study;
      recapture
cannibalized job, 62*f*
capital gains/losses, 57, 128, 129, 194
  casino effect on house/property price, 59,
      63, 107
  definition of, 197
casino
  allowed/banned, 15*t*, 16*t*, 17*t*, 34–35, 36
  "boat–to–nowhere", 15*t*, 34, 45,
      199 *(n 71)*
  definition of, 197
  licensing, 30–31
  riverboat (*see* riverboat casino/gambling)
Casino America of Biloxi, 35
casino expansion
  government role in, 47–49
      jurisdictional problems, 50–51
  opponent to, 53
  player role in, 45–47
  proponent for
      American Indian, 36–45
      casino owner, 28–32
      lobbyist, 32–36
  summary, 52–53
  see also social benefits, of casino
      expansion
casino gambling
  annual costs *vs.* drug abuse costs, 177, 186
  campaign spending/voting for, 35
  introduction in U.S., 26, 106, 181
  see also American Indian casino
CCCS, *see* Consumer Credit Counseling
      Services
charitable giving, effect of gambling on, 74,
      164
Charlotte Observer, 34
Chelius, James, 137
Chicago Sun Times, 138
Chicago Tribune, 29
citizen, definition of, 197
Clark County Residents Study, 39
Class I gambling, definition of, 197,
      206 *(n 89)*
Class II gambling, definition of, 197,
      206 *(n 89)*

Class III gambling
  definition of, 197, 206 *(n 89)*
  on Indian lands, 39–40, 44, 45
Clotfelder, Charles T., 46
Committee to Study the Impact of
      Gambling in Ohio, 6
constitutional provision against gambling,
      1900 vs. 2000, 15*t*–17*t*
Consumer Credit Counseling Services
      (CCCS), 140
consumer surplus, 127, 128, 194
  calculating, 115*f*
  cost–benefit analysis equation, 103, 104
  definition of, 198
  from casino competition, 209 *(n 190)*
  as price/convenience benefit, 63, 64,
      113
Cook, Philip J., 46
corruption, by government official, 20, 36
  see social costs taxonomy, campaign/
      official contribution example
cost–benefit analysis
  common mistakes in applying, 108–9
  definition of, 198
  need for future research on, 183–84
  need for theory in, 96, 182, 184
  vs. net export multiplier model, 92–93
  see also cost–benefit analysis, of sample
      regional casino; cost–benefit
      analysis, theoretical framework for
cost–benefit analysis, of sample regional
      casino
  cost *vs.* benefit, 193–95
  geography of casino, 189, 190*f*
  lessons from, 195
  regional income impact, 191–93
  revenue/profit/tax, 190–91
  see also cost–benefit analysis; cost–benefit
      analysis, theoretical framework for
cost–benefit analysis, theoretical framework
      for
  amenity benefit consideration, 98–99
  benefits of new business activity, 97
  calculating change in utility, 97–98
  consumer surplus equation, 103, 104
  cost–benefit summary, 107*t*
  distance consumer surplus equation, 103,
      104
  framework equation, 99
  gambling types, 98

income effects equation, 102, 104–5, 209 *(nn 179–81)*
  overall taxonomy equation, 105–7
  public good effect equation, 103–4
  relating utility to dollars, 99
  special issue in, 99–102
  transaction constraints equation, 102, 103
  utility function equation, 98, 208 *(n 175)*
  see also cost–benefit analysis; cost–benefit analysis, of sample regional casino
crime, associated with gambling
  example of *(see* social costs taxonomy, crime example)
  Index I, 133
  organized, 20, 134, 137–38
  pathological gambler rate of, 168

D
deadweight loss, *see* tax deadweight loss
demand substitution
  definition of, 197
  see also cannibalization
direct regulatory costs, of gambling, 144, 177, 178, 179, 182–83, 213 *(n 264)*
directly unproductive profitseeking (DUP), 136, 139, 198
distance benefits
  definition of, 197
  see also distance benefits, theoretical measurement of; distance consumer surplus
distance benefits, theoretical measurement of, 177
  approach used in, 114, 116
  calculating upper bound, 117, 118*f,* 121–23
  data source, 117*t*
  demand curve, 115*f*
  estimating demand using 30–35 percent rule, 117–18, 120*t,* 124–25, 190–91
  simulating benefits, 117, 119*t,* 123–24, 182, 183
distance consumer surplus
  as convenience, 63, 114
  cost–benefit analysis equation, 103, 104
  definition of, 98–99, 197, 198
  see also distance benefits; distance benefits, theoretical measurement of
distributive efficiency, 133, 210 *(n 196)*
dogracing, 178

dopamine, 21–22, 204 *(n 34)*
drug abuse
  annual costs *vs.* casino gambling, 177, 186
  relationship to casino gambling, 144
DUP, *see* directly unproductive profitseeking

E
economic base
  definition of, 198
  results of increasing, 64–65
  see also net export multiplier model
economic development
  contextual interpretation of, 8
  definition of, 56, 57, 198
  and growthless jobs, 58–59, 61*f*
  improved market functioning as, 63–64
  and jobless growthlessness, 57–58, 59, 60*f*
  and jobless growth, 59–60, 61*f*–62
  proposal for, 7
  using multiplier/cost–benefit analysis to determine, 62*f*–63
  see also job; net export multiplier model
economic growth, definition of, 198
economics, definition of, 8
Edwards, Edwin, 20, 36, 154
Edwards, Stephen, 154
employment, *see* economic development; job; job multiplier model
Encyclopedia Britannica, 19
Evans Group study, 88–92, 90*f,* 91*f,* 106
externality, 9
  definition of, 198–99
  negative, 25–26, 66, 101, 107, 198–99
  positive, 101, 198
  see also social costs; social costs taxonomy

F
factory, effect on local economy, 67–68, 69–70, 109
Fahrenkopf, Frank, 32
family costs, of gambling, 145
family costs example
  death of child, 146, 147, 158, 165
  domestic violence, 152
  food/rent/power bill problem, 159
  homelessness, 148
  marriage problem, 150, 159
  murder, 146–47, 165–66

Farrell, E., 211 *(n 225)*
Foxwoods Resort Casino, 36–37, 38,
    142
fraud, in casino gambling, 19
free entry, cost–benefit of, 126, 129*t*,
    209 *(n 184)*
Friedman, Milton, 44
Friedman's Law, 44

G
gambler
    gambling shares in Las Vegas, 45–46*f*
    vs. nongambler, 20–21, 45–47
    see also pathological gambler; problem
        gambler
gambler–anonymous group, 185, 187
Gamblers Anonymous, 141, 150, 156,
    157–58, 168, 211 *(n 226)*
gambling
    ancient evidence of, 18
    continual effect of, 18–19
    definition of, 199
    demographics of, 20–21, 23–24
    dogracing, 178
    horseracing, 14, 178
    need for government regulation of, 19–20
    psychological factors of, 21–22
    riverboat, 17, 21, 23–24, 28, 29, 31, 32, 33,
        178
    state allowing, 15*t*–17*t*
Gambling Impact Study Commission, 22
GAO, *see* U.S. General Accounting Office
Gerstein, Dean, 171
Goodman, Robert, 30, 32–33, 34
Goss & Associates, 71
gross profit, 80, 199

H
Hall, Matthew N., 176–77
Helms, Nat, 36
Hira, Tahira, 210 *(n 213)*
horseracing, 14, 178
household, definition of, 199

I
IGRA, *see* Indian Gaming Regulatory Act
illness costs, 143–44, 205 *(n 226)*
impact study
    as invalid assessment, 8
    see also net export multiplier model

import substitution, 68, 199
income–compensated demand curve, 115
    (n 1)
income *vs.* wealth, 57
Index I crime, 133
Indianapolis Star, 49
Indian casino, *see* American Indian
    casino
Indian Gaming Regulatory Act (IGRA), 30,
    39–40, 41, 42, 44–45
Indian tribe, *see* American Indian tribe
industry–sponsored research, on job
    gain/loss, 88–92, 90*f*, 91*f*, 106
International Game Technology (♠ IGT),
    see Evans Group study
Internet waging, fraud potential in, 19
Iowa Department of Human Services
    replication study, 178*t*–79
Iowa State University, 140
Iron Law of Economics, 169

J
job
    cannibalized, 62*f*
    casino effect on, 69, 106, 127, 128,
        129*t*
    effect of creation on utility, 59,
        61–62
    estimating with bathtub model, 70
    estimating with net export multiplier
        model, 67, 69–70, 182
    Indian casino effect on, 37, 38
    industry–sponsored research on
        gain/loss, 88–92, 90*f*, 91*f*, 106
    major league sports team effect on, 69,
        71–73, 128, 129, 194
    value of extra, to community, 64
    see also economic development; job
        multiplier model
job multiplier model
    as untrustworthy, 55
    see also net export multiplier model

K
Kindt, John, 33, 48

L
laissez faire
    definition of, 199
    see also free entry, cost–benefit of

Las Vegas Convention & Visitors Authority,
        39
Lazaroff, Michael, 36
Leakage, 78, 191–93, 199
    see also cannibalization; net export
        multiplier model, representative
        casino study; recapture
Lee, Barbara A., 137
Legalized Gambling as a Strategy for
        Economic Development (Goodman),
        30
legislation, gambling
    for American Indian casino, 30, 39–40,
        41, 42, 44–45
    in Illinois, 29
    in Indiana, 49
    in Iowa, 29
    in Massachusetts, 136, 138
    in Missouri, 30
    in New York State, 48–49
    in Pennsylvania, 138
    in South Carolina, 49, 186–87
Legislative Research Council (LRC), 7
Lesieur, Henry R., 22
licensing, casino, 30–31
lobbyist, 32–36
lottery
    allowed/banned, 15t, 16t, 17t
    definition of, 14
    household income of player, 150–51, 156,
        163
    willingness to overpay for ticket, 19
LRC, see Legislative Research Council

M
macroeconomics, 116
major league sports
    cannibalized revenues of, 73, 74
    job creating effects of, 69, 71–73, 128,
        129, 194
    leakage by, 78
    social cost–benefit of, 66
    tax benefit–cost of, 66, 73
market saturation, 126
Martin, Maryann, 42
Maryland Department of Health, 143–44,
        168
McCleary, Richard, 143
McConnell, K. E., 116
Miami Indians, 43

Missouri Gaming Commission, 36
multiplier model, 64–65
    industry–sponsored research on job
        gain/loss, 88–92, 90f, 91f, 106
    see also multiplier model, reliability of
        study based on; net export
        multiplier model
multiplier model, reliability of study based
        on, 71–73
    effect of cannibalization, 73–78, 75f, 77f
    effect of exaggerated multiplier, 79
    effect of leakage, 78

N
National Coalition Against Legalized
        Gambling, 33
National Gambling Impact Study
        Commission, 48, 88
    on cost–benefit research, 4–5
    on franchising gambling, 127
    limit to power of, 32
    on lottery player, 21
    on pathological/problem gambler, 22,
        145, 168, 179t–80
    on riverboat casino gambling, 23–24
    on spending at nearby casino, 185, 190
National Research Council, 71
Neely, Michelle Clark, 140
negative externality, 101, 107
    definition of, 25, 198–99
    example of, 66
net export multiplier model
    applying to regional casino, 191–93
    definition of, 55, 199–200
    estimating jobs with, 67, 69–70, 182
    vs. cost–benefit analysis, 92–93
    see also multiplier model; net export
        multiplier model, representative
        casino study
net export multiplier model, representative
        casino study
    conclusions, 87–88
    economic sectors for modeling, 80–81f
    effect of adjustments on outcome, 86–87
    effect of casino on local income flows,
        81–82t
    model for, 83, 84t
    social costs of casino gambling, 83, 85
    typical casino expenses, 80t, 82–83
    see also net export multiplier model

net exports
  definition of, 200
  see also net export multiplier model
New Jersey Casino Control Commission,
    137
New York Law Journal, 48
New York Times, 28, 29
Noll, Roger, 72

O
offtrack betting (OTB), effect on local
    economy, 2
organized crime, 20, 134, 137–38, 164

P
pathological gambler, 3, 7
  biological effects of gambling on, 21–22
  need for research on, 184–86
  as negative externality, 25
  percentage of casino revenues from, 46
  percentage of population, 22, 168, 177
  social costs of, 85, 96 (*see also* social costs,
      identifying by problem/pathological
      gambler study; social costs, of
      pathological/problem gambler;
      social costs taxonomy)
  see also problem gambler
pathological gambling, definition of, 167,
    200
Peiffer, Joe, 210 (*n 211*)
perfect competition, 125, 126–27, 200
perfect information, 126
Phillips, David P., 143
player, *see* gambler; pathological gambler;
    problem gambler
political economy, 8
positive externality, 101, 198
price effects, *see* capital gains/losses;
    consumer surplus
prisoner's dilemma, 4, 201–2, 203 (*n 3*)
private goods, 51, 98, 100, 101, 102, 116, 201
problem gambler
  need for research on, 184–86
  percentage of population, 22, 177
  social costs of (*see* social costs, identifying
      by problem/pathological gambler
      study; social costs, of
      pathological/problem gambler;
      social costs taxonomy)
  see also pathological gambler

problem gambling, definition of, 201
production externalities, 109
propensity to spend, definition of, 201
propensity to spend locally, definition of,
    201
public goods, 51, 201
  casino as not provider of, 66
  casino as provider of, 208 (*n 178*)
  feature of, 208 (*n 177*)
  see also cost–benefit analysis, theoretical
      framework for

Q
Quinn, Frank, 186

R
Racing and Gaming Commission, 78
recapture, definition of, 201
recaptured dollars, 81, 191–92, 193
  see also cannibalization; net export
      multiplier model, representative
      casino study
research, on gambling
  politics of, 6–7
  wider application of, 10–11
research need, on gambling
  distance benefits of increased casino
      gambling, 186
  effect of nearby casino on pathological/
      problem gambler, 184–86
  effect of treatment on
      pathological/problem gambler, 186
  on minimizing social cost, 186
  for uniformity, 183–84
resident, definition of, 199
restaurant
  effect of casino on, 23, 32, 39, 57–58, 74,
      192
  effect on local economy, 67–70
risk, 47
riverboat casino/gambling, 15*t*, 16*t*, 17, 21,
    23–24, 28, 29, 31, 32, 33, 178
Riverboat Gambling Act, 29
Ryan, Timothy P., 211 (*n 237*)

S
Samuelson, Paul, 139
Schwer, R. Keith, 170
Seminole Tribe of Florida v. Florida, 45
service, as value, 112–13

Shaffer, Howard J., 176–77
Shakopee (Minn) casino, 37, 38
Sherman, William, 41–42
Smith, Adam, 19
Smith, Gary, 134
Smith, M. M., 143
SMR Research Corporation, 140–41
social benefits, of casino expansion
    from Iowa replication study, 178*t*–79
    limiting, by limiting expansion, 209
        (*n 184*)
    price effects, 127–28, 209 (*n 191*)
    problem with generalization about,
        128–29
    profits/taxes, 125–27
    regional *vs.* entire economy, 129*t*
    see also casino expansion; distance
        benefits, theoretical measurement of
social costs
    of decision making (*see* casino expansion)
    definition of, 201
    see also social costs, identifying by
        problem/pathological gambler
        study; social costs, of pathological/
        problem gambler; social costs
        taxonomy
social costs, identifying by problem/
        pathological gambler studies
    annual cost per pathological gambler,
        171–73, 172*t*–73*t*, 211 (*n 237*)
    annual cost per problem gambler, 2003,
        174*t*
    background on gambler, 167–68
    identifying through levels of
        cost–creating activity, 168–69
    identifying through social costs, 168
    limitations, 169
    multiple causality concerns, 169–71, 211
        (*n 232*)
    sampling concerns, 171
    see also social costs, of
        pathological/problem gambler;
        social costs taxonomy
social costs, of pathological/problem
        gambler
    based on adjusted per–adult numbers,
        175, 177–78, 182–83
    based on casino in economy previously
        without, 175–76, 179–80
    based on direct statistical analysis, 168–69

based on implied national social cost,
    175, 176*t*, 177, 194–95
based on implied national social cost
    per–adult, 175, 177
of increased number in Iowa, 178*t*–79
of tax by casino, 176, 180–81, 212
    (*n 240*)
see also social costs, identifying by
    problem/pathological gambler
    study; social costs taxonomy
social costs–benefits
    of casino, 66–67
    of free entry, 126, 129*t*, 209 (*n 184*)
    of major league sports, 66
social costs taxonomy
    abused dollars, 66, 145–46, 197
    bankruptcy, 139–41, 210 (*nn 211, 213*)
    bankruptcy example, 152
    business/employment costs, 135–36,
        138–39
    campaign/official contribution example
        American Indian contribution, 157,
            161, 166
        campaign/candidate contribution, 153,
            157, 158, 159–60, 162, 164, 166
        government official payoff, 151
        lottery on ballot, 153
        payoff to official, 154, 160
    charitable giving example, 164
    church attendance example, 149
    conflict of interest example, 163
    crime, 133–35, 137–38
    crime example
        bad check writing, 158–59
        bribery, 158
        burglary, 156, 164
        crime of opportunity, 151
        check kiting, 160
        embezzlement, 147, 148, 150, 156, 157,
            160, 161, 163
        forgery, 158, 162–63
        hocked jewelry, 153
        insurance fraud, 146, 154, 165
        investment scam, 149–50
        loan fraud, 147
        loansharking, 154
        manslaughter, 147
        misappropriation of funds, 161
        murder, 146–47, 165–66
        organized crime, 164

robbery, 148, 149, 151, 153, 155, 160,
    161–62
siphoning funds, 155
shooting, 167
stealing, 148, 152, 153, 155, 158, 159,
    160, 162, 165, 167
stock share fraud, 161
taking money from mentally retarded
    adult, 164
theft, 152, 153–54, 157, 165
direct regulatory costs, 144, 177, 178, 179,
    182–83, 213 (n 264)
family, 145
family example
    death of child, 146, 147, 158, 165
    domestic violence, 152
    food/rent/power bill problem, 159
    homelessness, 148
    marriage problem, 150, 159
    murder, 146–47, 165–66
Gambler Anonymous increase example,
    150, 156, 157–58
illness/accident, 143–44, 211 (n 226)
household income of player example,
    150–51, 156, 163
overview of, 132–33
social services, 144
social services example, 155–56
suicide, 3, 134, 141–43
suicide/attempted suicide example, 151,
    152–53, 155, 156, 167, 210 (n 220)
social services costs, 144, 155–56
Societe des Casinos Du Quebec, 87
Speyrer, Jane, 73–74
Sports, Jobs & Taxes (Noll & Zimbalist), 72
A Study of the Economic Impact of the
    Gaming Industry through 2005, 89
suicide, 3, 134, 141–43, 151, 152–53, 155,
    156, 167, 210 (n 220), 211 (n 225)

T
"Task Forced to Study the Impact of a
    Maine–Based Casino", 6
tax, 185
    corrective, 183
    cost–benefit of casino, 25, 100–101,
        103–4, 106, 108–9, 127, 191,
        212 (n 240)
    cost–benefit of major league sports, 66, 73
    cost of casino vs. conventional, 51, 176,
        180–81

direct regulatory costs as, 144
Indian casino exemption from, 45
leakage of, 192, 193
on modern state lottery ticket, 19
see also net export multiplier model,
    representative casino study
tax deadweight loss, 132–33, 183, 194–95,
    201, 209 (n 181)
tax receipt data study, 74–78, 75f, 77f
Thompson, William, 70, 78, 170, 172t,
    173t, 204 (nn 19, 32, 46, 48), 211
    (n 233)
Time, 42
tollhouse, effect on local economy, 59, 68,
    69–70
transaction constraint
    definition of, 100, 201
    difficulty in estimating benefit, 128
    see also cost–benefit analysis, theoretical
        framework for
treatment, for gambling
    politics of funding, 5–6
    research need for, 186

U
U.S. General Accounting Office (GAO), 33,
    177
USA Today, 86
utility, 7, 9, 55, 57
    definition of, 201
    effect of job creation on, 59, 61–62
    see also cost–benefit analysis, theoretical
        framework for

V
value, 112–13
value added, 9, 202
Vander Bilt, Joni, 176–77

W
wealth, definition of, 57, 202
Wealth of Nations (Smith), 19
welfare, see utility
well–being, see utility
Welty, W. R., 143
Wolf, Frank R., 36
Wolfson, Robert, 36
World Book Encyclopedia, 23

Z
Zimbalist, Andrew, 72